# Acknowledgments

I wish to thank all the children and their families who have taught us what to teach and how to make it comprehensible. They are the ones who are truly responsible for the content of this book.

I also want to thank my colleagues, Andrea Footerman, Psy.D., Kenwin Nancoo, M.A., and Meryl Heller, who gave me many ideas for skill lessons. Lori Shery, president of ASPEN (Asperger Syndrome Education Network), also deserves my gratitude as she first encouraged me to start running groups for individuals with Asperger Syndrome in her relentless efforts to improve services for this population.

My wife Beth and our children, Jake and Lindsay, deserve many thanks for putting up with me and reminding me to have fun in everything you do, especially teaching.

– Jed Baker

# Table of Contents

**INTRODUCTION** . . . . . . . . . . . . . . . . . . . . . . . . . . . . . . . . . . . . . . . . . . . . . . . . . . . . .1
A Brief Overview of the Book

**CHAPTER 1** . . . . . . . . . . . . . . . . . . . . . . . . . . . . . . . . . . . . . . . . . . . . . . . . . . . . . .5
Social Skills Training Groups for Children with Asperger Syndrome

**CHAPTER 2** . . . . . . . . . . . . . . . . . . . . . . . . . . . . . . . . . . . . . . . . . . . . . . . . . . . . . .9
Overview of Asperger Syndrome
*Brenda Smith Myles*

**CHAPTER 3** . . . . . . . . . . . . . . . . . . . . . . . . . . . . . . . . . . . . . . . . . . . . . . . . . . . . .17
Assessment for Social Skills Training

**CHAPTER 4** . . . . . . . . . . . . . . . . . . . . . . . . . . . . . . . . . . . . . . . . . . . . . . . . . . . . .29
Strategies for Teaching Social Skills

**CHAPTER 5** . . . . . . . . . . . . . . . . . . . . . . . . . . . . . . . . . . . . . . . . . . . . . . . . . . . . .39
Where to Provide Skills Training: The Classroom, Small Groups,
or Play-Dates

**CHAPTER 6** . . . . . . . . . . . . . . . . . . . . . . . . . . . . . . . . . . . . . . . . . . . . . . . . . . . . .55
Behavior Management

**CHAPTER 7** . . . . . . . . . . . . . . . . . . . . . . . . . . . . . . . . . . . . . . . . . . . . . . . . . . . . .63
Promoting Generalization

**CHAPTER 8** . . . . . . . . . . . . . . . . . . . . . . . . . . . . . . . . . . . . . . . . . . . . . . . . . . . . .73
Skill Lessons and Activities

**CHAPTER 9** . . . . . . . . . . . . . . . . . . . . . . . . . . . . . . . . . . . . . . . . . . . . . . . . . . . . .219
Promoting Peer Acceptance Through Sensitivity Training and
Incentive Programs

**REFERENCES** . . . . . . . . . . . . . . . . . . . . . . . . . . . . . . . . . . . . . . . . . . . . . . . . . . .229

# Communication Skills

## Conversational Skills

1. Maintaining Appropriate Physical Distance from Others .................. 78
   ("Don't Be a Space Invader")

2. Listening Position ......................................... 80

3. Tone of Voice ............................................ 82

4. Greetings ................................................ 84

5. How and When to Interrupt ................................ 86

6. Staying on Topic .......................................... 88

7. Maintaining a Conversation ................................ 90

8. Taking Turns Talking ...................................... 92

9. Starting a Conversation .................................... 94

10. Joining a Conversation .................................... 96

11. Ending a Conversation .................................... 98

12. Asking a Question When You Don't Understand .............. 100

13. Saying "I Don't Know" ................................... 102

14. Introducing Yourself ..................................... 104

15. Getting to Know Someone New ............................ 106

16. Introducing Topics of Interest to Others ................... 108

17. Giving Background Information about What You Are Saying ........... 110

18. Shifting Topics .......................................... 112

19. Don't Talk Too Long ..................................... 114

20. Sensitive Topics ......................................... 116

21. Complimenting Others .................................... 118

22. Use Your H.E.A.D. ....................................... 120
    (Happy Voice, Eye Contact, Alternating Turns, Distance)

23. T.G.I.F. ................................................. 122
    (Timing, Greeting, Initial Question, Follow-Up Questions)

## Cooperative Play Skills

24. Asking Someone to Play . . . . . . . . . . . . . . . . . . . . . . . . . . . . . . . . . . . 124

25. Joining Others in Play . . . . . . . . . . . . . . . . . . . . . . . . . . . . . . . . . . . . 126

26. Compromising . . . . . . . . . . . . . . . . . . . . . . . . . . . . . . . . . . . . . . . . . 128

27. Sharing . . . . . . . . . . . . . . . . . . . . . . . . . . . . . . . . . . . . . . . . . . . . . . 130

28. Taking Turns . . . . . . . . . . . . . . . . . . . . . . . . . . . . . . . . . . . . . . . . . . 132

29. Playing a Game . . . . . . . . . . . . . . . . . . . . . . . . . . . . . . . . . . . . . . . . 134

30. Dealing with Losing . . . . . . . . . . . . . . . . . . . . . . . . . . . . . . . . . . . . . 136

31. Dealing with Winning . . . . . . . . . . . . . . . . . . . . . . . . . . . . . . . . . . . . 138

32. Ending a Play Activity . . . . . . . . . . . . . . . . . . . . . . . . . . . . . . . . . . . . 140

## Friendship Management

33. Informal Versus Formal Behavior . . . . . . . . . . . . . . . . . . . . . . . . . . . . 142

34. Respecting Personal Boundaries . . . . . . . . . . . . . . . . . . . . . . . . . . . . . 144

35. Facts Versus Opinions (Respecting Others' Opinions) . . . . . . . . . . . . . . 146

36. Sharing a Friend . . . . . . . . . . . . . . . . . . . . . . . . . . . . . . . . . . . . . . . . 148

37. Getting Attention in Positive Ways . . . . . . . . . . . . . . . . . . . . . . . . . . . 150

38. Don't Be the "Rule Police" . . . . . . . . . . . . . . . . . . . . . . . . . . . . . . . . . 152

39. Offering Help . . . . . . . . . . . . . . . . . . . . . . . . . . . . . . . . . . . . . . . . . . 154

40. When to Tell on Someone . . . . . . . . . . . . . . . . . . . . . . . . . . . . . . . . . 156

41. Modesty . . . . . . . . . . . . . . . . . . . . . . . . . . . . . . . . . . . . . . . . . . . . . . 158

42. Asking Someone Out on a Date . . . . . . . . . . . . . . . . . . . . . . . . . . . . . 160

43. Appropriate Touch . . . . . . . . . . . . . . . . . . . . . . . . . . . . . . . . . . . . . . 162

44. Dealing with Peer Pressure . . . . . . . . . . . . . . . . . . . . . . . . . . . . . . . . 164

45. Dealing with Rumors . . . . . . . . . . . . . . . . . . . . . . . . . . . . . . . . . . . . 166

46. Calling a Friend on the Telephone . . . . . . . . . . . . . . . . . . . . . . . . . . . 168

47. Answering the Telephone . . . . . . . . . . . . . . . . . . . . . . . . . . . . . . . . . 170

# Emotion Management Skills

## Self-Regulation

48. Recognizing Feelings . . . . . . . . . . . . . . . . . . . . . . . . . . . . . . . . . . . . . . . . . . . . . . . 172

49. Feelings Thermometer . . . . . . . . . . . . . . . . . . . . . . . . . . . . . . . . . . . . . . . . . . . . . 174

50. Keeping Calm . . . . . . . . . . . . . . . . . . . . . . . . . . . . . . . . . . . . . . . . . . . . . . . . . . . . 176

51. Problem Solving . . . . . . . . . . . . . . . . . . . . . . . . . . . . . . . . . . . . . . . . . . . . . . . . . . 178

52. Talking to Others When Upset . . . . . . . . . . . . . . . . . . . . . . . . . . . . . . . . . . . . . . 180

53. Dealing with Family Problems . . . . . . . . . . . . . . . . . . . . . . . . . . . . . . . . . . . . . . 182

54. Understanding Anger . . . . . . . . . . . . . . . . . . . . . . . . . . . . . . . . . . . . . . . . . . . . . . 184

55. Dealing with Making a Mistake . . . . . . . . . . . . . . . . . . . . . . . . . . . . . . . . . . . . . 188

56. Trying When Work Is Hard . . . . . . . . . . . . . . . . . . . . . . . . . . . . . . . . . . . . . . . . . 190

57. Trying Something New . . . . . . . . . . . . . . . . . . . . . . . . . . . . . . . . . . . . . . . . . . . . . 192

## Empathy

58. Showing Understanding for Others' Feelings: . . . . . . . . . . . . . . . . . . . . . . . . . . . 194
    Preschool-Elementary

59. Showing Understanding for Others' Feelings: . . . . . . . . . . . . . . . . . . . . . . . . . . . 196
    Preadolescent-Adulthood

60. Cheering up a Friend . . . . . . . . . . . . . . . . . . . . . . . . . . . . . . . . . . . . . . . . . . . . . . . 198

## Conflict Management

61. Asserting Yourself . . . . . . . . . . . . . . . . . . . . . . . . . . . . . . . . . . . . . . . . . . . . . . . . . 200

62. Accepting No for an Answer . . . . . . . . . . . . . . . . . . . . . . . . . . . . . . . . . . . . . . . . 202

63. Dealing with Teasing – K-4th Grade . . . . . . . . . . . . . . . . . . . . . . . . . . . . . . . . . . 204

64. Dealing with Teasing – 5th Grade and Up . . . . . . . . . . . . . . . . . . . . . . . . . . . . . 205

65. More Words to Deal with Teasing . . . . . . . . . . . . . . . . . . . . . . . . . . . . . . . . . . . . 207

66. Dealing with Being Left Out . . . . . . . . . . . . . . . . . . . . . . . . . . . . . . . . . . . . . . . . 208

67. Avoiding Being "Set Up" . . . . . . . . . . . . . . . . . . . . . . . . . . . . . . . . . . . . . . . . . . . 210

68. Giving Criticism in a Positive Way . . . . . . . . . . . . . . . . . . . . . . . . . . . . . . . . . . . 212

69. Accepting Criticism . . . . . . . . . . . . . . . . . . . . . . . . . . . . . . . . . . . . . . . . . . . . . . . . 214

70. Having a Respectful Attitude . . . . . . . . . . . . . . . . . . . . . . . . . . . . . . . . . . . . . . . . 216

## INTRODUCTION

# A Brief Overview of the Book

The impetus to write this book came from working with students with Asperger Syndrome and related pervasive developmental disorders. Inherent in these disorders is a profound difficulty with social interaction despite normal and sometimes superior intellectual ability. Each time a student with whom I was working experienced a problem with social interaction, I set out to create an explicit lesson to help the student know what to do and say to avoid the social difficulty.

After writing over 70 skill lessons I began to apply these strategies in my new job as director of social skills training for special education students in the Millburn School District in New Jersey. I realized that these skill steps were not just helpful to students with pervasive developmental disorders like Asperger Syndrome, but to any student who was having difficulty knowing what to do and say in social situations. Similarly, I urge other professionals to worry less about diagnostic issues and more about what social skills difficulties their students are encountering and then set out to implement skills training in the deficient areas. My philosophy about skills training is explained below along with a brief description of the organization of the book.

All social interaction and social problems involve at least two people. Social difficulties can be defined as both a skill deficit for the student with a social disability and a problem of acceptance of that student by his or her peers. Thus, intervention must focus on teaching skills to both the student with a disability and typical peers. All too often we strive to "fix" the child with the disability and virtually overlook the "typical" peers who may be ignoring, teasing or rejecting the child. Moreover, including typical peers as a focus for intervention may yield results much sooner, as typical peers may learn to be understanding of the child with a disability more quickly than the child with a disability can learn to interact more appropriately with peers.

1

Consistent with this view, I believe effective social skills training for individuals with Asperger Syndrome and related pervasive developmental disorders consists of at least the following four components:

## For Students with Special Needs

1. Skills training lessons for students who have social skill deficits
2. Activities and incentive programs to promote generalization and practice of skills in the situations where they are needed

## For Typical Peers

1. Sensitivity training lessons for typical peers to be more accepting of students with special needs
2. Activities and incentive programs to promote generalization and practice of sensitivity skills in the situations where they are needed

The majority of this book is dedicated to the first component through a series of 70 skill lessons and activities for children and adolescents who have skill deficits. Before we get to these step-by-step lessons and accompanying handouts, general information about social skills training and related issues will be presented.

Chapter 1 describes the background for developing social skills training groups. Keep in mind that training groups are not the only context in which to teach social skills. As discussed in Chapter 5, skills training can occur at home with a parent, on a play-date, or in a typical classroom. Chapter 2, written by Brenda Smith Myles, provides an overview of the symptoms of Asperger Syndrome with an emphasis on social skills. In Chapter 3 we look at what skills to target for social skills training and how to combine students if running a group. The centerpiece of this chapter is a Social Skills Menu listing all the skills covered in the book, for which detailed lessons are presented in Chapter 8. The menu is a place to begin assessing what skills to target with an individual child.

Numerous strategies for teaching skills are discussed in Chapter 4, with an emphasis on a technique called structured learning (McGinnis & Goldstein, 1997). "Structured learning" contains four components: (a) didactic instruction (verbal or pictorial explanation of the skill steps), (b) modeling (live demonstrations of how to perform the skill), (c) role-playing with feedback (having students physically go through the steps and providing them with corrective feedback until they can accurately perform the skill), and (d) practice assignments for outside the group.

Chapter 5 describes places where skills training may be provided – in a general education classroom, in a small group, or on a play-date. In the classroom, a structured skill lesson is conducted early in the week, then time to practice the skill is created by specific conversation and play activities scheduled during the rest of the week. During a small-group session, a formal lesson is conducted along with less structured times for practicing the skills more spontaneously. The schedule for small groups usually involves the following sequence:

- conversation time
- skill time
- playtime
- snack

For play-dates and other home-based activities, skill lessons are usually conducted prior to the get-together, then rehearsed just before the play-date and practiced on the play-date itself.

Chapter 6 describes behavior management strategies that can be used to run groups and to deal with challenging home and classroom behaviors. In Chapter 7, we take up the important topic of how best to promote generalization, beyond the generalization step built into the skills lesson. Chapter 8 contains the handouts of these skills broken down into their component parts. The handouts depict what to teach students and thus serve to guide those teaching the skills. An activity sheet accompanies each skill with tips for parents and teachers on how to practice and thus promote generalization of the skills at home and in the classroom. Finally, Chapter 9 deals with sensitivity training for typical peers and developing incentive programs to promote peer acceptance. Sample sensitivity lessons are included along with reward programs to help those skills generalize.

## CHAPTER 1

# Social Skills Training Groups
# for Children with Asperger Syndrome

As my co-therapist and I sat waiting one afternoon to begin the first session of a new social skills group for children with Asperger Syndrome (AS), three 12-year-old boys quietly entered the room. They avoided all eye contact and sat down without a word. The silence was broken as our youngest member, an 11-year-old, burst in and began (in a phony British accent), "It was 1944, the troops stormed Normandy…" My young friend's monologue continued as the other boys sat giggling, looking annoyed, apparently oblivious of the World War II lesson that was taking place. Our youngest member, fully aware of his AS diagnosis, framed the scene for the group: social skills as a "battleground" set in 1944 (perhaps not coincidentally the same year Hans Asperger wrote about the syndrome later to bear his name).

My original goal for the group was modest: to create a safe environment where the members developed a sense of belonging to help them combat the social isolation they felt outside the group. My co-therapist's goal was more ambitious: to create skill lessons from which the boys could learn, step by step, how to relate to others outside the group. The adoption of both goals proved fruitful. Skill lessons that make explicit what to do and say in different social situations were crucial to helping the boys develop the building blocks to connect with each other, in addition to developing relationships outside the group. For example, we taught our young World War II aficionado what to say to start a conversation during group (e.g., "How was your week?" "What are you going to do after group today?"). We practiced how to maintain a conversation "with" others (e.g., by asking on-topic questions and making on-topic comments) rather than talk "at" others. We also taught him to look for signs of others' interest and how to check to see if others want to hear more (see "Talking Briefly So Others Will Listen"). Without these specific lessons in "Talking Briefly" and "Starting a Conversation," he may have continued to alienate himself from the other group members by rambling on and on about his special interest.

Among the numerous approaches to social skills training advanced over the years, behavioral approaches tend to emphasize structured lessons in which the trainer tells and shows the student what to do in a class-like setting (e.g., McGinnis & Goldstein, 1997). In contrast, developmental approaches (e.g., Greenspan & Weider, 1998) stress following the lead of the student rather than directing the student in a more natural setting to facilitate the student's spontaneous use of skills. Allowing time for both structured skill lessons and more "natural" interactions continues to be my preferred format. Whether skill training occurs in a small group, during a play-date or in a large classroom, there needs to be time both for a skill lesson and to play or talk in less structured, naturalistic settings as a way of practicing the skills. For example, small groups usually involve a conversation time, a skill lesson, and a game/playtime.

Games might include standard board or card games appropriate for the age group, as well as activities geared to teaching verbal and nonverbal communication skills (e.g., charades, "20 Questions," and other guessing games). In brief, it is important that participants first learn a skill and then have a chance to practice it in "real" conversations or play situations with others. Thus, a group is a microcosm of the outside world, allowing members to experiment with new skills within an accepting atmosphere.

About seven years have passed since that first session. In that time, I have run and supervised over 40 groups for individuals with AS, from four-year-olds to young adults. With each session and each group, I created new skill steps or borrowed from other resources (e.g., Gajewski, Hirn, & Mayo, 1998; McGinnis & Goldstein, 1997) as dictated by participants' needs. These skills have now been compiled into a Social Skills Menu (see Chapter 3), which I use both to assess a prospective group member's social skills and to design an individualized curriculum.

## When Can You Expect to See Progress?

I run groups for 12 weekly sessions, after which participants can leave, new members can join the group, or members can continue for the next 12-week cycle. The average student attends for close to one year, with progress (based on parent and teacher ratings for each skill taught) typically shown after 12-24 weeks. In general, the better the child's conceptual ability and the more practice he or she receives, the sooner we see results as the child is better able to generalize skills outside of the group.

It is important to keep in mind that not all problems can be addressed through social skills training. Teaching students what to do and why does not guarantee that they will be able to perform the skills. For example, individuals with extreme impulsivity may need additional behavioral management programs and/or medication to allow them to implement the skills they have learned.

Although it is not 1944 and the troops are not storming Normandy, the social world continues to be a battleground for many students with AS. Social isolation, neglect, harassment, and direct rejection are frequent daily experiences for some in school settings. As a result, having a safe place – in the social skills group – to connect with other students and not be taunted becomes a very valuable experience.

From a parent's or educator's perspective, a crucial goal of a social skills group is that children will learn social skills that will help them gain greater acceptance. However, from the group member's point of view, having and being with friends in the group may be the most important issue, regardless of any skills learned. With this in mind, an effective group cannot just be a class, but must be a place where members feel safe and enjoy themselves.

Before launching into assessment and specifics of social skills training, Chapter 2, written by Brenda Smith Myles, gives a brief overview of the social skills challenges faced by children and youth with AS and how deficits in this area can prevent an individual from leading a successful and satisfying life.

# An Overview of Asperger Syndrome
## Brenda Smith Myles

**W**hile the awareness of Asperger Syndrome (AS) has increased since its inclusion in the *Diagnostic and Statistical Manual of Mental Disorders – 4th Edition* (American Psychiatric Association [APA], 1994), there is still much to learn about this exceptionality and interventions that can support children and youth with AS in school, home, and the community. Asperger Syndrome describes a cluster of related symptoms primarily involving problems with social interactions despite average to above-average intellectual and expressive language abilities. The structural aspects of language (e.g., grammar, vocabulary, and articulation) are often intact or even precocious, but the social use of language (e.g., conversational skills) is almost always impaired. In addition, often, but not always, individuals with AS have areas of interest that are atypical in either their intensity or focus. For example, students may be able to rattle off an incredibly long list of facts in a one-sided manner, but not easily engage with others in a two-way conversation. John, a 12-year-old with AS, knows numerous and obscure facts about weapons used in the Civil War and can talk nonstop for hours about this topic. His idea of conversation is directing comments on this special interest to someone within his proximity. If John's "conversation partner" attempts to talk about another topic, John ignores his peer's comments and keeps talking about weapons.

The current *Diagnostic and Statistical Manual of Mental Disorders – 4th Edition, Text Revision* (DSM-IV-TR; APA, 2000) describes AS as involving two symptom areas: (a) qualitative impairment in social interactions (e.g., impairment in nonverbal communication, or failure to form peer relationships); and (b) restricted, repetitive, and stereotyped patterns of behavior, interests or activities (e.g., preoccupation with a restricted pattern of interests, or inflexible adherence to nonfunctional routines or rituals). Moreover, the DSM-IV-TR specifies that AS does not involve a significant delay in language or cognitive development. This distinguishes it from more "classic" autism, which involves language and cognitive delays, but not from "high-functioning autism," in which individuals may have average to above-average intellectual abilities.

The boundaries between AS, autism, attention deficit hyperactivity disorder (ADHD), and nonverbal learning disability (NVLD) are not always crystal-clear. As a result, controversies abound over whether AS is at the high end of a continuum of autism spectrum disorders or whether it is a qualitatively different disorder from autism. Many children and youth with AS have attention problems. In fact, many individuals identified as having AS are initially diagnosed with ADHD (Myles, Simpson, & Becker, 1994-95). It is often difficult to determine whether the attention problems involve more of a selective attention to or an over-focus on obsessive interests, sensory issues and internal thoughts rather than difficulty sustaining attention as seen in ADHD.

For example, it is difficult to know whether Martha is attending in class. Although she seems to be attentive and looking at her teacher, when she is called upon, her teacher often has to say her name numerous times. At these times, Martha answers with the name of a hurricane, a topic of special interest. Sometimes Martha reorients herself constantly, turning her head and body from side to side. When asked what she is doing, Martha may tell her teacher that she is listening to birds singing or the construction going on outside. Her teacher is often surprised because she was not aware of outside noises.

Thus, the attention problems in AS may be different than in ADHD, yet individuals with AS may also have ADHD-like attention problems.

Finally, most individuals with AS present with NVLD, while those with more classic autism typically do not. To date, it is unclear whether NVLD is a part of AS or if it is the same as AS. It is beyond the scope of this chapter to fully review the controversies involved in defining AS and its overlap with other disorders. The interested reader is directed to current summaries of the research on these issues (Klin, Volkmar, & Sparrow, 2000).

Although diagnosis does suggest a range of problems and possible interventions that may help an individual with AS, it is ultimately that individual's specific pattern of strengths and weaknesses that best determines which services will be helpful. Even though researchers and practitioners have recognized that the social component of AS can be pervasive (Attwood, 1998; Barnhill, Cook, Tebbenkamp, & Myles, 2002; Wing, 1981), little emphasis has been placed on assessing social skills and formalizing curricula that can meet the unique needs of children and youth with AS. This may be attributed to the lack of focus on social skills instruction by communities who have developed academic standards and outcomes and mandate that educators exclusively address reading, mathematics, written language, and other core school-related areas. The absence of social skills instruction may also be related to a lack of understanding of how complex social skills are and how devastating social challenges can be for children and adults. Social skills pervade play, group interactions, work, and working with another student on a school report. In short, effective social skills are required across almost all tasks and activities. In fact, whenever there is more than one person in a room, social skills are required (Bieber, 1994).

This chapter will briefly overview the social skills challenges faced by children and youth with AS, highlighting how deficiencies in this area can prevent an individual from reaching his full potential. Many of the social skills problems experienced by persons with AS are related to difficulty in deriving meaning from the environment (Twachtman-Cullen, 1998; Winner, 2002). Although considered pervasive by those who understand the syndrome well, the social skills deficits of some students with AS are not easily recognized by those less familiar with its characteristics. In fact, some of the behaviors exhibited by children and youth with AS can mislead teachers, mental health professionals and parents into thinking that the child's skills are much more developed than they actually are (Myles & Southwick, 1999). Thus, the pedantic or "little professor" speaking style, advanced vocabulary, grammatically perfect responses, and use of rote phrases in seemingly meaningful ways often mask skill deficits (Wing, 1981). Social areas impacted by AS include problems with (a) nonverbal interactions, (b) reciprocal interactions, (c) inferring others' mindsets, (d) problem solving, (e) abstract or inferential thinking, (f) stress, and (g) lack of understanding of self.

## Nonverbal Interactions

Nonverbal cues provide as much understanding of a conversation or social situation as do verbal cues. Posture, gestures, facial expression, voice tone, proximity, and eye contact are all subtle forms of communication that support or sometimes contradict a person's verbal statements. An inability to process these cues during a conversation means that the child with AS is not receiving the entire message. Further, even when students appear to understand nonverbal cues, that may not be the case after all (Barnhill et al., 2002). That is, while individuals with AS may be able to name a facial expression and define it in isolation, they are often unable to integrate all of the components of nonverbal language and interpret them in the context of a conversation (Koning & Magill-Evans, 2001). Even when children and adolescents with AS attempt to seek out others, they encounter social isolation because of their failure to understand the rules of social behavior, including eye contact, proximity to others, facial expressions, gestures, posture, and so forth (Myles & Simpson, 2001).

## Reciprocal Interactions

Asperger (1944) reported in his clinical writings that the social relationships of the children he studied were fraught with difficulties. Specifically, a hallmark characteristic of these children was their inability to build and maintain social relationships; that is, they had problems with reciprocal social interaction. The inability to interact with peers is marked by (a) lack of understanding of social cues, (b) a tendency to interpret words and/or phrases concretely, and (c) language comprehension problems. In addition, persons with AS often exhibit a clumsy social style, engage in one-sided social interactions, and have difficulty accurately sensing the feelings of others or taking others' perspective. These children fail to take turns, either monopolize or have little to no participation in conversation, show abnormalities in inflection, and repeat phrases inappropriately and out of context.

The social rules considered second nature by many, such as not standing too close to somebody else or staring at somebody, are not innately understood by many persons with AS. Perhaps the problems in two-way social interaction occur because the person with AS fails to understand and use the rules governing social behavior. Often, individuals with AS do not know how to initiate and/or maintain a conversation, monitor others' interest in what is being said, use polite verbal and nonverbal cues or understand such cues when given by others. Research has shown that children with AS use fewer cues when trying to determine the emotional state of peers they are interacting with (Koning & Magill-Evans, 2001). That is, children and youth with AS may only look at a person's mouth to interpret what is being said but not take into account gestures, voice tone, and the remainder of the communicator's facial expression.

# Inferring Others' Mindsets

Children and youth with AS have difficulty in understanding and appreciating the thoughts and feelings of others (Barnhill, 2001). This is often referred to as mind blindness or theory-of-mind deficits (Howlin, Baron-Cohen, & Hadwin, 1999). Individuals who experience theory-of-mind problems (a) have difficulty determining the intentions of others, (b) lack understanding of how their behavior impacts others, and (c) experience difficulty with reciprocity.

Not understanding the impact of one's behavior on others may be thought of as a cause-and-effect problem. For example, the adolescent with AS does not understand that saying something he thinks of as a fact can hurt somebody else. As a result, he may say to a peer, "Your acne is really gross" or comment to a teacher, "You are really fat," failing to understand when these comments cause social ostracism and reprimands. In his mind, a sharing of facts is nothing more than an observation that anyone would make. Similarly, the child with AS may not comprehend that others won't want to play with her if she only talks about the construction of woodwind instruments, because she doesn't understand that her peers find that topic boring.

The pervasive nature of theory-of-mind deficits in children and youth with AS is not clearly understood. Some researchers have suggested that individuals with AS may have different degrees of theory-of-mind deficits and may be able to complete theory-of-mind simulations, but not be able to apply those skills in real-life situations (Ozonoff, Pennington, & Rogers, 1991; Ozonoff, Rogers, & Pennington, 1991).

# Problem Solving

Children and youth with AS often have difficulty generating multiple solutions to a given situation. As a result, they may select one problem-solving strategy and use it consistently regardless of the outcome. In other words, success or lack of success in using a strategy often does not (a) reinforce strategy use if the strategy was effective; or (b) deter the student from using a strategy, even if ineffective.

It is often assumed that students with AS can learn problem-solving skills with relative ease because of their good rote memory skills. The truth is that most can learn to recite problem-solving steps quite easily, but there is often no relationship between a child's ability to recite a problem-solving sequence and her ability to implement that strategy.

Retrieval of social problem-solving steps once learned is another challenge for many children and youth with AS. Because the student with AS often has difficulty searching his memory for particular facts, he may not be able to access them. That is,

although he is able to recite several problem-solving
can be generalized, he may not be able to recall any of
the student cognitively realizes that a problem exists
or disoriented, and these emotions further cloud the
lem-solving skills.

Todd had learned how to initiate playing with
recite the rules for social initiation and follow them i
had the opportunity to use his skills on the playground
seem to remember how to ask another child to play
that he hit his would-be friend – not because he was
he was too upset to do anything else.

## Abstract or Inferential

Children and youth with AS often misinterpret social situations when required to make inferences or drawing conclusions that are not carefully spelled out. Specifically, they frequently experience difficulty in:

- comprehending language related to describing abstract concepts
- understanding and correctly using figures of speech such as metaphors, idioms, parables, and allegories
- making inferences
- grasping the meaning and intent of rhetorical questions (Church, Alisanki, & Amanullah, 2000).

Since these conventions are commonly used by teachers, parents, and others, deficits in this area have a negative impact on the social interactions of students with AS (Myles & Southwick, 1999).

Because of well-developed rote memory skills, it is often difficult to determine that a child with AS does not understand higher-level concepts. Typically, the person with AS picks up from conversation certain words or phrases and uses them in a rote manner that mimics high-level comprehension, whereas comprehension is often only at the factual level. Meghan is a 16-year-old with AS who participates in a social skills group. Just prior to the beginning of the social skills lesson, she commented to her peers, "I am very concerned about my social skills. I think they may negatively impact my opportunity for a productive life." Meghan sounded extremely insightful; however, she was merely repeating sentences she had heard her parents say. In reality, she thought her social skills were just fine. She made the statements about her social skills because she was in a social skills group.

## Stress

Many individuals with AS experience stress and anxiety on an almost constant basis (Kim, Szatmari, Bryson, Streiner, & Wilson, 2000; Myles & Southwick, 1999). Wanting to play with another child but not knowing how, not understanding whether the teacher is pleased or displeased with an assignment, trying to follow teacher directions but not grasping what is being said, hearing children laugh around them and not getting the joke – these are all stressful situations that children and youth with AS experience daily.

en with AS become stressed by things that neurotypical people con-
tant. For example, they may become stressed by something as simple as
others as invading their private space in the lunch line or when they find
es in the midst of several social activities going on at the same time.

nally, excitement often causes the same reaction as stress. Many children
me overly excited about an upcoming event or worry excessively about a trip to a
ew restaurant because they don't know what is on the menu, for example. Such
excitement may lead to a meltdown or withdrawal. While the first example concerns
something pleasant and the second is somewhat negative, they may both look the
same to the child with AS.

# Lack of Understanding of Self

In addition to not understanding others' mindsets, evidence suggests that children
and youth with AS do not understand their own emotions and actions. For example,
Barnhill and others (2000) found that the self-perceptions of adolescents with AS dif-
fered markedly from those of their parents and teachers. Specifically, parents reported
that their offspring experienced significant symptoms of anxiety, depression, withdrawal, attention problems, and behavior problems. Teachers reported seeing similar behavior but found them to be less severe than reported by the parents. These perceptions
were in sharp contrast to self-reports of the students themselves, however, who lacked
awareness of having any difficulties in the areas identified by their parents and teachers. Similar findings were reported by Koning and Magill-Evans (2001), who stated that
the adolescents with AS whom they studied " … were less aware of difficulties in other
[social] areas and, as a group, were still relatively positive about their general social
skills" (p. 33), contrary to their parents' and teachers' perceptions. Lack of understanding of self has implications for self-management, for example. That is, if students do not
recognize that they are experiencing stress, how will they know that they need to calm
themselves or excuse themselves from an anxiety-provoking situation?

Self-awareness also affects interactions with others (Faherty, 2000). As mentioned,
social turn-taking is a problem for individuals with AS. In conversation, therefore, they
may become totally engrossed in talking about a topic of special interest to them without any concern for their communication partner, or a child may make what seems to
be an angry comment about a typical day-to-day happening, totally unaware that his
voice is causing others to think he is upset.

Self-awareness means knowing what you do well and what you need help on.
Many parents deliberate over whether to tell their child he has AS or not. Sharing the
characteristics common to this diagnosis seems to be preferable as it may lead to better self-awareness, among other things. For example, the child can learn that she has
trouble understanding lengthy sentences and therefore needs to attend more closely or
ask that directions be written down. Communication of the words *Asperger Syndrome*
is not important; understanding of self is the goal.

Some young people with AS are relieved to know they have a disorder that has
certain related strengths as well as challenges. Often students left with no information
about their disorder make globally negative statements about themselves based on
their emerging sense of rejection from others. Knowing that there is a name for the
challenges they face can help children and youth with AS accept themselves while
maintaining positive self-esteem.

This topic can be approached by discussing individual strengths and weaknesses – identifying the things that they do better than others their age and the skills that need some improvement. It is also beneficial to review the lives of famous people who were successful despite or because of some of the challenges they faced (see Chapter 9 – Promoting Peer Acceptance Through Sensitivity Training and Incentive Programs).

# Summary

Social skills impact every part of our daily lives. We use social skills at home, at work, in the homes of our friends and co-workers, in the grocery store, and at the post office. Children use social skills in all of these environments plus at school, on play-dates, and in their neighborhoods. Social skills seem innate to many children – they just naturally make and keep friends, for example. But the same is not true for children and youth with AS. Although they want to have friends, they don't seem to know how to interact with others. Since social skills are an important ingredient in life success, we need to make sure that children with AS acquire these skills or learn social rules to compensate for what does not come naturally. This curriculum provides a very important step in helping children and youth gain these skills, compensate for what does not come naturally and, as a result, lead successful lives.

## CHAPTER 3

# Assessment for Social Skills Training

**M**y assessment goal is rarely to arrive at a diagnosis, which by itself tells me little. Instead, my assessment objectives are to: (a) determine what social skills the student needs to work on, (b) what strategy would be most effective for teaching the social skills, and (c) what therapy modality (e.g., individual or group therapy) would be best to teach the social skills. Essentially, there are two pieces of information that I want to distill from the assessment to make these decisions: receptive language ability and level of attentiveness. *Language ability* tells me which strategy to use and the child's *level of attentiveness* determines whether to teach the child one-on-one or in a group setting.

## Receptive Language Ability

*Receptive language* refers to the ability to comprehend language. Difficulty with language comprehension is often called a semantic language disorder and involves trouble understanding the meaning of words. Many individuals with AS do not have difficulty comprehending others, but have a pragmatic language problem. *Pragmatic language* refers to the social use of language as is involved in sustaining or initiating conversation. For example, individuals with AS may appear to have perfectly intact language based on their ability to express themselves and understand others, yet have great trouble with social conversation, talking at people instead of with people and relaying factual information or phrases memorized from TV shows without responding to what their listener is saying or doing.

Some individuals with AS do have a semantic language problem involving difficulty understanding the meaning of words, especially abstract words, metaphors, or sayings.

17

For example, they may hear the saying, "Don't let the cat out of the bag" and search for a cat and bag rather than grasp the symbolic meaning regarding not spoiling a surprise. Or they may not understand basic words like "up and down," "here or there," "big and small," "on top," and "below." Failure to comprehend what these words refer to means that children are not easily able to follow verbal instructions.

As part of an evaluation for special education supports in public schools, a psychologist may conduct an intellectual evaluation of a student yielding several IQ scores (a full-scale IQ, verbal IQ, and performance IQ). A verbal IQ score along with an interview with the child is often adequate for determining receptive language ability. Students with a verbal IQ in the average to above-average range and who can follow verbal directions can benefit from a conceptual approach, in which we use words to explain why and how to perform a skill. If a verbal IQ score is not available, an interview with the child can help determine if the child can follow verbal directions.

For example, if Joe is able to follow directions such as "Walk over to your mother, say hello, and shake her hands," we know he can follow simple verbal directions. We might then ask him to follow more abstract directions like, "Tell us what you ate for breakfast this morning." (This is abstract because breakfast is not right in front of him; he must remember or symbolize breakfast in his mind before he answers the question.) If he is able to respond, we know he can not only follow verbal instructions, but can imagine things that are not right in front of him. This will make it easier to use verbal concepts to teach him social skills, because verbal concepts refer to things that are not right in front of you but must be imagined in your mind. For example, when we ask someone to wait until people stop talking (a "pause") before interrupting, this is an abstract concept that cannot be easily seen. For those who understand what these words refer to, comprehending this skill through verbal instruction is possible.

If, on the other hand, we give verbal instructions to Joe and he repeats them back like an echo without knowing what to do or what we said, he will not easily be able to learn skills from verbal instructions. For example, telling him to wait for a pause before interrupting would be meaningless. He may instead benefit from an approach that relies on visual aids (e.g., pictures, videos and direct modeling of how to interrupt) and from methods that help him learn prerequisite language skills (e.g., learning to identify what the word "pause" means). Discrete trial methodology (see Chapter 4) may be used to help children build prerequisite language skills so that they can later respond to verbal instruction.

# Level of Attention

As mentioned in Chapter 2, many children with AS present with inattention, impulsivity, and hyperactivity consistent with an attention deficit/hyperactivity disorder. However, many students with AS do not have a true attention deficit/hyperactivity disorder in which they cannot sustain their attention. Rather, their "inattention" may be due to perseveration on an irrelevant aspect of a situation. For example, a student may be sitting in class obsessively reviewing every dinosaur he has learned about instead of listening to the teacher. He may appear to have an attention deficit, but in fact his ability to attend is not the issue. His problem is that he has thoughts that he cannot turn off, causing him to obsess over topics that are irrelevant to the context at hand.

As a result of their inattention, some students are not ready to maintain the necessary focus in a group. Instead they may benefit from individual therapy or from being paired off with one other child until they have developed the attending skills necessary to participate in a group. My rule of thumb regarding readiness for group participation relies heavily on the child's response to efforts to get redirected to task. That is, if the student can be redirected by verbal prompts or with the help of a token economy in which tokens are dispensed for returning to task, I will consider him ready for group.

For example, I might say to an adolescent who is not attending and not following instructions, "Eyes up here; here's what I want you to do . . ." If he still does not follow directions, I might say, "Eyes up here. You will get one of these pretend dollars when you listen, and when you get 10 of these dollars you can have that reward you said you wanted." If he returns to listening to me after these efforts, I will have faith that I can help that young man listen in a group as well. On the other hand, if during typical one-on-one situations, neither I nor the parent can redirect the child back to task through verbal means, gentle physical prompts (e.g., a tap on the shoulder), or a token system (e.g., pretend dollars that add up to buy a reward), I will not consider that child ready for group work.

## Grouping Members

In private practice, my groups are usually quite homogenous with respect to diagnostic issues because few "typically functioning" children are referred for social skills training. Most children I see have AS, a related pervasive developmental disorder, or ADHD with social skill difficulties.

What we miss in not having typical peers is more than made up for in the advantages of a homogenous group, however. I continue to be amazed at how quickly students with related disabilities accept each other. They have many common experiences of being teased or rejected, as well as share similar "obsessive" interests. For many it is the first time they have felt part of a peer group.

An important consideration is to keep the level of receptive language ability relatively consistent in the group. Otherwise, the required teaching strategies become too disparate, resulting in one member becoming frustrated if things are too complex, or another becoming bored when the strategy is too simplistic. I have found that grouping by ability is far more important than grouping by age. Thus I might have children up to two years apart in the same group, as long as their ability to comprehend language is similar. For example, if John is two years older than Mary, yet both can follow my verbal explanation of skills, they may benefit from being in the same group. However, if John does not understand my verbal instructions because he does not know what many of the words mean, but Mary does understand my instructions, they would not be a good match because they require different teaching strategies.

Almost all the group members are boys, which is not surprising given the much higher prevalence of AS in boys (Ehlers & Gillberg, 1993). Thus when I do have a girl with AS, she remains a minority. In adolescent groups where dating is a common concern, this becomes complicated as many of the boys may vie for that one girl's attention. Special care must be taken to teach group members about personal boundaries, on the one hand, and interpersonal assertiveness, on the other, to prevent potential conflicts.

# Determining What Skills to Target

Once a student has been identified by parents or teachers to receive social skills training, it is helpful to request that the student's parent(s) and teacher(s) fill out a Social Skills Menu (see menu pp. 23-25) to help determine what skills to teach that student. The menu lists 70 different skills related to language pragmatics (conversational skills), cooperative play, dealing with one's own feelings, dealing with others' feelings, dealing with conflicts and teasing, and friendship management (e.g., knowing when to "tell," getting attention in positive ways, or not acting as the "rule police").

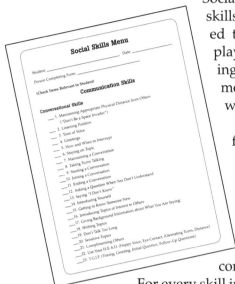

Typical problems identified for students with AS often fall into two categories: behavioral excesses and behavioral deficits. *Excess behaviors* include interrupting, perseverating on a topic despite the listener's obvious disinterest, off-topic comments, violating others' personal space, refusing to compromise, and imposing rules on others. *Behavioral deficits*, on the other hand, might include failing to greet or respond to others' questions, failure to initiate or maintain conversation or play with others, and ignoring others' feelings. For every skill in the menu, there is a corresponding handout that shows each step of the skill (see Chapter 8).

## Working with a student individually rather than in group

When parents and teachers have filled out the Social Skills Menu, I ask them to prioritize which 10-12 skills on the menu are most crucial to teach, and then I put together a curriculum of these skills to work on for a specified period of time; usually, 12 weeks. The following is a sample curriculum put together for a nine-year-old student named Jason. These skills were considered priorities by his parents:

1. Listening Position
2. Maintaining a Conversation
3. Starting a Conversation
4. Joining a Conversation
5. Sensitive Topics
6. Playing a Game
7. Asking Others to Play
8. Compromising
9. Keeping Calm
10. Dealing with Mistakes
11. Understanding Others' Feelings
12. Dealing with Teasing

The skills are laid out in a specific order because some are prerequisite for others. For example, "Listening Position" is a prerequisite for the student to listen and understand all other skills, and thus was selected first. Next come the conversational skills "Maintaining, Starting and Joining a Conversation," and "Sensitive Topics," so that we can lay down the foundations for talking with each other, as we will practice conversations in every session when we discuss how things went between sessions. For this student I chose to do play skills next because he was not initiating play with other students and this was a priority. Related to that, I typically prefer to do "Keeping Calm" before dealing with the other frustration skills (e.g., "Dealing with Mistakes" and "Dealing with Teasing") so that students learn a general means to stay calm before learning ways to deal with specific triggers to upset. In this way, they have a chance to keep calm when presented with triggers for which we have not yet prepared them. Finally, I chose to do "Showing Understanding for Others' Feelings" prior to "Dealing with Teasing," as having some understanding of others' feelings may help in not taking teasing personally or retaliating with hurtful statements to others.

For many students we can cover one new skill per week for a 12-week program depending on the student's ability to understand and generalize the skills. When we move on to new skills, we still continue to practice the old skills to maintain and further refine them. While this timeframe is pretty typical, with children with receptive language difficulties, we may work on the same skill for at least a three-week period before moving on to another. In these cases, 10-12 skills may be taught over an entire school-year curriculum.

## Working with a small group of children

When a small number of students are going to be grouped together to work on social skills (e.g., 4-7 students), we ask that a Social Skills Menu be filled out for each child by the child's parent and teacher, if possible. In reality, we may not be able to get a Social Skills Menu from each child's teacher depending on the teachers' schedules. However, we will at least have one menu for each child. I then put together an initial curriculum for the group, made up of the 10-12 skills that were most frequently checked across the Social Skills Menus of the group members. We may cover about one new skill per week for a 12-week program depending on the students' ability to understand and generalize the skills. As mentioned earlier, with groups of children with receptive language difficulties, we may work on the same skill for at least a three-week period before moving on to another one.

## Working with a whole class

If a whole class is targeted to receive training, the classroom teacher can fill out one Social Skills Menu for the entire class rather than for each student, indicating the skills she feels the whole class needs to learn. I ask the teacher to prioritize which 10-12 skills are most crucial to teach, and then put together a curriculum of these skills to work on for a specified period of time. Again, for many classes we can cover about one skill per week for a 12-week program. However, with groups of children with receptive language difficulties, we may work on the same skill for a three-week period such that 10-12 skills may be taught over an entire school-year curriculum.

Once a curriculum has been established for an individual, a small group or an entire class, it is helpful to rate students on the skills before and after social skills training has taken place in order to track progress. Parents and teachers can be asked to rate the students on just those 10-12 skills before training and again after every 12 weeks of

**Sample Skill Rating Form**

School: Lincoln

Teacher: Mrs. Smith                         Date: 2-24-02 (pretraining)

Directions: Based on your observations in various situations, rate each child's use of the following skills according to the following scale:

1 = the child **almost never** uses the skill
2 = the child **seldom** uses the skill                4 = the child **often** uses the skill
3 = the child **sometimes** uses the skill             5 = the child **almost always** uses the skill

| Skills | Names | | | | |
|---|---|---|---|---|---|
| | John | Gary | Sam | Lisa | Carla |
| 1. Listening Position | | | | | |
| 2. Maintaining a Conversation | 2 | 5 | 1 | 5 | |
| 3. Starting a Conversation | 2 | 2 | | 5 | 2 |
| 4. Joining a Conversation | 5 | 2 | 2 | 2 | 2 |
| 5. Sensitive Topics | 1 | | 1 | 2 | 2 |
| 6. Playing a Game | 4 | 4 | 1 | 2 | 2 |
| 7. Asking Others to Play | 5 | 2 | 2 | 4 | 4 |
| 8. Compromising | 5 | 5 | 2 | 5 | 5 |
| 9. Keeping Calm | 5 | 5 | 2 | 5 | 5 |
| 10. Dealing with Mistakes | 5 | 5 | 1 | 4 | 5 |
| 11. Understanding Others' Feelings | 5 | 5 | 2 | 5 | |
| 12. Dealing with Teasing | 2 | 2 | 4 | 5 | 2 |
| | | | 1 | 2 | 2 |

training to assess progress (see Sample Skill Rating Form on p. 26). This can help determine which skills to repeat in another 12-week cycle. In reality, it may be difficult for a general education teacher of 20 plus students to rate each student in the class. Instead, the teacher may choose to rate certain students who she knows are in need of social skills training and whose parents have requested that progress be tracked. In a small group or in individual therapy, each student can be rated by the parent and teacher every 12 weeks to track progress. A blank Skill Rating Form is provided on page 27 for your use in rating students before and after each 12-week period.

# Social Skills Menu

Student: _____ Date: _____

Person Completing Form: _____

**(Check Items Relevant to Student)**

## Communication Skills

### Conversational Skills

____ 1. Maintaining Appropriate Physical Distance from Others ("Don't Be a Space Invader")

____ 2. Listening Position

____ 3. Tone of Voice

____ 4. Greetings

____ 5. How and When to Interrupt

____ 6. Staying on Topic

____ 7. Maintaining a Conversation

____ 8. Taking Turns Talking

____ 9. Starting a Conversation

____ 10. Joining a Conversation

____ 11. Ending a Conversation

____ 12. Asking a Question When You Don't Understand

____ 13. Saying "I Don't Know"

____ 14. Introducing Yourself

____ 15. Getting to Know Someone New

____ 16. Introducing Topics of Interest to Others

____ 17. Giving Background Information about What You Are Saying

____ 18. Shifting Topics

____ 19. Don't Talk Too Long

____ 20. Sensitive Topics

____ 21. Complimenting Others

____ 22. Use Your H.E.A.D. (Happy Voice, Eye Contact, Alternating Turns, Distance)

____ 23. T.G.I.F. (Timing, Greeting, Initial Question, Follow-Up Questions)

## Cooperative Play Skills

___24. Asking Someone to Play

___25. Joining Others in Play

___26. Compromising

___27. Sharing

___28. Taking Turns

___29. Playing a Game

___30. Dealing with Losing

___31. Dealing with Winning

___32. Ending a Play Activity

## Friendship Management

___33. Informal Versus Formal Behavior

___34. Respecting Personal Boundaries

___35. Facts Versus Opinions (Respecting Others' Opinions)

___36. Sharing a Friend

___37. Getting Attention in Positive Ways

___38. Don't Be the "Rule Police"

___39. Offering Help

___40. When to Tell on Someone

___41. Modesty

___42. Asking Someone Out on a Date

___43. Appropriate Touch

___44. Dealing with Peer Pressure

___45. Dealing with Rumors

___46. Calling a Friend on the Telephone

___47. Answering the Telephone

# Emotion Management Skills

## Self-Regulation

____48. Recognizing Feelings

____49. Feelings Thermometer

____50. Keeping Calm

____51. Problem Solving

____52. Talking to Others When Upset

____53. Dealing with Family Problems

____54. Understanding Anger

____55. Dealing with Making a Mistake

____56. Trying When Work Is Hard

____57. Trying Something New

## Empathy

____58. Showing Understanding for Others' Feelings: Preschool-Elementary

____59. Showing Understanding for Others' Feelings: Preadolescent-Adulthood

____60. Cheering up a Friend

## Conflict Management

____61. Asserting Yourself

____62. Accepting No for an Answer

____63. Dealing with Teasing – K-4th Grade

____64. Dealing with Teasing – 5th Grade and Up

____65. More Words to Deal with Teasing

____66. Dealing with Being Left Out

____67. Avoiding Being "Set Up"

____68. Giving Criticism in a Positive Way

____69. Accepting Criticism

____70. Having a Respectful Attitude

# Sample Skill Rating Form

School: <u>Lincoln</u>                                    Date: <u>2-24-02 (pretraining)</u>

Teacher: <u>Mrs. Smith</u>

Directions: Based on your observations in various situations, rate each child's use of the following skills according to the following scale:

1 = the child **almost never** uses the skill          4 = the child **often** uses the skill
2 = the child **seldom** uses the skill               5 = the child **almost always** uses the skill
3 = the child **sometimes** uses the skill

| Skills | Names | | | | |
|---|---|---|---|---|---|
| | John | Gary | Sam | Lisa | Carla |
| 1. Listening Position | 2 | 3 | 1 | 3 | 2 |
| 2. Maintaining a Conversation | 2 | 2 | 2 | 2 | 2 |
| 3. Starting a Conversation | 3 | 3 | 2 | 2 | 2 |
| 4. Joining a Conversation | 1 | 1 | 1 | 2 | 2 |
| 5. Sensitive Topics | 4 | 4 | 2 | 4 | 4 |
| 6. Playing a Game | 3 | 2 | 2 | 3 | 3 |
| 7. Asking Others to Play | 3 | 3 | 3 | 3 | 3 |
| 8. Compromising | 3 | 3 | 2 | 3 | 2 |
| 9. Keeping Calm | 3 | 3 | 1 | 4 | 3 |
| 10. Dealing with Mistakes | 3 | 3 | 1 | 3 | 2 |
| 11. Understanding Others' Feelings | 3 | 3 | 4 | 3 | 3 |
| 12. Dealing with Teasing | 2 | 2 | 1 | 2 | 2 |

# Skill Rating Form

School: _____ Date: _____

Teacher: _____

Directions: Based on your observations in various situations, rate each child's use of the following skills according to the following scale:

1 = the child **almost never** uses the skill     4 = the child **often** uses the skill
2 = the child **seldom** uses the skill         5 = the child **almost always** uses the skill
3 = the child **sometimes** uses the skill

| Skills | Names | | | | |
|--------|---|---|---|---|---|
| 1. | | | | | |
| 2. | | | | | |
| 3. | | | | | |
| 4. | | | | | |
| 5. | | | | | |
| 6. | | | | | |
| 7. | | | | | |
| 8. | | | | | |
| 9. | | | | | |
| 10. | | | | | |
| 11. | | | | | |
| 12. | | | | | |

## CHAPTER 4

# Strategies for
# Teaching Social Skills

**M**ost children younger than eight years old and those whose verbal IQ is well below average benefit more from teaching strategies that rely on pictures, physical prompts, and direct modeling than strategies that rely primarily on verbal explanation. For older children, and those with good receptive language ability, social skills training strategies can include explanations of why to act in certain ways along with the more concrete strategies that rely on pictures, physical prompts, and direct modeling.

For example, certain students benefit from using the concept of time (past, present, and future) to help them remember good conversation starters like, "How was your week?" (*past*), "What are you playing?" (*present*), and "What are you going to do this weekend?" (*future*). They may be able to think of several conversation starters simply by remembering to ask questions about the past, present or future. For other students, the concept of asking about the past, present and future would not be understood. Instead, those students need a more concrete strategy like memorizing specific sentences to start a conversation.

The following describes an array of social skill training strategies – from the more concrete to the most conceptual.

## Discrete Trial

Most children with AS have good receptive language ability and would not generally need as structured an approach as discrete trial methodology. However, discrete trials are extremely helpful for children with limited receptive language ability by helping them learn basic words so that they can later respond to verbal instructions and questions. The discrete trial method can also help students attend to a task when they do not respond to verbal instructions to pay attention. Among other things, discrete trial can be used to help students maintain eye contact, and to identify objects, actions, or adjectives. For example, consider Amy who does not understand how to respond to instructions like "walk over to the big ball and give it to your teacher." She might go through a series of discrete trials to learn the meaning of words like "big," "ball," "teacher," and "walk." Then she will better understand instructions that contain these words.

A full description of discrete trial training is beyond the scope of this book. Instead, I will offer a brief overview.

A discrete trial consists of at least four components: a cue, prompt, behavior, and reinforcement. As an example, consider teaching Amy the word "big." A *cue* might be the words "touch the big ball" (presenting Amy with a picture of several small and one big ball). The *prompt* might be to physically move Amy's finger to the big ball. Her *behavior* would be to touch the picture of the big ball or the smaller one. Finally, the *reinforcement* would come as praise and perhaps a material reward whenever she accurately chooses the big ball. One might do many trials working with different items (balls, toys, pencils) with one big object mixed in with smaller ones until she always accurately picks the big item indicating her understanding of the concept of big.

Discrete trial is highly structured and relies heavily on the trainer cueing the child. As such it does not typically foster spontaneous social interaction, but it can be crucial in building prerequisite language and attention in preparation for other kinds of training that may facilitate greater social interaction.

# Incidental Teaching

The term "incidental" refers to teaching a student about a social situation as it is occurring rather than in a structured lesson. The goal is to amplify the social environment as it is unfolding so the student picks up on social cues, rules, others' feelings and perceptions that are all part of the social situation. This can be accomplished by explaining to a child what is happening in a social situation through words or visual aids, and by coaching and praising the child's behavior.

For example, during recess, a teacher points out to her student with AS, Larry, that someone looks physically hurt. She coaches Larry to stop playing and ask the other student if he is okay. She is amplifying an important social cue (*someone else is hurt*) so that Larry does not continue to play, oblivious to others' feelings. Similarly, another student with AS, Andy, gets upset when people bump into him in the hallway. When he gets bumped, his aide explains how and why the bump was accidental so that Andy will not get as angry. The aide points out a hidden social cue (i.e., the other person's intentions) to help Andy respond more appropriately.

This incidental lesson is quite conceptual as it relies on abstract information (i.e., others' intentions). Incidental teaching can also be made very concrete, depending on the child's needs. For example, to help a child understand when it is her turn in a game, a visual aid (e.g., using a turn card to denote whose turn it is) or physical prompts (e.g., tapping the child's shoulder) may be used when it is her turn. Another example of a visual aid to amplify the social environment is the use of red and green cards to indicate when it is and is not okay to talk in class. Red cards are placed on the child's desk to indicate that it is not okay to talk during a particular activity. When it is time to talk, the card is turned over to reveal the green side. Such visual supports can be very helpful to children and adults with AS, who do not always know when and where it is and is not okay to talk

Incidental teaching represents the basis for facilitating groups during unstructured conversation and playtime (see Chapter 5). For example, during conversations, the group leader may point out that a group member looks sad or upset and coach the others to ask if the student is okay. Or if a boy is talking nonstop about his obsession with light fixtures during conversation time and his peers are starting to get restless, the group leader might say, "Juan, look how the other children are yawning and squirming in their seats. What do you think they are feeling? Why? Can you ask them if they want to hear more?" In followup to this incidental lesson, the leader might later do a formal class lesson on "Talking Briefly So Others Will Listen."

During both conversation and playtimes the group leader uses incidental teaching methods by acting like a coach: prompting and rewarding behaviors as they occur. During playtime, the leader may prompt and praise the students for compromising, sharing, taking turns, deciding who will go first, and dealing with mistakes and losing. For example, if Joe and Sam are arguing about what game to play, the leader might say, "You guys obviously want to play different games, how can you solve this problem?" If the boys do not respond, the leader can go on to say, "Can you compromise?" The leader can again give the students time to create a compromise. If one is not forthcoming, the leader may suggest a way to compromise. Once the students have begun to compromise, the leader can comment, "I really like the way Sam and Joe are compromising." If they are not compromising, the leader can say, "How does it feel when you cannot decide what to do? Sam, how does Joe feel if you refuse to play what he wants? Joe, how does Sam feel if you refuse to play what he wants? How can you help each other feel better?" All these comments serve to highlight what is happening and how people are feeling in the unfolding play situation. If Sam and Joe cannot work out their conflict through incidental teaching methods (i.e., prompts to compromise and comments that highlight their feelings), the group leader may have to impose a compromise for the moment, and then at the next session provide a formal lesson on compromising.

Incidental teaching must always be part of social skills training because it involves teaching children in the real situations where they need the skills. However, incidental teaching is often not enough. When coaching a child in the moment does not help her understand the situation or alter her behavior, it is time to teach her in a more structured way to prepare her to deal with the social situation before it arises again. More structured, formal training lessons may include all of the methods described in the following sections (i.e., Social Skill Pictures, Cognitive Picture Rehearsal, Social Stories, and structured learning).

## Social Skill Picture Stories

Social Skill Picture Stories are mini-books that depict, step by step, children demonstrating various social skills (Baker, 2003). Each skill is presented like a cartoon strip, composed of digital pictures of actual children combined with text and cartoon bubbles to denote what the children are saying – and sometimes thinking – as they engage in the skills. Included is the correct (and sometimes the incorrect) way to act with accompanying text that explains what the children are doing.

Each skill is accompanied by several pages of pictures to illustrate each skill step. When using the Social Skill Picture Stories, the instructor can go through each page of a particular skill numerous times and then return to the first page and ask the student to relate what is happening in each picture. The instructor might ask questions such as, "What is happening here? What is the first step? How is he feeling? What is he saying? What happens next?" Students who cannot describe what is happening can be asked to show each step (e.g., "Show me the picture where they make eye contact. Now show me where they wait for a pause. Is this the right way or wrong way to say excuse me?").

Children can actively participate in the creation of Social Skill Pictures by posing for pictures and assembling the books on paper or a computer. The benefits are doubled for students who help to create their skill pictures. That is, they have the opportunity to role-play the skills during the picture taking and have their attention drawn to a permanent, highly appealing record of themselves engaged in the skill. In making your own Social Skill Pictures, four areas are considered:

- what skill to target
- how to break up the skill into simpler steps (also known as "task-analyzing" a skill)
- what perceptions, thoughts, or feelings you want to include in the cartoon bubbles to highlight for the student
- how to put the book together

Social Skill Picture sets can be created in several ways. Once a skill has been targeted and the accompanying perceptions and verbalizations have been thought through, map out the skill steps and what pictures will be needed. As often as possible, use the student as the model for the photographs. Pose students for the pictures while going through each skill step, first modeling what to do for each step. Do not worry if the student does not understand the skill fully at first, as learning will be reinforced after the picture set is created. Pictures can be taken with a digital camera and then imported into a Microsoft Power Point presentation or a variety of photograph software or desk-top publishing/ layout programs where the bubbles and text can be added. Alternatively, pictures can be taken with a nondigital camera and pasted to paper. Bubbles and text can then be handwritten or typed onto colored paper and pasted onto the pictures. Be consistent in using one color for bubbles that express verbalizations and another color for thought/perception bubbles, so as not to confuse the student. In addition to posing for the pictures, students can also participate in the cutting, pasting and assembling of the skills. With some students, the exercise of sequencing the skill in the correct order can be made into a game to further enhance the understanding of the individual steps.

Using Social Skill Picture Stories results in less reliance on verbal instruction and instructor modeling as is involved in some of the other methods described below.

## Cognitive Picture Rehearsal

This strategy utilizes cartoon-like drawings on index cards combined with positive reinforcement principles (Groden & Lavasseur, 1995). Cognitive Picture Rehearsal always includes drawings or pictures of three components: the antecedents to a problem situation, the targeted desired behavior, and a positive reinforcer. The pictures are displayed on index cards. On the top of each card (or on the back of the card) is a script describing the desired sequence of events. Children are shown the sequence of cards until they can repeat what is happening in each picture, and the sequence is reviewed just before the child enters the potentially problematic situation.

# Example of a
# Cognitive Picture Rehearsal

Unlike Social Skill Picture books, which were designed to model general social skills, Cognitive Picture Rehearsal is used for a specific problem situation. For example, the sample Cognitive Picture Rehearsal above was created for Matt, a seven-year-old who was having a specific problem getting off the computer. When his teacher told him it was time to leave the computer, Matt would tantrum and refuse to get off.

Cards 1 and 2 illustrate the *antecedent* to the problem situation: Matt is playing at the computer and then the teacher tells him it is time to get off the computer. Cards 3 and 4 show Matt engaged in the desired *target behavior*. The first desired behavior (Card 3) involves Matt thinking that the teacher will be happy if he gets off the computer and give him a chance to use the computer later. We want Matt to learn that he will get some of what he wants if he gets off the computer. The second desired behavior (Card 4) shows Matt being compliant and saying, "Okay, I'll get off the computer." Cards 5 and 6 show the *positive rewards* of engaging in the desired behavior. Card 5 shows Matt receiving a point on a reward chart for complying with the teacher's request to get off the computer. Matt happened to be on a reward chart for compliance in his classroom, so we incorporated this in these illustrations. Card 6 shows the teacher letting Matt use the computer again later that day because he had cooperated earlier when asked to get off the computer.

Matt's teacher would read the cards to him several times a day until Matt could explain what was happening in each picture. Matt's mother also read the cards to him as a bedtime story to reinforce the learning at home. Most important, the cards were read to Matt just prior to him getting on the computer in school and at home. Within two days of implementing this procedure, Matt no longer tantrumed or refused to get off the computer when asked to do so.

## Social Stories

Developed by Carol Gray and colleagues (Gray et al., 1993), this strategy uses stories written in the first person to increase students' understanding of problematic situations. Beginning with the child's understanding of a situation, a story is developed describing what is happening and why, and how people feel and think in the situation. While the story contains some directive statements (i.e., what to do in the situation), the focus is on understanding what is happening.

I often use this strategy with students with AS who believe they are being teased in a situation where they are not actually being teased. Peter was a 13-year-old who frequently got into fights at lunchtime because he believed that other students in the cafeteria were teasing him. He said that several other boys who sat on the other side of the cafeteria always laughed at him. He would give them "the finger" and then they would start a fight with him. When Peter was observed at lunch, it was apparent that the other boys were laughing, but not at him. They were at least 50 feet from Peter, not looking him, and laughing with each other, presumably about some joke or discussion they were having.

We developed the following Social Story for Peter starting with his perspective that others might be laughing at him:

*"When I am in the cafeteria I often see other boys laughing and I think they are laughing at me. Lots of students laugh during lunchtime because they are talking about funny things they did during the day, or funny stories they heard or saw on TV, movies or books they read. Sometimes students laugh at other students to make fun of them. If they are making fun of other students, they usually use the student's*

*name, or look and point at that student. If the other students are laughing, but they do not look or point at me, then they are probably not laughing at me. Most students do not get mad when others are laughing, as long as they are not laughing at them. If they do laugh at me, I can go tell a teacher rather than give them the finger."*

This Social Story contained only one directive statement (i.e., a statement that directs a student to do something). It says to tell a teacher rather than give "the finger" if someone is teasing you. Most of the story simply highlights the social cues involved in understanding when and if someone is teasing you (i.e., they look or point at you). The goal is to increase Peter's ability to read the situation rather than just tell him what to do.

Like Cognitive Picture Rehearsal, Social Stories are read repeatedly to children until they have overlearned them, and are then read again just prior to the problematic situation. For example, Peter was read the story several times a day until he had memorized it. Just prior to going to lunch his aide would review the story with him. After a week, Peter no longer needed to review the story and was able to continue to avoid misinterpreting when others laughed at lunch.

# Structured Learning

This approach forms the core teaching model for the skills lessons used in my groups and classes, as reflected in Chapter 8. The term "structured learning" refers to the strategies of Goldstein and colleagues in their "Skillstreaming" series (McGinnis & Goldstein, 1997). The Skillstreaming series is an excellent resource for social skills training that articulates skill steps for numerous skills, yet it does not contain many of the pragmatic language skills that I believe are crucial for youngsters with AS. In addition, the current Skillstreaming curricula do not always spell out specifically enough the steps or scripts that might be useful for individuals with AS. I have adopted their structured learning model for teaching, but have written skill steps more suited to individuals with AS.

Structured learning consists of four teaching components:

- didactic instruction (explanation of the skill steps)
- modeling of skill steps
- role-playing skills with feedback
- practice in and outside the group

## Didactic instruction

Didactic instruction involves the instructor (teacher, aide, or parent) explaining the steps of a particular skill, often with the skill steps written on a poster or black board as a visual aid. The key to this approach, or any other approach that relies partially on verbal and written instruction, is to engage the child's attention. Explanation of a skill is inherently "dry" and needs to be spiced up with game formats and lively presentations. For example, many of the children I have worked with are game show fans (undoubtedly because they excel in memorizing factual information). Thus discussing and reviewing the steps in the form of shows like "Jeopardy," "Wheel of Fortune," or "Who Wants to Be a Millionaire?" is usually well received. When explaining the skill steps, I might say, "Listen carefully to these skill steps because afterward we will play a game to see how well you remember them, and if you get enough questions right I will give you a prize."

I find "Who Wants to Be a Millionaire?" to be the easiest game show format to use as you can ask the questions in a straightforward manner. To play this game, I pretend to be the host and invite members to sit across from me to answer one question at a time. We ask, "Where are you from? Who did you bring with you to the show today?" Then we say, "Are you ready to go for a million dollars?" (as they would in the show). Unlike the real game show where only one contestant answers a series of questions until he or she reaches the million dollar question, I have members of a group or a class take turns answering questions, and collectively they can reach the million dollar question. Also, as a group they share the following three lifelines (i.e., three opportunities to receive help with a question): (a) let the audience vote on which answer is correct, (b) ask one person in the room for the answer, or (c) fifty/fifty – where two of four multiple-choice response are removed, leaving just two from which to choose. Starting at $2000, I ask the first student a question about the skill lesson we just had. Then taking turns with all the students, we work through the $4000, $8000, $16,000, $32,000, $64,000, $125,000, $250,000, $500,000, and then the $1,000,000 question. As in the show, after each contestant responds, I ask, "Are you confident? Final answer? You're right."

I tell them that if they get to $30,000, they all get a snack, and if they get to a million dollars, they all get a prize. Although I encourage the use of lifelines, I always make sure the students are able to get to a million dollars. I will give hints so that they will not fail, but still have to think about the answer. The goal of course is just that – to keep them thinking about the skill.

Sometimes it is helpful to write the "game show" questions down ahead of time (e.g., see activity sheet for "Sensitive Topics," p. 116, or for "Starting a Conversation," p. 94), but much of the time you can easily improvise the questions by using the skill lesson sheets (see Chapter 8) as your guide. Each step on a skill lesson sheet can be turned into a question. Often each step has several parts that can also converted into questions. It is easier to create questions without providing four multiple-choice responses, thus requiring students to recall the answer rather than recognize the answer from several choices. For example, if discussing the skill "Complimenting Others" (see p. 118), one can ask a question about Step 1: "Why is it important to compliment others?" A second question could be, "Tell another reason why it is important to compliment others." Step 2 can be another set of questions regarding what to compliment others about: "What kinds of things can you compliment others about? Name another thing you can compliment someone about." Step 3 can yield another set of questions, like, "What is a nice tone of voice? Why is it important to use a nice tone when complimenting others? What would be a nice tone of voice to use when complimenting others about their looks? What would not be a nice tone of voice to use when complimenting others about their looks?"

## Modeling the skill steps

Once the skill steps have been explained, it is important to model them for the students before asking them to carry them out. To do this, the facilitator needs (a) a situation to act out and (b) co-actors. Students or teachers can serve as co-actors to help model the skills. Ideas for what situations to act out are provided for most skill lessons in Chapter 8.

Before the skill is modeled, it is important to give the students who are observing very specific instructions on what to look for to maintain their attention. One can say, "Watch what we do and at the end tell us if we did Step 1, which is . . ., and Step 2, which is . . ., and Step 3, which is . . . Give us a 'thumbs up' if we did it right or a 'thumbs down' if we did it incorrectly." Giving the observers a physical action to do such as making a thumbs up or down gesture often helps to keep their attention on the skills. After modeling the skill, ask the observers whether each step was performed, "Did we do Step 1, which is . . .? Thumbs up or down? Did we do Step 2, which is . . .? Thumbs up or down? Did we do Step 3, which is . . .? Thumbs up or down?"

We can model several more times to help students understand the nuances of the skill. Each time we will ask observers to notice whether each step was performed correctly and to provide a "thumbs up or down." Each demonstration can involve doing one step incorrectly in order to highlight the importance of each step. For example, in modeling "How and When to Interrupt" (see p. 86), one can say, "Excuse me" correctly, but forget to wait for a pause. Then one can ask the observers about how each step was performed, highlighting the step that was modeled incorrectly and why it is important to perform correctly.

Depending on the personality and nature of the individual student, the instructor may choose not to explain or show the wrong way to enact a skill step and instead just focus on the right way to engage in the skill. The potential disadvantage of reviewing the wrong way is that some students are so entertained by inappropriate behavior that they may continually perform the skill the wrong way for their own or others' amusement. On the other hand, the advantage of demonstrating the wrong way is twofold: (a) certain skills will be much better understood when both the right and wrong way are shown, and (b) students who are reluctant to role-play may be more likely to try if they can role-play the wrong way first because then they do not have to fear making a mistake. The bottom line is "know your student." Youngsters who show a lot of "silly" attention-seeking behaviors may not be good candidates for having the opportunity to observe or role-play a skill the wrong way.

## Role-playing the skill

During role-plays, the student is asked to act out the skill steps in the right order. Role-playing is often more effective when done with two instructors or one instructor and two students. This way, the instructor can avoid participating in the role-play directly and act as a coach to help the students through the skill steps. Just as described in the modeling situation, the observers of the role-play should be given instructions to see if each step is done correctly or not. If children are reluctant to role-play for fear of making a mistake, we can ask them to do something the wrong way and then guess what it was. This will relieve some anxiety about performing in front of others.

Ideas for role-plays are provided on the activity sheets that accompany most skill lessons in Chapter 8.

## Reviewing the skill/providing corrective feedback

After each role-play, the instructor provides feedback about how each step was enacted. Feedback should always begin by noting what was performed correctly and include ample praise. Observing students are asked to tell what the role-playing student did well. Avoid telling students directly that they performed a skill or step incorrectly. Instead, give corrective feedback, saying something like, "In this step, here is what I want you to do to perform the step even better." Observers can also be asked to tell what they would do to make the role-play "even better" rather than saying what was done poorly. If needed, model the correct way to perform the skill. Corrective feedback and practice should continue until the student is able to demonstrate the step correctly.

The process of teaching a particular skill – reviewing the steps, role-playing the skill, and providing corrective feedback – should be repeated over and over until the student is able to demonstrate the skill without prompting. At this point we can begin to promote generalization of the skill by assigning practice assignments.

## Practicing the skills

Ideally, before the students leave the session, we want them to decide with whom and when they will practice the skill sheets. Modeled after the Skillstreaming curriculum, there is a practice area at the bottom of each skill lesson sheet in which the student can indicate with whom he or she will practice and when. One can tell students that if they return the assignment sheet and indicate how they practiced the skill, they can receive a bonus prize at the next session/lesson. Chapter 7 provides more details on how to encourage practice and promote skill generalization.

# CHAPTER 5

# Where to Provide Skills Training: The Classroom, Small Groups, or Play-Dates

**S**kills training can take place in a large classroom, in a small group in or out of school, or before and during a play-date. In all settings the pattern is to allow time for a formal lesson, followed by less structured times to practice the skills in a more spontaneous fashion. In the classroom, the formal skill lesson may be conducted early in the week and the less structured practice times spread out during the rest of the week through specific conversation and play activities organized by the classroom teacher. For example, the teacher may use a daily "show and tell" or "morning meetings" to work on conversation skills like staying on topic and starting a conversation.

In the small group both structured and spontaneous activities occur within an hour-long session. Typically a 20-minute skill lesson is imbedded into the group along with less structured activities.

Finally for play-dates, formal skill lessons are conducted and reviewed just prior to the play-date, and then parents coach their children during the more spontaneous interactions of the actual play-date.

There are advantages and disadvantages to each of the three settings. The advantage of the classroom setting is that it leads to better skill generalization. Because the skills training is completed in front of the teachers and typical peers, it is easier for the skills to become part of the classroom expectations and routines. With a small group, more effort must be made to help the skills generalize to

**Schedule**

1. Talk Time

2. Skill Time

3. Game Time

4. Snack

the child's life outside the group because his teacher and peers do not automatically know or use the same skills. For example, if Sam learns ways to start conversations in a small group outside of school, there may be no one in school to remind him how to do this unless the group instructor has specifically communicated to his teacher or aide ways to prompt Sam to initiate conversations in school.

In terms of disadvantages, a large class is typically not conducive to building close friendships. Besides, the skills to be taught may not be relevant to all the students in the class. This is particularly the case in middle and high school, where students with AS and related disorders often have greater needs for conversation skills than their typical peers. In the younger grades, on the other hand, all the students may be able to benefit from similar skills because, in terms of their developmental level, they all need help with conversation, play, and emotion management. Another practical problem in middle and high school is that the students routinely switch from class to class, making scheduling of a large skills training class difficult. By comparison, the small-group setting is ideal for developing close friendships among the members and allows the facilitator to group students with similar skill training needs. Thus for the middle school and high school students, the small group setting is preferable.

Play-dates are perhaps the most ideal setting for developing the closest friendships. It is in the context of one-on-one play that children typically develop their "best friends." Parents can try to encourage and arrange play-dates for their children throughout their childhood into their teenage years. Much of the time, this occurs through parents meeting other amenable parents and arranging for their families to get together, thus bringing the children together. One means to find other families is through local support groups of parents whose children have AS, other autism spectrum disorders, and/or learning disabilities. Also, parents who have children participating in after-school social skill groups often get to know each other while waiting for the children to finish their session. The instructor for the children's group can encourage the parents to arrange play-dates outside of the group meetings to continue the children's socialization.

In the following, we will look at both the common elements and unique features of the most common settings for social skills training – small groups, classrooms, and play-dates.

# SMALL-GROUP SETTING

The small group can take place in or out of school. The groups can meet at lunchtime, during a special education support class, or after school depending on staff availability. In one school, I modeled the after-school groups for a graduate student intern and school psychologist who later took over the group. We had several groups running for different ages and receptive language ability. Groups met once per week all year long with meetings every 12 weeks with parents to review progress. In most cases we were able to get the school district to provide transportation to the program, which took place in one of the schools (the students were coming from several different schools in the district). Parents picked up their children from the groups, which gave us an opportunity to tell them what we worked on, review any skill assignments, and let them get to know each other to arrange play-dates. After-school groups are often ideal in that they allow students from several schools to come together at a time when most other children are socializing with their friends.

Materials needed for the small group include a board to write on, copies of the skill handouts (see Chapter 8), a token system (e.g., play money), snack items, and three posters. One poster lists the rules so they are visible during all sessions. Another poster is a visual cue for maintaining conversations (see "Keeping the Conversation Going" at the end of this chapter). The final poster lists the schedule of activities for the group.

# The First Session

The first session generally entails four components:

- review of the purpose of the group
- establishment of group rules and consequences
- getting to know each other through discussion of interests
- game or snack time

The following contains sample transcripts from a first session with a group of seven-year-olds with AS named Sam, Joe, Jenna, and Tommy.

## Review of the purpose of the group

Here we open the group and remind everyone why we are meeting. We need to establish motivation to learn new skills. For some children the motivation is not to make friends, but to gain some material reward. We must then link learning the skills as a means to getting what you want, as we did for Sam in the following transcript. (The group leader bases his comments on information gathered from an initial intake session where he met with the student and explained the group.)

Group Leader: "Welcome to the group, ladies and gentlemen. Let me introduce you to each other. This is Joe, Sam, Jenna, Tommy, and you know me, my name is Dr. Baker."

Sam: (looking at Joe who is carrying a Gameboy™) "Can I see it?"

Group Leader: "Guys, eyes up here.  That's great listening. We can see what every one brought in just a moment, but first I want to ask you if you remember what this group is about. Why are we here?"

Joe, Jenna: (simultaneously shout out) "To make more friends."

Group Leader: "That's right. Everything we learn in this group is to help make more friends and hold on to the friends we have."

Sam: "But I do not want any more friends."

Group Leader: "Didn't you tell me when we met that you wanted a new Gameboy?"

Sam: "Yeah."

Group Leader: "Well, all the skills you learn here will help you get along with friends and parents so they will let you borrow their Gameboy or buy you one of your own. So some of you want to make friends, and some of you want to learn how to get along with others to get a Gameboy. (Some kids may not be motivated by making friends, but rather to be nice to others so that they will lend them a materials item, like a Gameboy, or eventually parents may buy them a Gameboy because they have behaving so nicely.) You will need to learn and practice the skills we are going to go over to do that."

## Establishing group rules

The members are encouraged to develop their own group rules. However, I guide their choices so that we will at least include the following rules:

- Listen to each other (wait for a pause to talk during conversation time, raise your hand and wait to be called on during skill time)
- Talk nicely to each other (i.e., do not yell, tease or insult others)
- Keep hands and feet to yourself (i.e., do not push, hit, kick, pinch or grab others)

**Group Rules**

- Listen to each other (wait for a pause to talk during conversation time, raise your hand and wait to be called on during skill time).
- Talk nicely to each other (i.e., do not yell, tease or insult others).
- Keep hands and feet to yourself (i.e., do not push, hit, kick, pinch or grab others).

Most of the time these are the rules, in one form or another, that are suggested by the students themselves. Three to four rules are satisfactory, as more would be overly complicated to remember.

Group Leader: "Okay, eyes up here. Good listening. Guys, this is your group so you should decide what rules you might need so we can all get along. What rules would you like in this group?"

Tommy: "Don't yell at each other."

Group Leader: "Okay. That sounds good. Many people agree with that rule? Sam, Joe, Jenna, what do you think?"

Sam, Jenna, and Joe: "Okay."

Group Leader: "Let's call that rule, 'Talk nicely to others,' I will write it on this poster."

Jenna: "How about no put-downs?"

Group Leader: "Sounds great to me. Guys, what do you think?" The other students begin to look around the room. "Eyes up here. Good listening. Jenna suggested no put-downs. Do you guys agree?"

Tommy, Sam, and Joe: "Yeah, and no teasing."

Group Leader: "Okay. I think these are all ways of saying 'talk nicely to each other,' so I will write under talk nicely, 'no yelling, put-downs or teasing.'" (Teasing is a subject that can help the group begin to bond around their similarities. So when someone brings it up, I use it to help the group feel connected and safe.)

Group Leader: "I know I have been teased. Most everyone I know has been teased. How many people here have ever been teased? Raise your hand if you have been teased. I think we can all raise our hands."

(All raise their hands.)

Tommy: "This kid called me a geek when I was in gym because I couldn't kick the soccer ball."

Group Leader: "It is not nice or fair to be teased like that. Plus you are totally an expert in soccer. I remember you telling me all about soccer when we met. I know I have been teased like that a lot of times. Has that happened to anyone else? Does anyone else want to tell a time they were teased?"

Jenna: "This boy called me stupid because I did not get my math problems right."

Group Leader: "Well, I know you are not at all stupid. In fact, you are quite intelligent, like the rest of you guys. I am sorry that happened to you. You know, Albert Einstein, who was considered one of the smartest people ever, failed math when he was a kid. So just because you missed a math problem doesn't mean you are not smart. Does anyone else want to tell a time they were teased?"

Sam: "I was, but I do not want to talk about it."

Group Leader: "You do not have to. But I think we can all understand how it feels to be teased and it's not fun. We all have something in common. We are all very smart and we all have felt what it's like to be teased. Can we all agree not to tease each other here?"

Group members: "Yeah."

Group Leader: "That's great. We will be like a family here and try to make each other feel better. Now what other rules might we need?"

At this point we elicited the two other rules: "Listen" (i.e., waiting for a pause during talk time, and raising your hand during a skill lesson) and "Keep hands and feet to ourselves" (i.e., no hitting, pushing, kicking and grabbing).

I then describe any behavioral management system we may use for following rules – such as a reward system or timeouts for disruptive behaviors. I have rarely needed a behavioral management system with teens. But with younger groups I often use a token system with play money earned toward a previously discovered incentive. I find the play money to be an effective, concrete, visual incentive, quieter than tokens (which can sometimes disrupt conversation when students clang them together) and somewhat reinforcing by association (see Chapter 6). I say the following to the students about the token system:

Group Leader: "Now that you guys came up with the rules, I will help you to follow them by giving you these dollars (play money) as you listen to each other, talk nicely, and keep hands and feet to yourselves" (pointing to the rules listed on a poster board). "When you guys get enough dollars, you will get a snack or a prize."

I usually do not tell them how many dollars they need during the first session because I do not know how many they will earn. I want them all to earn enough for snack the first session to help them feel successful and motivated to continue the "dollar" system. If, for example, they have each earned nine dollars by the end of the session, I will tell them they need 10 dollars for their snack or prize and then offer the last dollar in exchange for cleaning up and getting ready to leave.

## Getting to know each other

Since most members are quite nervous entering the first session, we usually spend most of the time with familiar territory. Each member has the opportunity to tell about his current interest (or obsession) during a "Getting to Know You" period. This usually breaks the ice, allows members to identify with each other further, and sets the stage for conversation skills we will be working on.

My comments as the group leader first center on getting the members to listen to one member talking at a time. I direct them to the poster "Keeping the Conversation Going" and instruct them that they can make comments or ask questions about what others say. Depending on the members' age and language ability, I may give a minimal prompt like, "Does anyone have a question or a comment about what Joe is saying?" For students who need more help, I might give a more intensive prompt like, "Can you ask Joe a 'where' question, like 'Where did you get that?'"

**Keeping the Conversation Going**

| Follow-up Questions | On-Topic Comments |
|---|---|
| Who | |
| What | |
| Where | I also _____ |
| When | I like _____ |
| Why | I am going _____ |
| How | I went _____ |
| What else | I _____ |

The following excerpt is from the first session with Joe, Sam, Jenna, and Tommy:

Group Leader: "Okay, ladies and gentlemen, we usually have a talk time, skill time, game and snack time in each session," pointing toward the schedule poster. "But since this is our first session, instead of learning a skill, we are going to get to know each other. Does anyone want to say a little about what they like to do or what they are interested in? Did anyone bring something in to show the others to help explain what they are interested in?"

Tommy: "Yeah I did. I have my Pokémon™ card collection. I have . . ."

Jenna: "I brought in my roller skates because . . ."

Group Leader: "Okay, we need to take turns talking. Jenna and Tommy both want to talk. Can one of you let the other go first?"

Tommy: "Okay, Jenna can go first. Ladies first."

Group leader: "That was very nice of you. Letting others go first can help make friends." (The leader hands Tommy a dollar for letting others go first.) "Here is a dollar for letting others go first." Sam and Joe begin to lose their attention. "Eyes up here, everyone. I like the way Sam, Joe, and Jenna are listening now, you can get dollars too." (Leader hands the others a dollar.) "Okay, we are listening to Jenna now. As we listen, you can ask Jenna questions or say something about what she is saying" (leader points to the poster "Keep the Conversation Going"). "Let's all look at Jenna. Go ahead Jenna."

Jenna: "These are my roller skates."

Group Leader: "Do you want to say something about why you brought them."

Jenna: "I love roller skating. I go really fast and can beat my brother in a race."

Group Leader: (Leader hands Joe, Sam, and Tommy a dollar and whispers.) "Good listening guys." Then in a louder voice, "Does anyone have any questions or comments for Jenna?"

Tommy: "What are the wheels made of?"

Group Leader: (Although this is not a totally relevant questions in terms of Jenna's interests, it is on the topic of roller skates, so it should be supported in this first session.) "Tommy, that's a good on-topic question" (handing a dollar to Tommy).

Jenna: "I don't know what they are made of."

Joe: "Where did you get them?" (Leader hands Joe a dollar.)

Group Leader: (Leader also hands Sam a dollar, whispering.) "I like the way you were listening to Jenna also."

Jenna: "At the skating shop."

Group Leader: "Does anyone else like to skate?"

Sam: "I like to watch skating."

Group Leader: (In an attempt to bring the group together, the leader points out similarities in interests.) "So it looks like you have something else in common. Besides all agreeing that you do not like teasing, it looks like some of you like to skate and others like to watch skating. Maybe some time you might all go skating or watch skating together. Does anyone else have a question or comment for Jenna?" No response. "Jenna, did you want to say more about what you like, or should we go on to someone else?"

Jenna: "I'm done."

Group Leader: "Tommy, I think you wanted to tell us about your Pokémon card collection. Everyone, let's look and listen to Tommy."

Tommy: "I have 150 Pokémon cards that I brought in, including this rare 'Charizard' card." All the students gather round to see the card.

Joe: "Can I see it?" (Reaching out to touch it.)

Group Leader: "Joe, you have to wait for Tommy's permission to touch the card. Tommy, what do you want Joe to do, look at or touch the card?"

Tommy: "I think just look at it right now."

Joe: (Looking at the card) "I have a lot of Pokémon cards too."

Group Leader: (Handing Joe a dollar and whispering to Joe.) "That's a good on-topic comment that really shows you are listening to Tommy."

Sam: "I do not like Pokémon. I like Digémon better." (Leader hands Sam a dollar and whispers that it was a good on-topic comment.)

Group Leader: "What about you, Jenna, do you like Pokémon or Digémon or any animated cartoon shows?"

Jenna: "I like a lot of the shows on Nickelodeon, like Sponge Bob." (Leader hands Jenna a dollar and whispers to her that her comment was on-topic.)

Group Leader: "Wow, you all have something else in common, you all like animated cartoon shows. Does anyone else have a question or comment for Tommy?" No response. "How about a 'where' question . . . where did you . . ." (waiting for the group members to respond.)

Joe: "Where did you get the cards, Tommy?" (Leader hands Joe a dollar and whispers that Joe asked a good follow-up question.)

The group continues with each member getting a turn to discuss his or her interests, after which the group leader makes more comments to try to point out the members' similarities and ignore some of the differences. For example, if they all like different TV shows, the leader points out how they all like TV rather than highlighting the differences in the shows they like. Early on it is important for the members to see how they can relate to each other, only in later sessions should they explore their differences.

## Subsequent Sessions

Subsequent sessions follow the format described earlier: conversation time, skill time, playtime and snack time.

### Conversation time

This part of the session resembles any typical therapy group in which members discuss their week, including problematic situations, and gain support and advice from other members. However, the difference is that I am as concerned about how the group participants are conversing as I am about what they are saying. My main job as facilitator is to coach, prompt, praise, and highlight the social environment as it unfolds during group.

A core set of conversation skills typically needs to be taught before conversation time can run smoothly. These are:

1. "Maintaining a Conversation"
2. "Starting a Conversation"
3. "Shifting Topics"
4. "Talking Briefly "
5. "Editing Sensitive Topics"
6. "Showing Understanding for Others' Feelings"

Given that these skills will not have been taught formally prior to the group, I do not expect conversation time to flow smoothly for some time. I coach the students through these skills during conversation time by prompting them on what to say and do in the moment. Then during the skill time of each session, we have a formal lesson on one of these skills to review it more thoroughly. Often in the first two sessions, skill time actually precedes conversation time. This is to allow two skills – maintaining and starting a conversation – to be taught so that the group members have some idea of what to say during conversation time. In subsequent sessions, the conversation time can precede skill time.

To prompt *starting a conversation* (see "Starting a Conversation" on p. 94), I will tell them to ask each other questions about the past (e.g., "How was your week?"), present (e.g., "What are you doing?"), future (e.g., "What are you going to do this weekend?"), and their interests (e.g., "Have you been playing soccer recently," posed to a member who is known to play soccer). Then to prompt maintaining a conversation I remind them to ask follow-up questions and make on-topic comments (see "Maintaining a Conversation" on p. 90).

To address members who are *talking incessantly*, I prompt them to talk briefly and check if others want to hear more: "Look at the other guys, do they seem interested? Why don't you ask them if they want to hear more?" In addition, I remind them to take turns talking, wait for a pause (which is typically part of the rules of the group), make eye contact, keep an appropriate distance from each other, and modulate their volume and tone of voice as necessary.

*Topic management* is a major issue in conversation time as members may stray from the topic quite rapidly. For example, two members may be discussing a video game, and a third member asks, "What are you going to have for dinner today?" I respond to this inappropriate shift in topics by saying something like, "Was that on-topic? They were talking about video games and you asked about dinner. Wait until they are done talking about the video game and then say, 'Can I talk about something else?'"

I also prompt them to *edit sensitive remarks* (see "Sensitive Topics" on p. 116). Sensitive topics are words that insult, embarrass, or otherwise make others uncomfortable. For example, a student might say to another student, "Why do you talk with a lisp?" I explain, "That is a sensitive topic that might make someone feel upset. Even though there is nothing wrong with talking with a lisp, it might make him upset when you point that out. So you can think it, but do not say it." To prompt the members to show understanding when someone is upset, I might say, "He looks upset, what can you say?" If there is no response, I say, "Ask him if he is okay or if you can help him."

As described in the transcript of the first session, I often use play money to reward students as they spontaneously or with some prompting from me demonstrate a skill. You must train yourself to watch for and praise the use of these skills as they occur in order to shape more appropriate conversation. For example, we may not notice when someone is sitting quietly listening and making eye contact while another member is talking. That is the time to go over to the quiet student and whisper, "Nice listening," and hand her a dollar. The youngster who asks a good follow-up question can also be given a dollar. The student who, with my prompting, asks the other members if they want to hear more rather than going on about his special interests also receives a dollar. The student who says, "Can I talk about something else?" rather than just changing the topic can get a dollar. In this way, the dollars highlight the positive conversation skills the members are demonstrating and encourage more positive behaviors.

## Playtime

The group leader's role during playtime is similar to that during conversation time, highlighting for members how others are feeling and prompting and rewarding the use of appropriate play skills (e.g., compromising, sharing, taking turns, deciding who will go first, and dealing with mistakes and losing). For example, if members are having a conflict such as arguing about who will go first in a game, I prompt them to use a skill they have learned. I might say, "You both want to go first, what do we do to decide who will go first?" If members do not have the skills to handle the conflict and begin to raise their voices or position to fight each other, I try to solve the problem for them. I step between them to prevent any physical confrontation and then offer my own solution such as, "Sam, you go first this time and, Tommy, then you can go first next time. Tommy, I will give you an extra dollar if you can accept this." If tempers continue to flare despite my efforts to solve the problem, I try to use a distraction to calm the students. For example, I might say, "Hey, who wants some of this clay. Why don't you guys create your Pokémon and Digémon characters using this clay." Using the members' interests (in this case, Pokémon and Digémon), I try to get their minds off the conflict at hand. In a later group, I return to the problem of deciding who goes first and incorporate it in a social skills lesson or problem-solving discussion to prepare the students for similar situations in the future. In general, my rule of thumb for situations that may prompt temper outbursts is as follows:

- try to get students to solve the problem if they have been taught the skills ahead of time
- offer your own solution if they cannot work it out
- during moments of intense anger, use distraction as a calming technique
- after the individual is calm, try to prevent the temper outburst by teaching a skill that prepares the individual for how to handle the problematic situation (see Chapter 6, Rule of Thumb Regarding Meltdowns).

# CLASSROOM SKILLS TRAINING

A 30- to 40-minute structured skill lesson (i.e., didactic explanation, modeling, and role-plays) should be done in class as early as possible during the week. For example, each Monday, one can review or introduce a new skill lesson. That leaves the rest of the week for practicing the skills. Ideally, social skills training should occur on a daily basis, but it is not necessary for a formal skill lesson to take place daily as long as the students have a chance to practice the skills each day as described below.

The job as a facilitator of classroom skills training is to (a) conduct the skills training lesson that introduces the skill concept, and (b) consult with the classroom teacher and aides to conduct daily activities to practice the skills. Even if the classroom teacher is not the one who is going to do the skill lessons, it is important for the teacher to take ownership of the program in both selecting and practicing skills. One way to approach a busy teacher who may not always be open to yet another "nonacademic" activity in the classroom is to explain how social skills training will eventually reduce social conflicts in class, allowing more time for academic teaching. In other words, although the teacher will have to put some time and energy into practicing the skills, this will later free up more time when she is no longer constantly addressing peer conflicts in class.

At a minimum, the teacher should be present for the lessons so that he or she knows what the students are learning. In addition, the classroom teacher may be requested to reward children for demonstrating the skills and to conduct daily activities like "show and tell" or "morning meeting" to work on conversation skills as described below.

In "show and tell," students take turns bringing in an item or pictures of something they want to share or somewhere they have been. Other students are prompted by the teacher to make on-topic comments or follow-up questions. The "Keeping a Conversation Going" poster should be present in the classroom as a visual aid to this activity. For example, the teacher may direct a student to stand in front of the class and describe what he brought in. Then the teacher will ask, "Does anyone have a question or comment about what he brought in?" The teacher can point to the "Keeping the Conversation Going" poster and say, "Does anyone have a 'Where' question, like 'Where did you get it?' or a 'Who' question like 'Who got it for you?' or a comment like 'I like it' or 'I have one too.'"

In the "morning meeting" activity, students are split up into dyads or groups of three to four and told to ask each other a series of conversation-starter questions like, "What did you do yesterday?" or "What are you going to do after school today?" Questions are usually pulled from the skill lesson on starting a conversation (see Chapter 8). One fun way to do this is to ask the students to walk around the room until the teacher says, "freeze." At that point the students are instructed to turn to the nearest person and ask him or her a particular conversation starter like, "How was your weekend?" Other questions might involve students' plans for the upcoming weekend, after-school activities, or a special interest. Students are instructed to ask follow-up questions and make on-topic comments to keep the conversation going. Then they are free to walk around again until the teacher calls "freeze." Again, they must pick the closest (but a different) person and ask another question the teacher calls out, such as "What are you going to do for the upcoming vacation?" Each student is asked to report what they learned about their classmates.

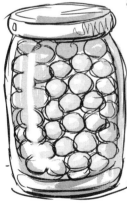

Stickers, points or other tokens can be given to each student who recalls what another student told them when they spoke. This activity promotes listening, starting conversations, staying on-topic, and general conversational skills.

Prior to conducting skill lessons, the teacher and the skills facilitator should decide on what incentive system to use to reward students for demonstrating the skills. Various versions are described in Chapter 7. However, the most user-friendly version for a large classroom is similar to the marble jar system used by Lee Canter (1987). Using this system, a marble or token is put into a jar every time a student exhibits the target skills. When the class accumulates enough marbles (typically 50 to 100), the whole class receives a reward (a party, extra art period, etc.). So as not to overwhelm the students and the teacher, it is wise to focus on no more than two or three skills at a time. In addition, avoid removing marbles for misbehavior so that students can maintain a positive attitude about the incentive system.

# PLAY-DATES

The first step in conducting play-dates is to arrange for one! This is not always easy for children with AS and related disorders, who may be isolated from peers (Wolfberg, 2003). Often teachers can be a great resource in helping to determine which classmates might be open to a play-date. In addition to asking the student's teacher, parents can seek out local support groups for parents of children with Asperger Syndrome, autism, and learning disabilities. Parents of children attending the same social skills group in school or in a private clinic are another option.

Once a play-date has been arranged, it is recommended that parents consider a couple of practical issues to increase the chances of a successful get-together. First, consider having the play-date at your house so that you can be on hand to coach and guide the activities. In addition, arrange to pick up and drop off your guest so that you can end the play-date early if the children begin to have conflicts they cannot resolve. (Warn the other parents that this may happen so arrangements can be made to ensure they are available to receive their child early.) Parents of multiple children may want to send their "typical" children to neighbors prior to the play-date to avoid a common problem whereby the invited guest ends up ignoring the child with disabilities to play with his or her siblings. Consider having short (e.g., 30-minute) play-dates at first, then gradually increasing to longer social times after having a chance to see how the children interact. Finally, parents may want to collect "cool" toys and games like having a trampoline in the front yard, great video games, and fun art project materials to increase motivation for peers to return.

Formal skill lessons can be conducted any time prior to the play-date (before bed, on the weekends). But the skill steps needed for the play-date should be reviewed just prior to the guest's arrival as well. Some of the more important rules and skills to consider teaching are to play with the guest rather than separately, play what the guest wants to play, compromise, take turns, deal with losing, and avoid sensitive topics. (See Chapter 8 for skill steps.) Parents can use the structured learning approach described in Chapter 4 to explain, model, and role-play the steps for these and other skills. Parents may negotiate a reward for their child for complying with the rules and skills steps. For example, parents may agree to buy the children ice cream (if that is truly rewarding for their child) after their child plays what the guest wants to play for the first 10 minutes and for the remaining time works to compromise with the guest over what else to play.

For children who have great difficulty taking turns and/or losing, it makes sense to initially avoid games and activities that require waiting for a turn and have a winner or loser. Most board games, video games, and outdoor competitive games fall into this category. Only after the child has had many chances to practice these activities with parents should they be introduced with peers. Instead, initial play-dates can focus on activities that students can do in parallel without any wait time, and with no winner or losers. Art and cooking projects fall into this category, with each child getting his or her own materials and putting the projects together side by side. Materials might include play-doh™, building materials (Legos™, blocks), paper maché, and ingredients for making food. Older children can create model ships, cars and other hobby items, sitting side by side with little interaction.

As children get accustomed to each other, you can progress to more interactive activities. For younger children, these might include pretend play with kitchen items, cars, building materials, and puzzles. Parents may facilitate this by helping their child notice what their guest is doing and trying to imitate it. For example, the parent might say, "Look at Sam, he is pretending to put out a fire with the fire truck. Can you put out the fire too?" Younger children can also learn to take turns by sharing materials. For example, children can be directed to take turns using a trampoline, going down a slide, or playing dress-up with a particular hat. For elementary-aged children, board and video games require more social interaction, patience, and the ability to tolerate frustration. Parents may decide to start with games with which the child already feels very competent so that she can tolerate taking turns and losing the game. New games that require great skill are not the best choice to introduce into a play-date for a child who gets frustrated easily. Instead, let the child learn the game ahead of time with her parent, and then when some level of comfort is established, incorporate the game into a play-date.

# Group Rules

- Listen to each other (wait for a pause to talk during conversation time, raise your hand and wait to be called on during skill time).

- Talk nicely to each other (i.e., do not yell, tease or insult others).

- Keep hands and feet to yourself (i.e., do not push, hit, kick, pinch or grab others).

# Keeping the Conversation Going

| Follow-up Questions | On-Topic Comments |
|---|---|
| Who<br>What<br>Where<br>When<br>Why<br>How<br>What else | I also _____.<br><br>I like _____.<br><br>I am going _____.<br><br>I went _____.<br><br>I _____. |

# Schedule

1. Talk Time

2. Skill Time

3. Game Time

4. Snack

## CHAPTER 6

# Behavior Management

**Y**ou cannot run a class or a group without some means of maintaining the students' attention and cooperation. A full description of behavior management techniques is beyond the scope of this book, and interested readers may want to refer to other sources (Canter, 1987; Durand, 1990; McGinnis & Goldstein, 1997). Instead I offer a few simple ideas and strategies that have been useful to me when leading a group or class.

## Relationship Is Key

No matter how difficult it is for a student to read nonverbal social cues, if you grow to dislike a student, he eventually picks up on that feeling. For example, frequent sighs of irritation or frowns can subtly communicate disdain for a student, creating even more defiance from a challenging individual. Students are much more likely to cooperate and attend to you if they know you genuinely care about them and are willing to work with them, despite any oppositional or defiant behaviors. You can demonstrate this by telling them this directly and sincerely. For example, "Mike, I like working with you. You are a terrific kid." If they do something wrong, like interrupt continually, you can say, "What can we do to work on the interruptions? I know you are not doing it on purpose and I really want you in the group, but I do not want you to keep interrupting because then I cannot explain the skill lesson. What do you think we could do?" The goal is to involve the student in the problem solving and work as a team member so that he is motivated to address the issue and does not feel attacked or ashamed by the problem. "Mike, would you like me to give you a signal, like a cough, when you interrupt so you know it is happening? I could also reward you for waiting to be called on instead of interrupting if that would help. For example, if you can wait to be called on without interrupting the skill lesson, I will give you 10 extra points. What do you think?"

Prior to the group or class, doing something fun with a student, including giving rewards, can build credit so the child sees you positively when it is time to teach. For a classroom teacher, this can be established by making lessons engaging and using a reward system as a regular part of class. Most important, for students who have difficulty controlling their emotions, it is critical to keep an accepting and calm attitude. There is no sense in fighting fire with fire. I have come to the conclusion that when I lose my temper it is because I was not prepared with a strategy to deal with some challenging behavior. That is, my anger was a reflection of my own feelings of powerlessness. If I am prepared with a strategy (even one that is not effective at that moment), I am less likely to get angry.

My interactions with Mike can serve as a good example of the importance of preparation. In my early group sessions with Mike, a 10-year-old with an "attitude," he often refused to cooperate with listening to skill lessons or participating in group games. His defiance made me feel ineffective as a teacher. My frustration with myself caused me to feel angry and raise my voice at him when he defied me. But my anger only made him more defiant. Once I realized what was happening, I made a plan to deal with his defiance. I gave him warnings followed by loss of rewards for being disrespectful or defiant. Although this too proved to be ineffective in reducing his defiance, the procedure allowed me to keep calm as I quietly gave him warnings and consequences. My calmness had at least stopped an escalating cycle in which his defiance was worsening due to my anger. Finally, after serendipitously discovering more information about Mike's school day prior to his coming to group, I realized what was contributing to his defiance. On days when he had behaved perfectly in school, his attitude was much worse in group. The opposite was also true; difficult days in school resulted in a generally positive attitude in group. Mike had just so much energy to meet the demands of school and group. He needed some downtime after school before he could follow directions in group. Once I acknowledged this to Mike and let him relax for the first 10 minutes of group, he was much more cooperative the rest of the time. He knew I was on his side, understanding of his stress, and willing to work with him to be successful in group.

## Maintaining Interest and Understanding

Most acting-out behavior can be avoided if the student is engaged in a lesson that is fun, interesting and taught at the correct level. So, rather than working hard to address an inappropriate behavior with rewards and consequences, it is more profitable to work on trying to make the activity more interesting and understandable in the first place.

Often I use the special interests of my students to teach them a skill. For example, we may work on conversation skills by pretending to interview famous people they like. After Mike Tyson, infamous boxer, bit Evander Holyfield's ear in a boxing match, my adolescent group members could focus on nothing else for a couple of sessions. So we practiced starting and maintaining a conversation by pretending to talk with Mike Tyson.

I also had several group members who were avid fans of the game show "Jeopardy." So to motivate attention to learning a new skill, I told the group that we would play "Jeopardy" to see who can remember the steps of the skill. The "Jeopardy" fanatics were upset if we in any way violated the rules of the actual show, which required contestants to phrase their responses in the form of a question. This proved difficult for some of the group members, so we agreed to play a new show called "Almost Jeopardy," in which you did not have to phrase your response in the form of a question. The "Jeopardy" fanatics would start the review of each skill by saying, "Live from the 'almost' Sony picture studios, it's 'almost' Jeopardy, with your host 'almost' Alex Trebek. Entering the studios today is John, a 12-year-old from Highland Park, New Jersey . . ." After they had introduced each group member, I would pose questions to review the skills and provide play money for their accurate responses (regardless of whether the response was phrased as a question).

# Rule of Thumb Regarding Meltdowns

Daniel Goleman in his book on emotional intelligence never mentions Asperger Syndrome or autism, yet his concepts are relevant for students with AS, who often get what Goleman describes as "hijacked" by their emotions (Goleman, 1997). That is, when extremely upset, they do not seem to have access to their reasoning abilities. Take for example, a six-year-old student named Zach, who came to my office with his mother for a therapy appointment. On the way to the office Zach saw a Toys-R-Us store and asked his mother to stop and buy him something. She said no because they were running late to our appointment. As a result, Zach arrived at the office furious that they did not go to Toys-R-Us. Efforts to calm him by explaining how they were late so they could not stop were useless. Threatening that if he did not stop he would not get to watch TV at home only made things worse. Even promises that they could go to the store after the appointment were futile. Zach could not be reasoned with and continued to boil.

Meltdowns like Zach's might include tantrums or moments when a child is "stuck" on an issue (talking incessantly about a situation that upset him or tantruming because he did not get something he wanted).

Rule #1: *During a meltdown, there is often no point in trying to reason with a child or threaten a loss of privilege. At these moments it is usually best to use some form of distraction to get the student's mind off whatever it is that triggered the upset.*

For Zach, a card game fan, his mother and I began to play "Uno" (a card game) in front of him during the session as a distraction. He yelled, "I am not playing!" His mother and I ignored his protest and continued to play. As his mother began to complain, somewhat theatrically, that she was losing and needed help, Zach began to look at her cards, and mumbled with much less vigor this time, "I am not playing." After a moment he picked up her cards and played for her. I was not going to work on the skill "Dealing with Losing" in that session and quickly arranged for Zach to win the game. He was now happy and available for the rest of our session. The total tantrum time was about 10 minutes. Without distractions in school, his tantrums sometimes lasted for two hours.

To help a student get out of a meltdown, you have to show him something that catches his interest. For students who love computer games, a good distraction may be to display a favored computer game in the child's line of vision. Like insulin for a diabetic, carry enticing distracters with you at all times in case of an emergency.

Distraction does not mean giving in to the tantrum. It means getting the students' minds off of what is upsetting them. In doing so, be careful not to develop a pattern of rewarding the child for tantrums, however. If the child tantrums because she did not get to watch TV, TV is not a good distraction. My two-year-old son tantrums if he does not get a piece of my dessert. Rather than giving him the dessert, I distract him with a favored toy.

Rule #2: *When the meltdown is over, you must develop a plan with the student to prevent the meltdown from happening again.*

This involves identifying the trigger to the meltdown. A simple way to do this is to keep a diary of behavioral meltdowns and record what was happening just before and after the behavior occurred (see Functional Assessment in the next section). Review of the diary can give you clues as to what precedes or triggers meltdowns. In Zach's case, the trigger was obvious – he did not get to stop at Toys-R-Us. Once he calmed down, I needed to teach him a skill to prepare him for the next time he cannot stop at Toys-R-Us.

Zach and I developed a Cognitive Picture Rehearsal (see Chapter 4) that shows what Zach will get if he accepts "no" when Mom tells him they cannot stop at Toys-R-Us. The cartoon pictures we created depict Zach asking to go to the store, Mom saying no, Zach saying okay and not getting mad, and then later Zach and Mom returning to Toys-R-Us to buy something as a reward for Zach because he accepted "no" earlier that day. We reviewed the sequence with Zach until he could tell us himself. Then before each trip to the session to see me, his mom reviewed the skill to prepare him for what to do when they pass Toys-R-Us. Zach was able to accept "no" on the way to the office, and his mother rewarded him with a stop after the visit. Eventually, she was able to help Zach wait longer and longer before going back to the toy store as Zach fully understood the rewards of waiting.

All the social skills training strategies described in this book (e.g., Cognitive Picture Rehearsal, Social Stories, Structured Learning, and Social Skill Picture Stories) are ways to teach skills and prepare students so they can avoid becoming upset or overwhelmed by problem situations. We call these methods "front-end approaches" because they teach what to do *before* a problem arises. "Back-end" approaches, like rewards and punishments, come into play *after* a behavior has occurred. Any good behavior plan must involve a "front-end" approach in which we try to prepare or prime children before they misbehave or encounter a problem. For example, creating and reviewing the Cognitive Picture Rehearsal with Zach before he comes to my office is a "front-end" approach, whereas rewarding or punishing Zach after he gets to my office for his behavior when he passes the toy store is a "back-end" approach.

## Teaching Alternatives: Functional Assessment

If we want to prepare students ahead of time to avoid a problem, we often need to teach them alternative ways to get what they want. For example, if Kevin always tantrums to avoid filling out his worksheet, it would be better to teach him how to ask for a break if he wants to avoid the situation rather than resort to tantruming.

A "functional assessment" asks the question, "Why is this inappropriate behavior occurring?" By observing when the behavior occurs, under what circumstances, and how others react to it, we can hypothesize about the function, or reason, for the behavior. A full description of how to conduct a functional assessment is beyond the scope of this book. (Readers who are interested in a more thorough treatment of this topic are referred to Durand, 1990.) However, I do want to take a look at the types of functions many disruptive behaviors serve in an effort to illustrate how to approach disruptive behaviors as opportunities to teach appropriate behaviors.

Durand (1990) describes four typical functions of "challenging" or "disruptive" behavior. Each function is listed below, along with suggested strategies for addressing disruptive behaviors that are associated with each function.

## Functions of Behavior

### Escape/avoidance of a feared, difficult, or boring task

- Teach how to ask for a break.
- Modify the task to make it more interesting or understandable, or less difficult.
- Increase incentives for engaging in the task.
- Use gradual exposure to feared situations (e.g., just watch the activity first, then do one part of activity, then two parts, etc.).
- Use incentives to motivate approaching the task. Desired rewards are likely to be reduced work.

### Attention-Seeking

- Teach better ways to get attention (e.g., how to start a conversation or ask others to play).
- Give the student a time to shine during group or class by letting her present information about which she has expertise.
- Teach the importance of being a good audience (e.g., being liked and being attended to are different; sometimes you are liked more when you are not the center of attention).
- Use a timeout.

### Tangible Reward

*(i.e., tantruming because students did not get something they wanted)*

- Teach how to delay gratification or wait for what they want. See the skill called "Accepting No for an Answer" (see p. 202).

### Self-Stimulation

*(e.g., body rocking, hand-flapping, twirling, repeating phrases heard from TV in an effort to soothe oneself)*

- Teach relaxation strategies like "Keeping Calm" (see p. 176).
- Provide less disruptive ways to soothe or stimulate (e.g., a ball to squeeze).

# Rule of Thumb Regarding
# Being Firm or Accommodating

The decision on when to be firm and when to be flexible has everything to do with the previous discussion about teaching alternative behaviors. We want students with Asperger Syndrome to be able to follow rules like everyone else, but we also want to accommodate some of their difficulties. So when should we be firm and when should we be flexible?

Rule #3: *If a child has been prepared by learning an appropriate way to get what she wants but chooses an inappropriate behavior, then I am firm and possibly impose a consequence. If a child does not know how to handle a situation and is becoming upset, I usually choose to be accommodating.*

For example, imagine Joe coming to my social skill class for the first time. Right from the start he refuses to participate, screaming that he wants to leave. Rather than using a negative consequence for refusing to participate, I am accommodating. I talk to Joe about ways to make the session more fun and allow him to leave if I cannot convince him to stay. For example, I may offer to play some games with him rather than just work on skills during this session. Then before the end of the session, I prepare him for the next session by teaching him an appropriate way to escape (e.g., asking for a break). We role-play how he can ask for a break instead of screaming if he wants to leave. I tell him I will give him three "break cards," which he can hand me if he wants a break. Each break will last 3 minutes. I tell him that we will make the session more fun for him with games at the end and explain that he will be rewarded for participating. We negotiate three rewards he would like for staying on task in the group, like a snack, a small toy, and a chance to play with the computer at home after the session (which we arrange with his mother).  I also point out that if he screams rather than asking for a break, he will get a warning. If he continues to scream or tantrum, he will get another warning. If he screams or tantrums a third time, he will lose the opportunity for snack. The fourth time he will lose the opportunity to have the toy, and the fifth time he will

**I need a break, Please**

lose the opportunity to play the computer after the group. Now that Joe is prepared for the skills class, and knows the *appropriate* way to escape, I will be firm and give warnings followed by taking away privileges if he chooses to demonstrate an *inappropriate* way to escape (e.g., screaming).

Upon Joe's return to group, I hand him his break cards and remind him that he can simply ask for a 3-minute break rather than scream if he does not want to participate. I remind him that if he screams, tantrums, or refuses to come back after a break, he will receive a warning. If he continues to be noncompliant, I will give him another warning followed by progressively taking away his rewards (i.e., the snack, toy, and computer). Joe tests the program by screaming during skill time. I give him a warning and tell him he can use a break card instead, but he continues to scream and falls to the floor. I give him another warning, saying, "You do not have to scream, all you have to do is ask for a break. That way you will not lose your snack." This time Joe uses the break card. I remind him that he must return in 3 minutes or he will lose his snack. He goes into the waiting area of my office and reads a book. After 3 minutes he returns and participates in skill time. Some of the other group members ask if they can take breaks too, and although I tell them that they can, I also share that I do not believe they need the breaks the way Joe does. The other students seem to accept this because they generally enjoy the group and want to cooperate.

# Use of a Token Economy

With groups of children about 10 years old or younger, I often use a token system with play money earned toward a small prize, or any other incentive that has been found to be effective. Money is a good, concrete, visual incentive, quieter than tokens, and somewhat reinforcing by association. For example, I give out dollars to individual children for following class rules, or as an incentive to use a skill (e.g., start a conversation, ask a follow-up question). I may give out a dollar as frequently as one per minute or as infrequently as one per 10 minutes during a 60-minute group. In Chapter 5, the transcript of the first session provides a good example of how to introduce this idea to the students and how to dole out the money during group session.

I attempt to give out dollars when there is no misbehavior – when the group is listening and following directions, for example. In other words, I must "catch them being good." If a child is quietly listening to another, I will say, "Good listening" and hand out a dollar to him. My other cue to give out dollars is when one child misbehaves. At that moment I turn to the others and give them dollars. For example, if Meagan is not listening and begins to wander out of her seat, I say, "Let's see who is in listening position," and then give dollars to everybody except for Meagan. When Meagan comes back to a listening position, I let her know that she will get a dollar too for holding the listening position a little longer (e.g., about 10 seconds). This method serves an important purpose – you avoid a power struggle with a misbehaving child because you are focusing on the children who are behaving. If, on the other hand, you focused on the misbehaving student, you would digress from the lesson plan and begin to lose the other children's attention as well.

If I have specified that the children need 10 dollars to get their reward, I often create a situation so everyone has received about nine dollars just before we end the session. That allows me to use the last dollar to get everyone ready to transition out of group (e.g., get their coat, shoes, skills sheets, and line up).

On rare occasions I take a dollar away as a consequence, but I never get into a physical tug of war over it. If a student does not want to give up the dollar, I just note that he has one less than what is actually in his hand. For some students the dollars are distracting if they hold on to them, so instead we put them in a cup with their name on them or ask their parents to hold the dollars (i.e., if the parents are in the session with us).

Typical rewards include snacks, stickers, use of special games or toys, or getting to go somewhere special after the group with their parents. Although seemingly obvious, in practice, people often forget that rewards are only effective if they are truly rewarding. That means we need to know what children like and be ready to alter our rewards as their preferences change. We need to ask the students, "What do you want to work for today?" Many students can readily tell us their preferences if asked.

Some adolescents resist the token system stating that they are "too old for rewards" or that they do not like "being controlled" by the rewards. Many adolescent groups do not need the token system and can demonstrate adequate self-control without the system. For those adolescents who do need constant redirection to stay focused, but who resist the idea of a token system, I often suggest using the dollars not for rewards, but as a means for them to keep track of their own on-task behavior. For example, I will agree with the students that they are too old for rewards, but suggest that I give out the dollars to help them see how well they are staying focused on what others are saying. When they get a dollar, they know they are staying focused. If they lose a dollar, there is no loss of reward or privilege, but just a nonverbal signal from me that they lost focus temporarily. In this way the dollars serve as a visual aid to help the students know how they are doing so they can better regulate their attention.

With most groups, I begin to fade the use of the token system after 12-24 weeks and start relying only on verbal praise. Some children will continue to need the token system because of extreme inattention, impulsivity, and hyperactivity. In these instances, I may use the system just with those students. To make the situation clear, I say, "I know it can be hard for you to stay focused, so I am going to start using the dollars with you again so you can see how you are doing. If you get enough dollars, you will get your rewards. Although the other students are not going to get the dollars, they still need to behave in order to get their rewards at the end of group."

Occasionally, students experience stressful situations or events outside of the group that make it difficult for them to maintain attention and readjust to the structure of school or group. In addition, as some students undergo medication changes, they may have periods of greater agitation or restlessness. These may be times when the token system will be reintroduced until the stressful period is over.

# CHAPTER 7

# Promoting Generalization

One of the goals of skills training is to improve social functioning outside the group. It is not enough to introduce a skill once a week in a social skills class. It is the constant repetition of a skill in real situations that facilitates learning in a meaningful way. High repetition rates may eventually allow a skill to become second nature rather than effortful. A good metaphor for this process is learning a new musical piece. When learning a new piece, most musicians have to consciously think about the notes they are playing, converting the written music into specific muscle actions to play the piece. After many repetitions of practicing the piece, however, they no longer have to think about the notes, everything just seems to flow. In the same way, social skills may eventually flow naturally when enough practice has occurred.

In addition to constant practice, the better a child's conceptual ability prior to training, the easier it will be to generalize skills outside of the group. As mentioned, some children learn a concept for starting conversations such as asking about the past (e.g., "How was your week?"), present ("What are you doing?"), and future (e.g., "What will you do after school?") to think of conversation starters. Learning such a concept allows the student to create new appropriate conversation starters for many different situations. For example, on a Monday they may ask people how their weekend was. On a Friday they may ask others what they will do for their weekend. And after a vacation they may ask others how their vacation was. Children who instead memorize a script for conversation starters (e.g., they might learn to say, "How was your weekend?") will have a more difficult time generalizing the skills to other situations because the script may not apply. For example, on Friday it would be odd to ask others, "How was your weekend?" Thus, children who cannot easily learn a concept but must memorize specific words and actions need to be trained and prompted to practice different versions of a skill in situations that are different from the original learning situation.

It is important to remember that not all problems can be addressed through social skills training. Teaching students what to do and why does not guarantee that they will be able to perform the skills. Individuals with extreme impulsivity may need a good behavioral management program and/or medication to allow them to implement the skills they have learned. For example, an individual with ADHD may learn how and why to wait for a pause before interrupting, but nevertheless be unable to wait consistently because of attention and impulse control problems. Providing a reward for waiting or possibly medication to control impulsivity may help. Similarly, some individuals are too anxious to implement the skills they have learned. Despite learning how to start and maintain conversations, they may be too frightened to do so, anticipating rejection or humiliation. Such individuals may need therapy to address and combat their self-defeating beliefs and possibly medication to reduce their anxiety.

# Role-Plays and Instructions to Practice

Several factors help promote generalization of skills beyond the training session. First, role-plays conducted in the groups should resemble, as best as possible, the actual situations that children will confront outside the group. For example, to role-play starting a conversation or joining into play at recess in school, one can serve a meal and play the actual recess games.

To facilitate practice outside of the group, each skill handout in Chapter 8 serves as a written practice sheet asking group members to consider with whom and when they will practice the skill. I typically offer rewards to children who return their practice sheets to me the next week indicating they have practiced the skills. With older students, snack can also be an incentive. However, special class or group privileges (e.g., a party or a field trip) can be earned for accumulating many practice assignments.

The key to practice is to successfully involve parents and teachers who can prompt practice during the week. Along with each skill handout is a set of suggested activities for parents and teachers to help their students practice and use the skills outside the group. Thus, parents and the teacher receive both the skill handout and the suggested activity after a lesson is conducted.

# Involving Parents

As a rule, in my clinic-based groups I include parents of children eight and younger. In schools, I often invite parents to come and observe any new skill that we are working on. This means that the parents may come for the 20 minutes or so of skill time, and then leave so as not to disrupt their children in their other school activities. This allows me to model for parents how they can prompt their students at home. In addition, the presence of a parent provides more support during the group to handle challenging behaviors. For older children, I review with parents after the group what skill the group learned.

Prior to the start of skills training, parents receive instructions on how to practice with their child (see sample letter at the end of this chapter). Parents can engage in four activities to encourage generalization:

- quiz the child about the skill steps
- model and role-play the steps
- prompt the child to enact the skill when needed (i.e., incidental teaching)
- provide a reward for enacting the skill

Moreover, parents are encouraged to set up get-togethers with other group members to continue the practice, and to foster growing friendships.

## Involving Teachers

Teachers and aides should also receive copies of the skill handouts so they too know what skills to prompt and praise in their students. If skills are taught in the classroom, this is easy as the teachers and aides are present for the lesson. For students in a small group, aides are often invited to accompany the child to group so they can see the skill lesson directly. In addition, a copy of the skill sheet is left for the general education teacher so she is kept aware of the skills covered.

Teachers, school counselors, or parents can also set up a behavior chart that targets some of these skills to promote skill generalization. Sometimes it is too difficult for the skills trainer or teacher to initiate creating a behavior chart because they may have too many students for which they are responsible. Instead, the parent or school counselor may ask for a brief meeting with the student's teacher to set up a behavior chart. If the behavior chart is created in advance, the teacher may be more open to implementing it than if the teacher is asked to create it him/herself.

A variety of behavior charts can be used to facilitate generalization of skills. Recognize that charts are not just recording devices to determine when a student should be rewarded, they are also visual aids that remind students, parents and teachers what skills the student is trying to practice. Two sample charts are presented. One is for an individual child for whom we may set up a school/home chart (see Individual Behavior Chart and Instructions for Using Individual Behavior Chart, pp. 68-69). Here the child can earn rewards at home for gaining a certain number of points during the school day. For example, in order to watch TV or use the computer at home each night, the child must get a certain number of points that day. It is best to select just two or three skills at a time to target for generalization even though the student may be learning many skills in the social skills training class. For example, the child might need to work on following class rules and doing class work every day, all year long. However, a third target, "social skill of the week," would change once in a while. This target could be how and when to interrupt. If the student seems consistently to get high scores on the chart for this skill for several weeks, we might decide to change the target to a different skill the student has learned, such as compromising with others. Perhaps this skill will only be charted for lunch/recess time and group work. If after several weeks the student consistently demonstrates high scores for compromising, we may again change the target to another skill he is learning in the social skills training class.

The second chart (see Social Skill Class Behavior Chart, p. 70) is used for an entire class that is learning social skills. Here individuals or the entire group can earn rewards when they get points for demonstrating the skills. For example, we might target the following two skills that were taught in a skill lesson, "Accepting No for an

Answer" and "Compromising." As children either "Accept No" or "Compromise" during the class day, a point is written by their name. Explain that when they get a certain number of points, they will get a reward. We might want to set the points equal to the number of times the children might demonstrate the skills each day. For example, if the students accept no and compromise about five times per day, then we can say when one child gets 5 points by their name, he or she can receive a reward (e.g., snack or privilege). Alternatively, we may decide that when the entire group combined gets enough points (e.g., a value of five times the number of students in the class), the whole group can have a reward (e.g., pizza party, movie, or free play).

A more user-friendly way to reward a large classroom of children is based on the "marble jar" system used by Canter (1987). In this system, a marble or token is put into a jar every time any student exhibits the target skills. When the class accumulates enough marbles (typically 50 to 100), the whole class gets a reward (e.g., a party, extra art period, etc.). So as not to overwhelm the students and the teacher, it is wise to focus on no more than two or three skills at a time. In addition, avoid removing marbles for misbehavior so students can maintain a positive attitude about the incentive system.

# How to Create Instances to Reward: Shaping and Correcting

Both teachers and parents must be vigilant to reward any positive demonstration of the skills being charted. In many instances, adults must learn how to draw the skills out of their children and not just wait for them to display the skills. To this end, it is necessary to be able to shape and correct behavior.

In *shaping* behavior, we may not see a complete demonstration of the skill. We may have to prompt a student to engage in a part of the skill and then reward this partial demonstration. For example, a child may forget to introduce himself to someone new and therefore will need to be reminded of the steps. When he introduces himself the next time, he may not completely sustain eye contact. Nevertheless, we may reward this behavior because it demonstrates progress for this particular student.

In *correcting* behavior, we can use instances of inappropriate behavior to prompt and reward a skill. For example, if a child interrupts, we can tell her to "Wait for a pause, then say excuse me" and then reward her for doing so.

If points are not being earned on a behavior chart, we must create a way for the students to earn them. We must draw the target behavior out of the child, sometimes in partial steps, and sometimes after the child has misbehaved rather than wait for the skill to be demonstrated. As teachers, parents, facilitators, and aides, it is our job to create situations so that students must use the skills and can then be rewarded for doing so.

To do this, we may "bait" the skill. This means doing something that requires the student to show how to use the skill. For example, with the skill "Accepting No for an Answer," you might tell students that they will be tested on their ability to accept no. Show them a favorite food, game, or toy and wait for them to ask for it. Then say, "No, you cannot have it." If they accept no, then say, "Great job, you accepted no so you can have a point on your chart." Another example, with the skill "Showing Understanding for Others' Feelings," you might fall down and loudly pretend to be hurt in front of a child. Then wait for him or her to say, "Are you okay?" If the child does not, you might say, "what can you say if I look hurt?" For conversation skills, we can direct them to start conversations with each other by breaking them up into pairs and giving them a conversation starter to use (see "Starting a Conversation" and "Maintaining a Conversation," pp. 90 and 94). Then we can give them the point for starting the conversation.

For most of the skills presented in the next chapter, ideas for how to bait the skills, correct misbehavior and generally practice the skills to increase generalization are presented after the skill lesson itself.

# Instructions for Using Individual Behavior Chart

1. Each student has a daily behavior chart and gets rated for each period on three different target behaviors: "Following Rules," "Doing Classwork," and "Social Skill of the Week" (i.e., a particular skill that is a focus for the week).

2. This chart follows the student from class to class and must be filled out by the student's teacher or aide each period.

3. During the first week of classes, the chart is to be filled out each day to get a one-week baseline to determine the average daily points the student gets.

4. Based on the average daily points students receive, we can determine how many points to expect students to get each day. The average daily point value, plus or minus 5 points, can be set as the "points needed to get daily privileges."

5. When a student gets the "points needed to get daily privileges," he may receive daily privileges in school or at home. Daily privileges in school may include a homework pass, snack, and free time during the last period. At-home daily privileges may include TV, computer, and going outside to play.

6. Any points in excess of "points needed to get daily privileges" can go into savings for special privileges. Savings can be accumulated over weeks or months and might be recorded by a number posted on the refrigerator at home, a jar filled with pennies or any other means the student and parent may desire. Special privileges might include material items like music CDs, computer games, or going to movies.

7. If possible, this program should be coordinated with parents so students receive their daily and special privileges at home for points earned in school. If parents are willing to participate, the daily student rating must go home every day and be presented to parents in order for the child to receive privileges. Student failure to give the sheet to the parent is the same as not getting enough points for privileges that day. This prevents the potential for a child to hide the ratings from a parent who wants to participate.

# Individual Daily Behavior Chart

Name: _____ Date: _____

Please rate this student in each target area for each period using the following scale:

1 = try harder        2 = good        3 = excellent

| Target Behaviors | Period 1 | Period 2 | Period 3 | Period 4 |
|---|---|---|---|---|
| Following Class Rules | | | | |
| Doing Classwork | | | | |
| "Social Skill of the Week" | | | | |

| Target Behaviors | Period 5 | Period 6 | Period 7 | Period 8 |
|---|---|---|---|---|
| Following Class Rules | | | | |
| Doing Classwork | | | | |
| "Social Skill of the Week" | | | | |

Average daily points earned during baseline:        _____

Points needed to earn basic privileges:        _____

Points in savings needed to earn special privileges:  _____

# Social Skill Class Behavior Chart

Instructions: Please award 1 point to each student
each time the student demonstrates a particular skill.

| Skills | Names | | | | |
|---|---|---|---|---|---|
| 1. | | | | | |
| 2. | | | | | |
| 3. | | | | | |
| 4. | | | | | |
| 5. | | | | | |
| 6. | | | | | |
| 7. | | | | | |
| 8. | | | | | |
| 9. | | | | | |
| 10. | | | | | |

When a student gets _____ points, he or she can have _____.

When the whole class gets _____ points, they can have _____.

# Sample Parent Letter

Dear Parent(s) or Guardian(s):

As you may already have heard, your child will be receiving social skills training as part of his/her class curriculum. Each Monday at 10:00 a.m., for the next 12 weeks, a skill will be introduced or reviewed and your child will be rewarded for practicing the skill throughout the week. Your child will receive a written summary of the skill to share with you and to use as a reminder to practice the skill. Please look for this skill sheet each Monday as that is when your child should receive it.

One of the biggest obstacles to teaching social skills is making sure the skills generalize beyond the training session. In order for your child to learn and be able to use the skill on his/her own, it is important that he or she practices at home as well as in school. To help your child learn the skills, we ask you to participate in the following ways:

1. If possible, attend the skills training session on Monday mornings to see what skill your child is learning. This will enable you to better understand how to coach your youngster in displaying the skill at home.

2. When you receive the skill sheet, you can help your child practice each night by:

    a. **Quizzing** the child about the skill steps. Make a game of it and give rewards for correct answers.

    b. **Modeling** and role-playing the skill with the child. Use rewards if your child is reluctant to try the skill with you.

    c. **Coaching** the child to use the skill when it would be appropriate to do so. For example, if the skill is "interrupting" and your child did not wait for a pause before interrupting, remind him or her to wait for a pause. You can use stars or stickers to motivate use of the skills. For example, every time your child interrupts the correct way, give him or her a star. When the child has accumulated five stars, he or she can get a special snack, privilege, or other reward.

Please feel free to call me or ask your child's teacher if you have any questions.

Sincerely,

*Jed Baker, Ph.D.*

## CHAPTER 8

# Skill Lessons and Activities

The skill handouts are organized in the order listed below. An activity sheet listing ways to demonstrate, practice, and reinforce the skill at home and in the classroom accompanies most skills. The activity sheets along with the skill handouts are designed to guide teachers and parents in how to teach and practice the skills.

## Communication Skills

### Conversational Skills

1. Maintaining Appropriate Physical Distance from Others ("Don't Be a Space Invader")
2. Listening Position
3. Tone of Voice
4. Greetings
5. How and When to Interrupt
6. Staying on Topic
7. Maintaining a Conversation
8. Taking Turns Talking
9. Starting a Conversation
10. Joining a Conversation
11. Ending a Conversation
12. Asking a Question When You Don't Understand

13. Saying "I Don't Know"
14. Introducing Yourself
15. Getting to Know Someone New
16. Introducing Topics of Interest to Others
17. Giving Background Information about What You Are Saying
18. Shifting Topics
19. Don't Talk Too Long
20. Sensitive Topics
21. Complimenting Others
22. Use Your H.E.A.D. (Happy Voice, Eye Contact, Alternating Turns, Distance)
23. T.G.I.F. (Timing, Greeting, Initial Question, Follow-Up Questions)

## Cooperative Play Skills

24. Asking Someone to Play
25. Joining Others in Play
26. Compromising
27. Sharing
28. Taking Turns
29. Playing a Game
30. Dealing with Losing
31. Dealing with Winning
32. Ending a Play Activity

## Friendship Management

33. Informal Versus Formal Behavior
34. Respecting Personal Boundaries
35. Facts Versus Opinions (Respecting Others' Opinions)
36. Sharing a Friend
37. Getting Attention in Positive Ways
38. Don't Be the "Rule Police"
39. Offering Help
40. When to Tell on Someone
41. Modesty
42. Asking Someone Out on a Date
43. Appropriate Touch
44. Dealing with Peer Pressure
45. Dealing with Rumors
46. Calling a Friend on the Telephone
47. Answering the Telephone

# Emotion Management Skills

## Self-Regulation

48. Recognizing Feelings
49. Feeling Thermometer
50. Keeping Calm
51. Problem Solving
52. Talking to Others When Upset
53. Dealing with Family Problems
54. Understanding Anger
55. Dealing with Making a Mistake
56. Trying When Work Is Hard
57. Trying Something New

## Empathy

58. Showing Understanding for Others' Feelings: Preschool-Elementary
59. Showing Understanding for Others' Feelings: Preadolescent-Adulthood
60. Cheering up a Friend

## Conflict Management

61. Asserting Yourself
62. Accepting No for an Answer
63. Dealing with Teasing – K-4th Grade
64. Dealing with Teasing – 5th Grade and Up
65. More Words to Deal with Teasing
66. Dealing with Being Left Out
67. Avoiding Being "Set Up"
68. Giving Criticism in a Positive Way
69. Accepting Criticism
70. Having a Respectful Attitude

# Teaching the Skills

Each skill is designed to be taught using the structured learning approach (see Chapter 4). As mentioned, structured learning consists of four components:

- didactic instruction (verbal or pictorial explanation of the skill steps)
- modeling (live demonstrations of how to perform the skill)
- role-playing with feedback (having students physically go through the steps and providing them with corrective feedback until they can accurately perform the skill)
- practice assignments for outside the group

*Didactic instruction* can be accomplished by writing the skill steps on a blackboard or poster and describing each step to the students. The adult then *models* the skill – both the correct and the incorrect way – asking students for feedback after each step to see if it was conducted correctly or incorrectly (see Chapter 4). In the third step, the students are guided in *role-plays* of the skill. As the last step, the skill sheet is handed out as a homework assignment to encourage the student to *practice* the skill outside the lesson time and to return the sheet to the facilitator with information about the practice time.

The *activity sheets* for each skill provide ideas for how to "spice" up the presentation of the skill (e.g., by using an attention-engaging activity like a game show format) and makes suggestions for situations to model and role-play. The activity sheets also provide exercises to promote generalization of skills.

Typically, four to five activities are described on each activity sheet:

1. Situations to use for modeling and role-plays.
2. Ways to "bait" the skill. This means doing something that requires the student to show how to use the skill. For example, with the skill "Accepting No for an Answer," you might tell students that they will be tested on their ability to accept no. Show them a favorite food, game, or toy and wait for them to ask for it. Then say, "No, you cannot have it." If they accept no, then say, "Great job, you accepted no so you can have it now."
3. Redirecting inappropriate behavior to the correct skill. This involves instruction in how to use misbehavior as an opportunity to teach the appropriate skill.

4. Praising and rewarding skill enactment. This involves setting up incentives to increase the probability of the student choosing to use the skill.
5. Special note/activity related to the specific skill. This section may include a special tip that applies only to a given skill. For example, for the skill "Accepting No for an Answer," it is suggested that you offer the students double of what they want if they can accept no for an answer so they can see the payoff to waiting.

Although you can use the skill sheet and activity sheet alone to guide a skill lesson, it is recommended that you read the other chapters, particularly Chapters 4 and 5, to better understand how to conduct the lessons. Also, Chapter 3 on assessment issues is crucial in understanding what skills to teach and in what order. Focus only on the skills that are relevant to your students, making sure to first teach those skills that are prerequisites for other skills you will teach.

# Don't Be a Space Invader

1. Stand at least an arm's length away.

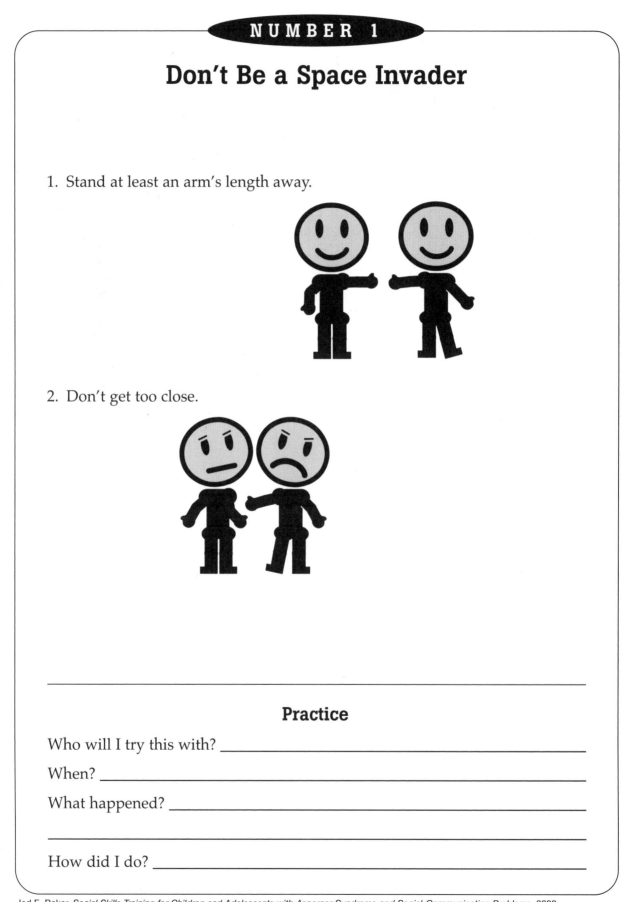

2. Don't get too close.

_____

## Practice

Who will I try this with? _____

When? _____

What happened? _____

_____

How did I do? _____

# Suggested Activities for
# Don't Be a Space Invader

1. Role-play situations in which a student must modify his personal space. For each situation, ask the student or observers to say when the actors get too close and when they are the right distance. Suggested role-plays:

    a. Greeting others the first time you see them and saying goodbye when you leave.
    b. Standing in line at school or in public (e.g., a movie, a store).
    c. Riding public transportation (e.g., not sitting or standing too close to others).
    d. Using a public restroom (e.g., not using the urinal right next to somebody else if there are others available).
    e. Requesting something from someone (e.g., asking for a snack or other food item that someone is holding, asking to play with someone's toy or game).
    f. Interrupting someone to ask a question about what was said, or to ask permission to do something.

2. Bait the skill. This means doing something that requires the student to maintain appropriate distance. Tell her you are going to test her ability to stay at least an arm's length away. Then get too close to her as you talk to her or stand in line with her.

3. Correct inappropriate distance. Say, "Don't be a space invader because it will make others uncomfortable and then they will not want to play with you. Keep an arm's length away."

4. Provide rewards for appropriate distance.

    a. Give verbal praise for correct or partially correct distance.
    b. Give tokens, pennies, or points for periods in which the student maintained an appropriate distance from others. When the student gets an agreed-upon number of tokens (e.g., five tokens), give a special reward (e.g., snack, stickers, or privileges to play special game).

Jed E. Baker, *Social Skills Training for Children and Adolescents with Asperger Syndrome and Social-Communication Problems*, 2003. Shawnee Mission, KS: Autism Asperger Publishing Company; www.asperger.net

# Listening Position

1. Make eye contact.

2. Stay still. Quiet hands and feet.

3. Don't interrupt. Do not talk while others are talking.

4. If you are in class and you want to say something, raise your hand and wait to be called on.

---

## Practice

Who will I try this with? _____

When? _____

What happened? _____

_____

How did I do? _____

Jed E. Baker, *Social Skills Training for Children and Adolescents with Asperger Syndrome and Social-Communication Problems*, 2003. Shawnee Mission, KS: Autism Asperger Publishing Company; www.asperger.net

# Suggested Activities for Listening Position

1. Role-play the steps for LISTENING POSITION. As a parent or teacher, model the correct and the wrong way and ask the student to tell what you did right or wrong. Suggested role-plays:

   a. Listening to a story time or lesson in class
   b. Listening to a parent give instructions
   c. Listening to another student during "show and tell"
   d. Raising your hand to ask a question about a lesson or to ask permission to go to the bathroom during class time

2. Correct inappropriate listening. Have student demonstrate a good listening position.

3. Provide rewards for appropriate LISTENING POSITION.

   a. Give verbal praise for correct or partially correct LISTENING POSITION.
   b. Give tokens, pennies, or points for periods in which the student demonstrates a good listening position. When he gets an agreed-upon number of tokens (e.g., five tokens), give a special reward (e.g., snack, stickers, and privileges to play special game or watch a special show).

Jed E. Baker, *Social Skills Training for Children and Adolescents with Asperger Syndrome and Social-Communication Problems*, 2003. Shawnee Mission, KS: Autism Asperger Publishing Company; www.asperger.net

# Tone of Voice

1. Use just enough volume in your voice so others can hear you.

   a. Your voice should be softer when you are inside and there are few other noises around. We call this an "inside voice."

   b. Your voice may need to be louder when you are outside or there are many other noises around.

2. Try not to speak too fast or others will not understand you.

3. Unless you are angry with someone, use a happy, respectful tone of voice.

## Practice

Who will I try this with? _____

When? _____

What happened? _____

_____

How did I do? _____

Jed E. Baker, *Social Skills Training for Children and Adolescents with Asperger Syndrome and Social-Communication Problems*, 2003. Shawnee Mission, KS: Autism Asperger Publishing Company; www.asperger.net

# Suggested Activities for
# Tone of Voice

1. Model and role-play different types of VOICE TONE. You can make this into a game by giving tokens or prizes for correct responses. Prizes can be given to the student acting out the tone of voice, or to observers who accurately indicate whether the voice tone was appropriate for the situation.

   a. Have the student communicate a message to another using the appropriate volume for each of these situations.
      (1) Inside the class or home where no one else is talking (quiet voice).
      (2) Inside the class or home where many others are talking (louder voice).
      (3) Inside the class or home where you are right next to the listener (quiet voice).
      (4) Inside the class or home where you are far from the listener (louder voice).
      (5) Outside on the playground (louder voice).
      (6) Outside watching a performance where the audience is quiet (quiet voice).

   b. Have the student communicate a message using an **angry** or **respectful/happy** tone of voice. A respectful tone usually has softer articulations of the consonant sounds, whereas an angry tone usually uses a more staccato, precise pronunciation. Try using a tape recorder so the child can listen to her own tone in the following situations:
      (1) The student asks permission to go somewhere or have something (respectful tone).
      (2) The student tells someone to stop yelling at her or hitting her (angry tone).

   c. Have the student communicate a message in a fast rather slower pace. Again, use a tape recorder so the student can hear herself. Make up intricate messages to see if others can hear and remember what the student said. Give points or prizes when the communication is received clearly.

2. Bait the skill. This means doing something that requires the student to use an appropriate tone.

   a. For example, purposely stand far away or create background noise to see if the student adjusts his volume.

3. Provide corrective feedback when the student's tone is inappropriate.

4. Provide rewards for appropriate tone of voice.

   a. Give verbal praise for correct or partially correct tone of voice.
   b. Give tokens, pennies, or points every time, or for periods in which the student uses an appropriate tone. When he gets an agreed-upon number of tokens (e.g., five tokens), give a special reward (e.g., snack, stickers, and privileges to play a special game).

Jed E. Baker, *Social Skills Training for Children and Adolescents with Asperger Syndrome and Social-Communication Problems*, 2003.
Shawnee Mission, KS: Autism Asperger Publishing Company; www.asperger.net

# Greetings

1. The first time you see someone during the day, you say, "Hi, how are you?"

2. When you pass someone in the hallway, you say, "Hi."

3. When someone is leaving for the day, you say, "Goodbye."

## Practice

Who will I try this with? _____

When? _____

What happened? _____

_____

How did I do? _____

Jed E. Baker, *Social Skills Training for Children and Adolescents with Asperger Syndrome and Social-Communication Problems*, 2003.
Shawnee Mission, KS: Autism Asperger Publishing Company; www.asperger.net

# Suggested Activities for Greetings

1. Model and role-play the skill using the following situations.

   a. Pretend it is the first time a student sees his teacher and classmates in the morning. Role-play the correct way in which you say hello and good morning. Point out the wrong way in which you either do not say hello or say it over and over to the same person.

   b. Pretend to pass someone in the hallway. Practice saying, "hello" or waving hello.

   c. Pretend it is the end of the school day or guests at your house are leaving. Role-play the correct way in which you say goodbye. Point out the wrong way in which you either do not say goodbye or you say it over and over to the same person.

2. Bait the skill. Purposely walk close to the person first thing in the morning and do not say anything, waiting for the student to say hello first. Do the same thing when students are leaving for the day and it is appropriate to say goodbye. If nothing is said, make the greeting and wait for them to respond. If nothing is said again, prompt them to make the greeting.

3. Provide corrective feedback when the student does not make a greeting.

4. Provide rewards for appropriate greetings.

   a. Give verbal praise for correct or partially correct greetings.

   b. Give tokens, pennies, or points every time the student makes an appropriate greeting. When he gets an agreed-upon number of tokens (e.g., five tokens), give a special reward (e.g., snack, stickers, or privileges to play a special game).

Jed E. Baker, *Social Skills Training for Children and Adolescents with Asperger Syndrome and Social-Communication Problems*, 2003. Shawnee Mission, KS: Autism Asperger Publishing Company; www.asperger.net

# How and When to Interrupt

1. Decide if you need to interrupt.

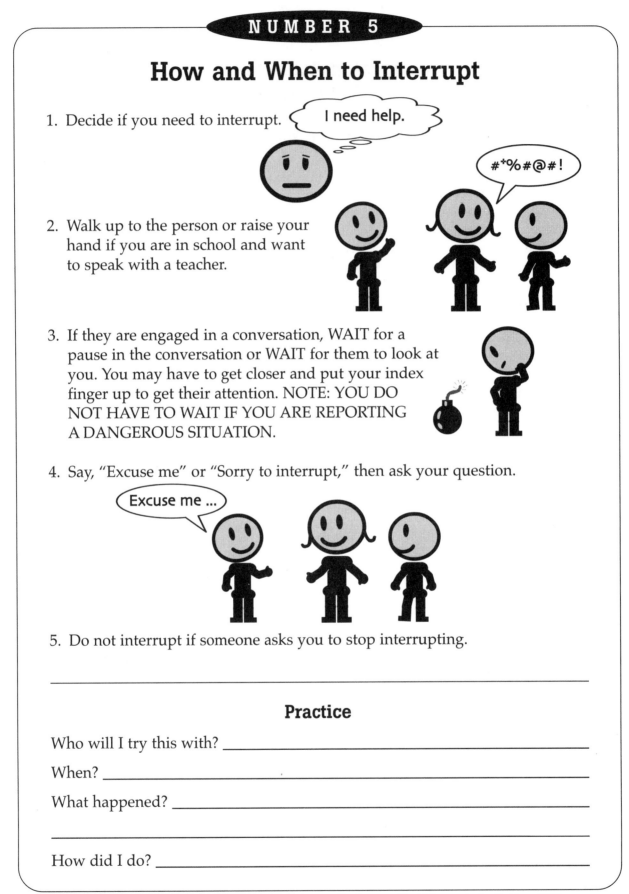

I need help.

#*⁺%#@#!

2. Walk up to the person or raise your hand if you are in school and want to speak with a teacher.

3. If they are engaged in a conversation, WAIT for a pause in the conversation or WAIT for them to look at you. You may have to get closer and put your index finger up to get their attention. NOTE: YOU DO NOT HAVE TO WAIT IF YOU ARE REPORTING A DANGEROUS SITUATION.

4. Say, "Excuse me" or "Sorry to interrupt," then ask your question.

Excuse me ...

5. Do not interrupt if someone asks you to stop interrupting.

_____

## Practice

Who will I try this with? _____

When? _____

What happened? _____

_____

How did I do? _____

Jed E. Baker, *Social Skills Training for Children and Adolescents with Asperger Syndrome and Social-Communication Problems*, 2003.
Shawnee Mission, KS: Autism Asperger Publishing Company; www.asperger.net

# Suggested Activities for
# How and When to Interrupt

1. Role-play the steps for HOW AND WHEN TO INTERRUPT. Suggested role-plays involve the following scenarios:

   a. Asking permission in class/camp (e.g., to use bathroom, get a drink of water, or borrow something).

   b. Needing help with something (e.g., schoolwork, getting a zipper up, tying a shoe, opening a jar).

   c. Being asked to be a messenger from one class to another, or from one parent to another.

   d. If hearing people talking about something the student is interested in (e.g., a popular TV character, video game, weekend plans). After the student says, "Excuse me," he can say, "Were you talking about ___?" and then ask a question about it. (See JOINING A CONVERSATION.)

   e. If coming to tell a parent or teacher about a dangerous situation (e.g., if someone is hurt, something is on fire, or a sibling ran away). Reinforce that the student should not wait, but interrupt immediately in these situations.

2. Bait the skill. This means doing something that requires the student to interrupt.

   a. For example, take the student's pencil and then say, "Everyone, please take out a pencil."

   b. Purposely ignore when you see a child needing something so that the child must interrupt to ask for what he or she wants.

3. Correct inappropriate interrupting. Have student interrupt again the right way if he interrupts incorrectly.

4. Provide rewards for appropriate HOW AND WHEN TO INTERRUPT.

   a. Give verbal praise for correct or partially correct HOW AND WHEN TO INTERRUPT.

   b. Give tokens, pennies, or points every time students interrupt appropriately. When they get an agreed-upon number of tokens (e.g., five tokens), give a special reward (e.g., snack, stickers, privileges to play special game or watch special show).

Jed E. Baker, *Social Skills Training for Children and Adolescents with Asperger Syndrome and Social-Communication Problems*, 2003. Shawnee Mission, KS: Autism Asperger Publishing Company; www.asperger.net

# Staying on Topic

| Topic: |
|--------|

| On-Topic 🙂 | Off-Topic 😠 |
|---|---|
| **ASK** <br><br> Who _____? <br><br> What _____? <br><br> Where _____? <br><br> When _____? <br><br> Why _____? <br><br> How _____? <br><br> What else _____? <br><br> **TELL** <br><br> I like _____? <br><br> I also _____? <br><br> I went _____? <br><br> I am going _____? | |

## Practice

Who will I try this with? _____

When? _____

What happened? _____

_____

How did I do? _____

Jed E. Baker, *Social Skills Training for Children and Adolescents with Asperger Syndrome and Social-Communication Problems*, 2003.
Shawnee Mission, KS: Autism Asperger Publishing Company; www.asperger.net

# Suggested Activities for Staying on Topic

1. Pick a topic and write it at the top of the page where it says "topic." Then ask students to ask a question or make a comment on the topic.

   a. Start with concrete topics like a "show and tell" object that the students can see. Graduate to using more abstract topics like a picture of a past event. Then try to fade out the pictures and use the words to describe a past or future event (e.g., topic might be "What I did yesterday").

   b. Use flash cards with questions or comments written on them for students who cannot initially generate their own questions or comments with the prompts provided on the skill sheet.

   c. Give points for all on-topic utterances and no points for off-topic comments. When students get enough points, they may get a prize.

2. Correct off-topic comments or questions by saying, "That's off-topic, we were talking about ____." Tell students to stay on topic until people stop talking, then they can ask to talk about something else.

3. Provide rewards for STAYING ON TOPIC.

   a. Give verbal praise for correct or partially correct on-topic utterances.

   b. Give tokens, pennies, or points for periods in which students stay on topic. When they get an agreed-upon number of tokens, give a special reward (e.g., stickers, and privileges to play special game or watch special show).

Jed E. Baker, *Social Skills Training for Children and Adolescents with Asperger Syndrome and Social-Communication Problems*, 2003. Shawnee Mission, KS: Autism Asperger Publishing Company; www.asperger.net

# Maintaining a Conversation

1. Show a good listening position:

   a. Make eye contact. Look at their eyes.
   b. Face them.
   c. Stay at least an arm's length away.

2. Wait for a pause before talking. Don't interrupt.

3. Ask follow-up questions about the topic they are discussing.
   "Who _____?"
   "What _____?"
   "Where _____?"
   "When _____?"
   "Why _____?"
   "How _____?"

4. Make on-topic comments.  Say something that is on topic.

   "I like that too."
   "I also _____."
   "I went _____."

_____

## Practice

Who will I try this with? _____

When? _____

What happened? _____

_____

How did I do? _____

Jed E. Baker, *Social Skills Training for Children and Adolescents with Asperger Syndrome and Social-Communication Problems*, 2003.
Shawnee Mission, KS: Autism Asperger Publishing Company; www.asperger.net

# Suggested Activities for
# Maintaining a Conversation

1. Role-play the steps for MAINTAINING A CONVERSATION. Suggested role-plays involve the following scenarios:

   a. Asking a parent, peer, or teacher about his or her day and trying to keep the conversation going on-topic. Give out tokens for every question and comment that is on-topic.

   b. Someone presenting a "show and tell" item while others must ask questions and make comments about the item.

   c. Creating a mystery bag with hidden items inside the bag (like a ball, food, or other familiar items). Have the students ask questions or make comments until they can guess what is in the bag.

   d. Playing a "guess who" game where someone pretends to be someone famous and the other person has to guess who it is by asking follow-up questions.

   e. Doing a mock interview of a famous person.

   f. Picking a topic and writing "on" and "off" on a piece of paper. Ask the student to make on-topic comments and questions. Give points for all on-topic utterances and minus points for off-topic comments. When students get enough points, they may get a prize.

2. Correct inappropriate listening and shifts in conversation. Have the student show LISTENING POSITION and say something ON TOPIC. Repeat what the topic is, if necessary, to help the student generate an on-topic question or comment. See SHIFTING TOPICS for information on how and when to shift topics.

3. Bait the use of the skill. Using the mystery bag (see above) or some other surprise, try to motivate the child to want to ask or tell until she can guess what information you have withheld.

4. Provide rewards for appropriate listening.

   a. Give verbal praise for correct or partially correct listening.

   b. Give tokens, pennies, or points for periods in which the student listens appropriately. When she gets an agreed-upon number of tokens, give a special reward (e.g., snack, stickers, and privileges to play special game or watch special show).

Jed E. Baker, *Social Skills Training for Children and Adolescents with Asperger Syndrome and Social-Communication Problems*, 2003. Shawnee Mission, KS: Autism Asperger Publishing Company; www.asperger.net

# Taking Turns (Two-Question Rule)

1. When others greet you, greet them back.
   a. If they say "Hello," then say "Hello" back to them.

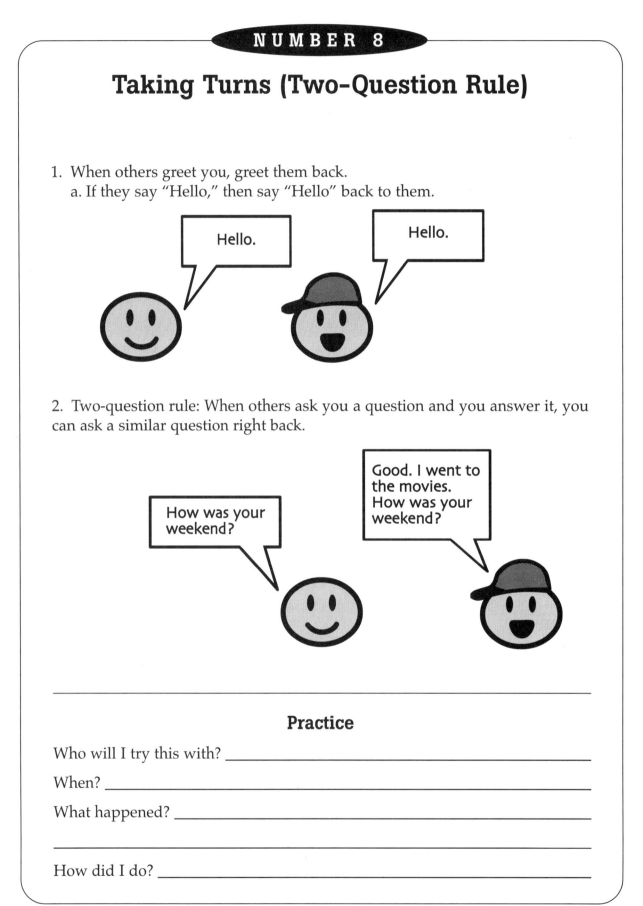

2. Two-question rule: When others ask you a question and you answer it, you can ask a similar question right back.

---

## Practice

Who will I try this with? _____

When? _____

What happened? _____

_____

How did I do? _____

Jed E. Baker, *Social Skills Training for Children and Adolescents with Asperger Syndrome and Social-Communication Problems*, 2003. Shawnee Mission, KS: Autism Asperger Publishing Company; www.asperger.net

# Suggested Activities for Taking Turns Talking

1. Role-play the steps for TAKING TURNS TALKING. Suggested role-plays involve the following scenarios:

   a. Greet the students and prompt them to greet you back. Do the same for goodbyes.

   b. Ask them how they are and what they have been doing. After they respond, prompt them to ask back. Repeat with questions about future plans (e.g., what are you doing this weekend) and present-oriented questions (e.g., what are you playing, eating, doing?).

   c. Pick topics about which people have different preferences (movies, TV shows, food, school subjects, etc.). Prompt students to take turns sharing their preferences about each topic (e.g., "I like pizza, what food do you like?"). This activity can also be used to find out what students have in common as a basis for conversation and friendship.

   d. Use two colors of tokens, one for questions and one for comments. During conversations dispense the tokens as students form questions and comments. The goal is for each student to end up with an equal number of tokens from each color, and to have equal number of tokens compared to each other.

2. Correct inappropriate turn taking by pointing out when one student dominates the conversation. Prompt them to ask others a question to maintain turn taking.

3. Bait the use of the skill. Ask a student a question or share information about something you did and gesture for him or her to ask or share back. For example, say, "I went to the zoo this weekend." Instead of asking where the student went, simply wait for the student to share back what he did over the weekend.

4. Provide rewards for appropriate turn taking.

   a. Give verbal praise for correct or partially turn taking.

   b. Give tokens, pennies, or points for periods in which the student takes turns talking. When he gets an agreed-upon number of tokens, give a special reward (e.g., snack, stickers, and privileges to play special game or watch special show).

Jed E. Baker, *Social Skills Training for Children and Adolescents with Asperger Syndrome and Social-Communication Problems*, 2003. Shawnee Mission, KS: Autism Asperger Publishing Company; www.asperger.net

# Starting a Conversation

1. Greet the person.

   Say, "Hi" or "How are you?" the first time you see a person during the day.

2. Ask questions about what the person is doing in the PRESENT SITUATION.

   "What are you [doing] [talking about] [eating] [reading]?"

   "How do you like this [class, lunch, project, game]?"

   "Where did you get the [shirt, hat, sneakers, watch]?"

3. Ask questions about the PAST.

   "How was your [day, week, weekend, vacation, holiday]?"

   "Did you hear about [what happened in the news, the new TV show, a sports game]?"

4. Questions about the FUTURE.

   "What are you going to do [after school, this weekend, this week, for vacation]?"

5. Ask about one of THE PERSON'S INTERESTS.

   "Have you been [doing a favorite activity, playing a favorite game, watching a favorite TV show, working on a favorite project] lately?"

6. Remember to ask follow-up questions and make on-topic comments.
   WHO, WHAT, WHERE, WHEN, WHY, HOW, WHAT ELSE …?

---

## Practice

Who will I try this with? _____

When? _____

What happened? _____

_____

How did I do? _____

Jed E. Baker, *Social Skills Training for Children and Adolescents with Asperger Syndrome and Social-Communication Problems*, 2003. Shawnee Mission, KS: Autism Asperger Publishing Company; www.asperger.net

# Suggested Activities for Starting a Conversation

1. Activities to review or generate STARTING A CONVERSATION include:

   a. Ask students what they would say to start a conversation in each of the situations listed below. Use a quiz show format with points or play money for appropriate responses.

   b. When students are in their language arts classes, see if they can be assigned to write sentences and paragraphs that are conversation starters for various situations. In other words, when students are working on grammar or paragraph formation, they can also be working on STARTING A CONVERSATION.

   c. Make a list of people you know and things that they do. For example, write down what jobs they have, their hobbies or interests, and what classes they take. Use this as the basis for conversation starters. For example, if you know that a fellow group member likes basketball, then ask, "Have you seen any good basketball games lately?"

2. Role-play STARTING A CONVERSATION. Suggested role-plays include:

   a. Use the situations listed below or ask the students to tell you actual situations they have experienced. Let each conversation continue for several minutes so the students also work on maintaining a conversation.

   b. Play the conversation freeze game. Have students wander the room until the teacher says freeze. Each student must then turn to the nearest student and ask one of the conversation starters. The teacher can give them the question (e.g., what are you going to do after school?). Then they must exchange the information. The teacher then asks each student what they learned from the other student. In this way the students must actually listen to each other. Tokens can be given out for remembering what their partner says. Then the teacher can ask students to wander again until the next "freeze" where a new question will be posed to a new partner. The teacher (or a parent) can do this daily with the same set of conversation starters until the students have memorized the questions.

   c. A variant of the above game is to list conversation starters on posters in various places. Students are asked to go to an area with a partner and ask the conversation starter that is posted on the wall in that area. The teacher or parent then asks the students what they learned from their partner to test if they listened to each other.

3. Bait the skill. This means doing something that requires the student to "Start a Conversation."

   a. For example, purposely stay quiet when you see the student for the first time during the day or when you have something in your hand you know might be interesting to the student (e.g., a picture of something, a new game, or a book). Then prompt or wait for him to start the conversation.

4. Correct inappropriate ways to start a conversation, such as launching into a monologue about a subject of little interest to others. Prompt by saying, "First ask how the other person is doing or how she has been. Then ask if she wants to hear about what you want to talk about." (Also see the skill called TALKING BRIEFLY.)

5. Provide rewards for appropriately STARTING A CONVERSATION.

   a. Give verbal praise for correct or partially correctly STARTING A CONVERSATION.

   b. Give tokens, pennies, or points every time students start a conversation appropriately. When they get five tokens, give a special reward (e.g., snack, stickers, or privileges to play special game).

## Situations for STARTING A CONVERSATION

**Past:**
   1. You overhear someone talking about her vacation.
   2. You see your friend on a Monday morning.
   3. You see your classmates after a school break.
   4. A friend just came back from taking a hard test.

**Present:**
   5. You are eating lunch with your classmates.
   6. You see someone playing with a Gameboy™ or some electronic toy.
   7. You see someone wearing a T-shirt that has the name of a school on it.
   8. You are in line at a movie theater and you see someone from school who is also on line.

**Future:**
   9. It's Friday before school lets out for the weekend and you are with your classmates.
   10. It's the end of the school day on Wednesday and you are saying goodbye to your friends.
   11. You overhear your friends talking about their school break plans.

Jed E. Baker, *Social Skills Training for Children and Adolescents with Asperger Syndrome and Social-Communication Problems*, 2003. Shawnee Mission, KS: Autism Asperger Publishing Company; www.asperger.net

# Joining a Conversation

1. Listen to what the people are talking about to identify the topic of conversation.

2. Walk up to the people talking.

3. Wait for them to look at you or wait for a pause in their conversation.

4. Say, "Excuse me, were you talking about _____?"
   (Topic)

5. Ask a question about the topic:
   Who … What … When … Where … Why … How … What else?

## Practice

Who will I try this with? _____

When? _____

What happened? _____

_____

How did I do? _____

Jed E. Baker, *Social Skills Training for Children and Adolescents with Asperger Syndrome and Social-Communication Problems*, 2003. Shawnee Mission, KS: Autism Asperger Publishing Company; www.asperger.net

# Suggested Activities for
# Joining a Conversation

1. Role-play the steps for JOINING A CONVERSATION. Suggested role-plays involve the following scenarios:

    a. Have two students start a conversation about what they did over the weekend, or what they will do after school or group, or any other topic you choose (e.g., favorite movies, sports teams, food, TV shows, something in the news, video game, vacation spot, etc.). Have a third student join the conversation by listening for the topic and asking or telling something relevant. Have one of the original two students leave, and begin a new conversation with the pair that remain. Then have yet another student join in. Continue until all students have had a chance to join a conversation between two people.

    b. Have a group conversation and give out tokens for any student who asks or tells on-topic, thus participating and joining in the conversation. This can occur in a small group, where students review their week or discuss a specific topic such as those listed above.

2. Prompt those who withdraw from conversation to join in. Prompts can be simple (e.g., Can you ask or tell something about what they are saying?") or more scripted (e.g., "They were talking about movies, can you ask them what movie they liked best?").

3. Bait the use of the skill. Talk about students' favorite topic or interest in front of them until they spontaneously join in with a question or comment.

4. Provide rewards for joining in.

    a. Give verbal praise for correct or partially correct joining in.

    b. Give tokens, pennies, or points for instances in which the student joined a conversation. When she gets an agreed-upon number of tokens, give a special reward (e.g., snack, stickers, and privileges to play special game or watch special show).

Jed E. Baker, *Social Skills Training for Children and Adolescents with Asperger Syndrome and Social-Communication Problems*, 2003. Shawnee Mission, KS: Autism Asperger Publishing Company; www.asperger.net

# Ending a Conversation

1. Decide if you need to end the conversation.

    a. Is it because you have to do something else or because you are late in getting somewhere?

    b. Is it because you are bored?

2. Ask one more follow-up question or make one more on-topic comment to show you care about what the person is saying. For example, say "That's interesting."

3. Decide what to say to end the conversation.

    a. If you are late, say, "Well, I have to go because I am late."

    b. If you have to do something else, say, "Well, I have to go because I have other things to do."

    c. If you are bored, do not tell the other person you feel bored. Make an excuse that you have other things to do. Say, "I have to go because I have other things to do."

4. Say, "See you later," and then leave or walk away.

_____

## Practice

Who will I try this with? _____

When? _____

What happened? _____

_____

How did I do? _____

Jed E. Baker, *Social Skills Training for Children and Adolescents with Asperger Syndrome and Social-Communication Problems*, 2003. Shawnee Mission, KS: Autism Asperger Publishing Company; www.asperger.net

# Suggested Activities for
# Ending a Conversation

1. Role-play the steps for ENDING A CONVERSATION. Suggested role-plays involve the following scenarios:

    a. A student is talking with another student about their favorite video game, food, movie, TV show, sport, or other activity. One of the students realizes he is late for class and therefore must end the conversation.

    b. Again two students discuss one of the topics above. One of the students begins to go on and on about his interests while the other student is getting bored. The bored student must end the conversation appropriately.

    c. This time one of the students has homework to do, which he will not be able to finish unless he stops talking. He must end the conversation appropriately.

2. Correct inappropriate or abrupt endings. Have the student show interest with a question and then make an appropriate excuse to end the conversation.

3. Bait the use of the skill. Purposely talk on and on in a boring way, or start talking when the student wants to play or leave, then prompt the appropriate ending.

4. Provide rewards for appropriately ending the conversation

    a. Give verbal praise for correct or partially correct ways to end the conversation.

    b. Give tokens, pennies, or points in instances in which the student ended the conversation appropriately. When she gets an agreed-upon number of tokens, give a special reward (e.g., snack, stickers, and privileges to play special game or watch special show).

Jed E. Baker, *Social Skills Training for Children and Adolescents with Asperger Syndrome and Social-Communication Problems*, 2003. Shawnee Mission, KS: Autism Asperger Publishing Company; www.asperger.net

# Asking a Question
# When You Don't Understand

1. When you do not understand what someone is saying, say, "I do not understand."

2. If the person repeats what he said and you still do not understand, you can:

   a. Say, "I still do not understand. Can you explain it in a different way?"
   b. Ask someone else to explain it to you.

---

## Practice

Who will I try this with? _____

When? _____

What happened? _____

_____

How did I do? _____

Jed E. Baker, *Social Skills Training for Children and Adolescents with Asperger Syndrome and Social-Communication Problems*, 2003.
Shawnee Mission, KS: Autism Asperger Publishing Company; www.asperger.net

# Suggested Activities for
# Asking a Question When You Don't Understand

1. Role-play the steps for ASKING A QUESTION WHEN YOU DON'T UNDER-STAND. Suggested role-plays involve the following scenarios:

    a. The teacher or parent gives the student instructions for completing typical class work, but says it in another language or uses a fancy word to describe an action. For example, "Please circle all the 'corpulent' words in the following sentences." One can then prompt the student to ask for clarification, and explain that the student should circle any word with more than four letters.

    b. Give vague instructions like, "Please put your name on your paper and then write about the thing or the stuff" (with no reference to what the stuff or thing refers to).

2. Prompt students to ask for clarification when they do not respond to questions or instructions.

3. Bait the use of the skill. Tell students that they can receive a great reward when they complete a task or answer a question. Then ask them something they will not understand or give vague instructions so they will have to ask for clarification to get the reward.

4. Provide rewards for appropriate listening.

    a. Give verbal praise for correct or partially correct asking for clarification.

    b. Give tokens, pennies, or points for instances in which the student said he does not understand. When he gets an agreed-upon number of tokens, give a special reward (e.g., snack, stickers, and privileges to play special game or watch special show).

Jed E. Baker, *Social Skills Training for Children and Adolescents with Asperger Syndrome and Social-Communication Problems*, 2003. Shawnee Mission, KS: Autism Asperger Publishing Company; www.asperger.net

# Saying "I Don't Know"

1. When others ask you questions that you understand, but you do not know what the answer is, say something to respond to their question. You can say,

   a. "I don't know" – if you do not have the answer.
   b. "Let me think about it" – if you need more time to think about the answer.

2. Do not just keep silent. Let the other person know that you are thinking about the question or do not know the answer.

_____

## Practice

Who will I try this with? _____

When? _____

What happened? _____

_____

How did I do? _____

Jed E. Baker, *Social Skills Training for Children and Adolescents with Asperger Syndrome and Social-Communication Problems*, 2003.
Shawnee Mission, KS: Autism Asperger Publishing Company; www.asperger.net

# Suggested Activities for
# Saying I Don't Know

1. Role-play the steps for SAYING I DON'T KNOW. Suggested role-plays involve the following scenarios:

   a. The teacher or parent asks factual questions of the student in simple language. For example, the teacher might ask how many pairs of socks the student's mother owns, or the name of his teacher's dentist. Prompt students to say they do not know rather than be nonresponsive.

   b. Sometimes children do not know how they feel or what they prefer when choosing food, TV, or other activities. Prompt them to say "I do not know," or to pick one choice rather than remaining quiet.

2. Prompt students to say "I do not know" when you have asked a straightforward question and they do not respond.

3. Bait the use of the skill. Tell students that they can receive a great reward when they correctly answer a question. Explain that one correct answer may be "I do not know." Then ask them something they do and something they do not know, prompting them to accurately say they do not know when that is the case.

4. Provide rewards for appropriate listening.

   a. Give students verbal praise for correct or partially correct sharing that they do not know.

   b. Give tokens, pennies, or points for instances in which students say they do not know when, in fact, they do not know. When they get an agreed-upon number of tokens, give a special reward (e.g., snack, stickers, and privileges to play special game or watch special show).

Jed E. Baker, *Social Skills Training for Children and Adolescents with Asperger Syndrome and Social-Communication Problems*, 2003. Shawnee Mission, KS: Autism Asperger Publishing Company; www.asperger.net

# Introducing Yourself

1. Decide if this is a person you want to meet.

    a. Maybe you have something in common with the person and could be friends.

2. Wait for a pause before talking.

3. Try to get the person's attention with a gesture or by saying, "Excuse me."

4. Make eye contact and use a strong, positive tone of voice.

5. Say, "My name is _____. What's your name."

6. Then say, "It's a pleasure to meet you."

# Introducing Others

1. When you are with several people you know, but who do not know each other, it is your job to introduce them to each other.

2. Say to Person #1, "_____, I would like you to meet _____."
                          Person #1                                    Person #2

3. Say to Person #2, "_____, I would like you to meet _____."
                          Person #2                                    Person #1

4. Then you can explain who each person is to you.  For example, "_____ is my friend," or "_____ is my mother."

---

## Practice

Who will I try this with? _____

When? _____

What happened? _____

_____

How did I do? _____

Jed E. Baker, *Social Skills Training for Children and Adolescents with Asperger Syndrome and Social-Communication Problems*, 2003. Shawnee Mission, KS: Autism Asperger Publishing Company; www.asperger.net

# Suggested Activities for Introducing Yourself and Others

1. Role-play the steps for INTRODUCTIONS. Suggested role-plays involve the following scenarios:

   a. Have students pretend to introduce themselves to new children in class, or to children they meet in the park, or in the cafeteria.
   b. Have students pretend to meet adult friends of their parents, teachers, or community leaders.
   c. Have students pretend to introduce their friends to their parents and vice versa.
   d. Have students pretend to introduce their old friends to new friends.

2. Prompt students to introduce themselves to any new individual in class or at home. Prompt students to refrain from introducing themselves to the same people more than once, or to strangers with whom they will have no continuing relationship or no basis for friendship.

3. Bait the use of the skill. Have new people purposely come to the classroom or home, and then prompt the use of the skill.

4. Provide rewards for appropriate introductions.

   a. Give verbal praise for correct or partially correct introductions.
   b. Give tokens, pennies, or points for instances in which the student appropriately introduces himself. When he gets an agreed-upon number of tokens, give a special reward (e.g., snack, stickers, and privileges to play special game or watch special show).

Jed E. Baker, *Social Skills Training for Children and Adolescents with Asperger Syndrome and Social-Communication Problems*, 2003. Shawnee Mission, KS: Autism Asperger Publishing Company; www.asperger.net

# Getting to Know Someone New

1. Start the conversation by asking a question about something you see in the present moment or about something you might have in common with the person:

   a. Ask, "What are you [doing, reading, eating, playing]?"

   b. If you are in the same class or in the same place ask, "So how do you like this [class, place]?"

2. Introduce yourself.

   a. Say, "By the way, my name is _____, what's your name?"

3. Ask questions to get to know the person.

| OKAY TOPICS | OKAY QUESTIONS |
| --- | --- |
| SCHOOL | Where do you go to school? <br> What grade are you in? <br> Who are your teachers? |
| AGE (for kids only) | How old are you? (do not ask an adult) |
| NEIGHBORHOOD | Where do you live? <br> What's it like there? |
| INTERESTS | What do you like to do for fun? <br> What games do you like? <br> What TV shows do you watch? <br> What kind of music do you like? |
| FAMILY | Do you have a big family? <br> Do you have brothers and sisters? |

4. Do not ask about "sensitive topics" unless the other person brings it up first. Sensitive topics are subjects that can make others upset. For example,

   a. Don't ask about someone's race or religion when you first meet them.

   b. Don't ask about something that makes the person look different or sound different.

   c. Don't ask the person about any problems she may have.

## Practice

Who will I try this with? _____

When? _____

What happened? _____

_____

How did I do? _____

Jed E. Baker, *Social Skills Training for Children and Adolescents with Asperger Syndrome and Social-Communication Problems*, 2003. Shawnee Mission, KS: Autism Asperger Publishing Company; www.asperger.net

# Suggested Activities for
# Getting to Know Someone New

1. Role-play the steps for GETTING TO KNOW SOMEONE NEW. Suggested role-plays involve the following scenarios:

   a. Have students pretend to meet a new child in class. For example, they can start by asking how the new student likes the new class or school.

   b. Students can pretend to meet someone at the park, asking if they like the park or playground equipment they are using to begin (e.g., "Do you like the swings? Me too. My name is . . .").

   c. Students can pretend to meet someone in the cafeteria. They can begin, "What are you eating?" or "The lunch room is pretty loud, right?"

   d. Students can pretend to meet someone at a party. They can begin with, "So how do you know . . . ?" referring to the host of the party.

2. Prompt students to get to know any new individual in class or at home. Correct the use of any sensitive topics during this first encounter.

3. Bait the use of the skill. Have new people purposely come to the classroom or home and then prompt the use of the skill.

4. Provide rewards for appropriate GETTING TO KNOW SOMEONE NEW.

   a. Give verbal praise for correct or partially correct attempts to get to know others.

   b. Give tokens, pennies, or points for instances in which the student is willing to try to talk with and get to know new students. When he gets an agreed-upon number of tokens, give a special reward (e.g., snack, stickers, and privileges to play special game or watch special show).

Jed E. Baker, *Social Skills Training for Children and Adolescents with Asperger Syndrome and Social-Communication Problems*, 2003. Shawnee Mission, KS: Autism Asperger Publishing Company; www.asperger.net

# Introducing Topics of Interest to Others

1. When you want to tell someone something, wait for a good time to talk, like when there is a pause in the conversation or the person is not busy with something else.

2. Then ask if it is okay to talk. You could say:

    a. "I have something I would like to talk about. Is this a good time?"
    b. "Excuse me. May I ask you something?" "Did you hear about …?"

3. Try to pick a topic that others might be interested in. Examples might be:

    a. Telling about something that **happened to you** or something you did recently.
    b. Telling about something that **happened in the news**, like a breaking story or a sporting event.
    c. Asking about something you might have **in common** with the other person. For example, discussing a TV show, game, place or food you both like.
    d. Asking others for **advice or opinions** about something. For example, if you have a problem, you could ask others what they think you could do about it.

_____

## Practice

Who will I try this with? _____

When? _____

What happened? _____

_____

How did I do? _____

Jed E. Baker, *Social Skills Training for Children and Adolescents with Asperger Syndrome and Social-Communication Problems*, 2003. Shawnee Mission, KS: Autism Asperger Publishing Company; www.asperger.net

# Suggested Activities for
# Introducing Topics of Interest to Others

1. If you have a small group, have students first review different topic areas such as TV shows, foods, hobbies, books, games, sports, school subjects, etc. Find out which topics are of common interest and post them. This will serve as a basis for students introducing interesting topics to each other.

2. For middle-schoolers and older students, have them keep track of current news events in a journal. They can use this later as a basis for discussion.

3. Role-play the steps for INTRODUCING TOPICS OF INTEREST TO OTHERS. Suggested role-plays involve the following scenarios:

    a. Have students introduce a common interest for discussion. Contrast this with students introducing a topic only of interest to them and lecturing others about it.
    b. Have students discuss an experience they had and then ask others if they ever had a similar experience. For example, "I went to the museum yesterday and saw . . . Has anyone else ever gone to the museum?" Contrast this with talking about an experience without asking others and demonstrate how this would grow boring to others after a while.
    c. Have students introduce topics from the news. "Did you hear about . . .?"
    d. Have students ask other students for advice. Point out that for older students this can be especially helpful in engaging the opposite sex. One can ask advice on dating or clothes or hair styles. This can help typical peers take a "big brother or sister role" with a student with a disability, allowing the student to have a recognized place in a social grouping.

4. Correct inappropriate introductions of topics, as when a student talks at others about their interest with little sensitivity to the audience. Redirect the students to talk about a common interest, event or experience, or to ask for advice.

5. Provide rewards for introducing interesting topics.

    a. Give verbal praise for correct or partially correct introductions of appropriate topics.
    b. Give tokens, pennies, or points for instances in which the student appropriately introduced topics of interest. When she gets an agreed-upon number of tokens, give a special reward (e.g., snack, stickers, and privileges to play special game or watch special show).

Jed E. Baker, *Social Skills Training for Children and Adolescents with Asperger Syndrome and Social-Communication Problems*, 2003. Shawnee Mission, KS: Autism Asperger Publishing Company; www.asperger.net

# Giving Background Information about What You Are Saying

## Steps

1. If no one else is talking, tell people that you are going to talk about a new topic.

Can I tell you something?

2. If someone is talking and you want to change the topic, ask if you can talk about something else.

Can I talk about something else?

3. Explain what you are talking about.

  a. If you are talking about people, tell who they are.
  Is it a FRIEND, FAMILY MEMBER, TEACHER, OR A FAMOUS PERSON?

  b. If you are talking about a thing, explain what it is.
  Is it a GAME, TV SHOW, A PLACE, OR A TOY?

---

## Practice

Who will I try this with? _____

When? _____

What happened? _____

_____

How did I do? _____

Jed E. Baker, *Social Skills Training for Children and Adolescents with Asperger Syndrome and Social-Communication Problems*, 2003. Shawnee Mission, KS: Autism Asperger Publishing Company; www.asperger.net

# Suggested Activities for Giving Background Information about What You Are Saying

1. On a large poster or writing board, draw a line down the middle creating two columns. Label the first column EXPLAINED and the second column, UNEXPLAINED. Take turns with students beginning various topics and decide if the information shared was explained (there is appropriate background information) or unexplained (there is missing background information). For every comment that was explained, put a check mark under EXPLAINED. For every unexplained comment, put a check mark under UNEXPLAINED. Make a game of it with rewards for getting a certain number of "explained" check marks.

   a. Talk about an event you experienced. For example, "I went to see John yesterday." Decide if you explained enough; do they know who John is? Repeat it the correct way, "I went to see my brother John yesterday." Decide again if you have explained enough.

   b. Talk about an interest of yours. "I like the really old ones. They are worth more." Repeat it with more information, "I like coin collecting. I like the really old ones. They are worth more."

   c. Talk about a preference for food, entertainment, or games. For example, "I like it with peppers" is unexplained. In contrast, "I love pizza. I like it with peppers" is explained.

2. Pick different individuals with whom the students interact: fellow students, teachers, their parents, and grandparents. Have them pick topics like names of students in the classroom, names of siblings, or names of characters in a video game. Then have them pretend to discuss each topic with the various people with whom they interact, noting that parents and grandparents may not know names of classmates or video game characters, and teachers or peers may not know names of siblings. Have them decide which group of people would need what kind of background information when introducing certain topics.

3. Correct students when they leave out background information. Prompt them with the question, "Would the other person know who or what you are talking about? What do you need to tell them?"

4. Bait the use of the skill. Talk to students without giving them the necessary background information and then prompt them to tell you whether it is EXPLAINED or UNEXPLAINED.

5. Provide rewards for GIVING BACKGROUND INFORMATION.

   a. Give verbal praise for correct or partially correct attempts to give background information.

   b. Give tokens, pennies, or points for instances in which the student gives necessary background information. When he gets an agreed-upon number of tokens, give a special reward (e.g., snack, stickers, and privileges to play special game or watch special show).

Jed E. Baker, *Social Skills Training for Children and Adolescents with Asperger Syndrome and Social-Communication Problems*, 2003. Shawnee Mission, KS: Autism Asperger Publishing Company; www.asperger.net

# Shifting Topics

1. Wait for the right time to change the topic. This includes:

   a. When the other person stops talking, or says he is done.

   b. After the other person had a chance to talk about a topic and you showed you were interested by asking at least one follow-up question.

2. Prepare the other person for a change in topic by asking if it is okay to change the topic or by using a transition phrase.

   a. Examples of ways to ask if it is okay to change the topic:

   "Can I change the topic?"
   "Can I talk about something else?"

   b. Examples of transition phrases:

   "By the way, did you hear about . . . ?"
   "Speaking of . . ."  (Here you are referring to something the other person said and using it to start a new topic.)

3. Begin discussing the new topic.

---

## Practice

Who will I try this with? _____

When? _____

What happened? _____

_____

How did I do? _____

Jed E. Baker, *Social Skills Training for Children and Adolescents with Asperger Syndrome and Social-Communication Problems*, 2003. Shawnee Mission, KS: Autism Asperger Publishing Company; www.asperger.net

# Suggested Activities for
# Shifting Topics

1. Role-play the steps for SHIFTING TOPICS. Suggested role-plays involve the following scenarios:

   a. Pretend others are talking about a topic, like their favorite TV shows, and someone wants to talk about what they are going to do over the weekend. In the first role-play have them just start talking about the new topic without making any comment to indicate the shift in topic (the wrong way).

   b. Role-play a similar situation but with an appropriate transition statement.

   c. Role-play the scene again using appropriate transition statements, yet do not wait for the former topic to end. In other words, keep shifting the topic without asking any questions about the former topic as if you are not interested. Discuss the importance of waiting before shifting the topic.

2. Have students compose transition statements to get from one topic to another. Give them a list of two topics and have them compose the transition statement. For example:

   a. From going to the zoo to going to a museum (say, "Speaking of trips . . .").

   b. From watching a baseball game to playing soccer (say, "Speaking of sports . . .").

   c. From being teased to having a test (Say, "Speaking of stressful experiences . . .").

3. Correct abrupt shifts in conversations. Prompt students to wait until there is a pause, then make a transition statement or ask to talk about something else.

4. Bait the use of the skill. Talk endlessly about a boring topic until students feel compelled to shift the topic.

5. Provide rewards for appropriate shifts in conversation.

   a. Give verbal praise for correct or partially correct topic shifts.

   b. Give tokens, pennies, or points for instances in which the student shifted the topic appropriately. When she gets an agreed-upon number of tokens, give a special reward (e.g., snack, stickers, and privileges to play special game or watch special show).

Jed E. Baker, *Social Skills Training for Children and Adolescents with Asperger Syndrome and Social-Communication Problems*, 2003. Shawnee Mission, KS: Autism Asperger Publishing Company; www.asperger.net

## Don't Talk Too Long
### (K-3rd Grade)

1. When you are talking about a topic, look at others' faces to see if they are interested or bored.

Bored    Interested

2. If they look bored say, "Do you want to hear more?"

> Do you want to hear more?

> What do you want to talk about?

3. If they say no, stop talking or ask, "What do you want to talk about?"

## Talk Briefly So Others Will Listen
### (4th Grade and Up)

1. Remember, when you take a long time to talk and add too many details, listeners often become bored.

2. Look for signs that listeners may be bored or interested while you are talking.
   a. <u>Signs of interest:</u> the listener is looking at you, leaning toward you, or asking you questions.
   b. <u>Signs of boredom:</u> listeners are looking away from you, yawning, sighing, or appear interested in something else.

3. If you see signs of boredom, check to see if that is how others feel.
   a. Say "Am I going on too long, or are you interested in hearing more?"

4. If others are bored, think about your choices for dealing with it.
   a. Stop talking and give the other person a chance to talk.
   b. Ask the listener what she would like to talk about or hear about.
   c. Change the topic.
   d. Give a summary of what you wanted to talk about without all the details.

## Practice

Who did I do this with? _____

When? _____

What happened? _____

_____

How did I do? _____

Jed E. Baker, *Social Skills Training for Children and Adolescents with Asperger Syndrome and Social-Communication Problems*, 2003. Shawnee Mission, KS: Autism Asperger Publishing Company; www.asperger.net

# Suggested Activities for
# Don't Talk Too Long

1. It is equally important when practicing this skill for talkers and listeners to respond appropriately. Talkers must read the signs of boredom and ask if others want to hear more, and listeners must politely indicate they do not want to hear more, shift the topic, or end the conversation (see ENDING A CONVERSATION). If asked by the talker whether they want to hear more, listeners can be instructed to say, "Maybe another time," rather than saying, "No, I do not want to hear more."

2. Role-play the steps for talking briefly. Suggested role-plays involve the following scenarios:

   a. Since many students with AS and related disorders tend to talk obsessively about their interests, it may be useful to use their interest in the role-play to emphasize that this could be tedious for listeners. Pick an interest of one student that is not shared by the others and ask him to begin talking. Have other students first show interest and then gradually subtle signs of disinterest. Subtlety is important, as we do not want the listeners learning how to demonstrate extreme boredom. Have the student identify when the other listeners become bored and have him ask if they want to hear more. Prompt the listeners to say, "Maybe another time."

   b. Role-play the same situation with the student starting a conversation as others are indicating they have to leave. Often students launch into a discussion as the class or group is over. Help them to see that this is not the time to begin a lengthy discussion.

   c. If you have a small-group discussion as a regular part of a group, you can do the following activity to demonstrate to certain members how much talking they actually do. Give out tokens for every comment or question each student makes. At the end, review who has the most tokens. If one student has more than everyone else, then he or she is doing too much talking. This exercise is often helpful for students who complain that they do not get enough time to talk, not realizing that they dominate every conversation.

   d. Have students practice shortening their description of an experience into three sentences, leaving out all details, unless someone asks a follow-up question.

3. Correct lengthy talking by drawing students' attention to their audience. Prompt them to ask others if they want to hear more and perhaps stop talking, or ask the others a question to engage their interests.

4. Bait the use of the skill. As students are talking to you, begin to look bored or fidgety until they ask if you want to hear more.

5. Provide rewards for talking briefly.

   a. Give verbal praise for correct or partially correct talking briefly.

   b. Give tokens, pennies, or points for periods in which the student spoke briefly or checked to see if others wanted to hear more. When she gets an agreed-upon number of tokens, give a special reward (e.g., snack, stickers, and privileges to play special game or watch special show).

Jed E. Baker, *Social Skills Training for Children and Adolescents with Asperger Syndrome and Social-Communication Problems*, 2003. Shawnee Mission, KS: Autism Asperger Publishing Company; www.asperger.net

# Sensitive Topics

1. "Sensitive topics" are things you should not talk about because they may make others feel bad, upset, hurt, sad, or mad.

2. When you think of something you want to say, decide if it is a sensitive topic like:

   a. Something negative about how the person looks.
   b. How old the person is. (Okay to ask children but not adults.)
   c. A physical difference (uses wheelchair, missing limb, blind, or deaf).
   d. A learning difference (difficulty reading or understanding class work).
   e. A behavioral difference (difficulty paying attention or sitting still, saying odd things).
   f. A loss of a job or death of a family member or friend.

3. If it is a sensitive topic:

   a. Do not talk about it unless the other person brings it up.
   b. Except for questions about looks, you may be able to ask permission to discuss a sensitive topic. For example, "Can I ask you a question about a sensitive topic?"

---

## Practice

Who will I try this with? _____

When? _____

What happened? _____

_____

How did I do? _____

Jed E. Baker, *Social Skills Training for Children and Adolescents with Asperger Syndrome and Social-Communication Problems*, 2003. Shawnee Mission, KS: Autism Asperger Publishing Company; www.asperger.net

# Suggested Activities for Sensitive Topics

1. One way to begin teaching this skill is to walk into the room with something odd-looking like a bag for a hat, or a fake huge pimple on your nose. Do not say anything about it unless a student asks. Pretend that you do not know what the student is talking about until other students also point it out. Then begin a discussion about "sensitive topics," pointing out that we may see something different about someone but may not want to say anything to protect the person's feelings.

2. This skill is difficult to role-play because the right response is to do nothing. Thus, the rehearsal necessary is entirely a thought process rather than an outward behavior. As such, it is helpful to discuss numerous situations rather than act them out. You may decide to adopt a "game show" format to review situations with play money for prizes. For each situation, students can indicate whether they think it is a sensitive topic and if they would say anything. Example situations:
   a. You think someone has nice sunglasses. (not sensitive)
   b. You think someone has really thick glasses. (sensitive)
   c. Someone says it's a nice day. (not sensitive)
   d. A student asks how old his teacher is. (sensitive)
   e. A teacher asks how old a student's little brother is. (not sensitive)
   f. You ask your friend if he gets any special help for math and reading. (sensitive)
   g. You wonder why the boy in your class is so strong. (not sensitive)
   h. You wonder why the boy in your class is fat. (sensitive)
   i. You wonder why the girl in your class is so good at gymnastics. (not sensitive)
   j. You wonder why the girl in your class cannot read her assignment. (sensitive)
   k. Your friend's grandfather died. (sensitive, but you can say "Sorry to hear that")
   l. Your teacher has a large belly and you wonder if she is pregnant. (sensitive)
   m. You heard that your friend's dog died. (sensitive)
   n. You heard that your friend won a spelling bee. (not sensitive)

3. Bait the skill. For example, purposely do something to change your appearance (e.g., wear an odd piece of clothing or use makeup to make a fake blemish), or make a mistake (e.g., with work, or household chores) and see if the student can refrain from saying anything negative.

4. Any time the student makes an insensitive remark, label it a "sensitive topic" and explain how the remark can hurt others' feelings.

5. Provide rewards and possibly negative consequences
   a. Consider using warnings followed by loss of privileges for making insensitive remarks **only if** you are certain the student knew the remarks were hurtful.
   b. Give tokens, pennies, or points for periods in which students refrained from making sensitive remarks or asked an adult for guidance about whether it is okay to say something. When they get an agreed-upon amount of tokens (e.g., five tokens), give a special reward (e.g., snack, stickers, or privileges to play special game).

Jed E. Baker, *Social Skills Training for Children and Adolescents with Asperger Syndrome and Social-Communication Problems*, 2003. Shawnee Mission, KS: Autism Asperger Publishing Company; www.asperger.net

# Complimenting Others

1. Think about the reasons for complimenting others:

   a. Others will view you positively.
   b. Others will want to spend time with you.

2. Notice positive things about others. These might include:

   a. How they look, what they are wearing, or a new haircut.
   b. Something good that they did.
   c. Some ability they have.

3. Tell them, in a sincere tone of voice, the positive thing about them.

   a. For how they look, say: "You look great." "That's a beautiful [dress, tie, shirt, pair of shoes, new haircut]."
   b. For something they did, say, "You did that really well."
   c. For some special ability they have, say, "You are really good at [math, English, this game, sports, dancing, singing]."

## Practice

Who will I try this with? _____

When? _____

What happened? _____

_____

How did I do? _____

Jed E. Baker, *Social Skills Training for Children and Adolescents with Asperger Syndrome and Social-Communication Problems*, 2003. Shawnee Mission, KS: Autism Asperger Publishing Company; www.asperger.net

# Suggested Activities for Complimenting Others

1. Role-play the steps for COMPLIMENTING OTHERS. Suggested role-plays involve the following scenarios:

   a. In a small group or classroom, take turns complimenting the person to your left until everyone has had a turn. Switch the category of compliments so that some are about appearance, some about abilities, and some about actions.

   b. Demonstrate sincere versus insincere tone of voice with a compliment and ask the group if they can discern which comments were sincere and which were not. For this exercise, do not direct you compliments to a person in the room so as not to hurt anyone's feelings.

2. Prompt students to compliment others when peers accomplish something, have a new haircut or "look" or demonstrate their work.

3. Bait the use of the skill. Tell or show students your accomplishment or your new clothing or haircut, or demonstrate a talent. Remind them that they could compliment to make you feel good.

4. Provide rewards for COMPLIMENTING OTHERS.

   a. Give verbal praise for correct or partially correct COMPLIMENTING OTHERS.

   b. Avoid material rewards for complimenting, as the person being complimented will not see it as sincere if others were rewarded for saying something nice to him or her.

Jed E. Baker, *Social Skills Training for Children and Adolescents with Asperger Syndrome and Social-Communication Problems*, 2003. Shawnee Mission, KS: Autism Asperger Publishing Company; www.asperger.net

# Using Your H.E.A.D.
# When You Are Involved in a Conversation

| | |
|---|---|
| **H**APPY VOICE: | Use a happy, medium-volume voice when having a conversation. Don't scream or whisper. |
| **E**YE CONTACT: | Look at people's eyes when talking or listening to them. |
| **A**LTERNATE: | Alternate between talking and listening. Take turns talking. |
| **D**ISTANCE: | Keep about an arm's length away from people when talking. Don't be a "Space Invader" by getting too close. |

## Practice

Who will I try this with? _____

When? _____

What happened? _____

_____

How did I do? _____

Jed E. Baker, *Social Skills Training for Children and Adolescents with Asperger Syndrome and Social-Communication Problems*, 2003. Shawnee Mission, KS: Autism Asperger Publishing Company; www.asperger.net

# Suggested Activities for Using Your H.E.A.D.

1. For many students with good verbal rote memories, the acronym H.E.A.D. can serve to remind them of several important skills related to having a conversation. All of the skills imbedded into this acronym appear as separate skills elsewhere in the book. For example, "happy voice" is the skill entitled TONE OF VOICE, "eye contact" is part of LISTENING POSITION, "distance" is part of DON'T BE A SPACE INVADER, and "alternate" is part of the TWO-QUESTION RULE.

2. Role-play each part of this skill separately:

   a. **Happy Voice** (see TONE OF VOICE)
      Consider using a tape recorder so the student can hear himself trying each of the following types of voice.
      (1) Use an "outside" (high volume) rather than an "inside" (regular volume) voice.
      (2) Use an angry rather than a pleasant tone of voice.
      (3) Use a fast or slow rather than an appropriate pace of speech.

   b. **Eye Contact** (see LISTENING POSITION)
      (1) Make eye contact in class with the teacher.
      (2) Make eye contact with a peer in conversation.
      (3) Make eye contact when greeting others and saying goodbye.

   c. **Alternate** (see TWO-QUESTION RULE)
      (1) Role-play exchanging greetings (e.g., say, "Hi" and ask the student to say "Hi" back).
      (2) Role-play conversation starters (e.g., ask the student what she did over the weekend and prompt her to ask back).
      (3) Tell a story about what you are going to do after school and prompt the student to tell you what he will do after school.

   d. **Distance** (see DON'T BE A SPACE INVADER)
      (1) Role-play getting too close and too far. Have student give you a thumbs-up sign when you are an "okay" distance apart and a thumbs-down sign when you are too far.
      (2) Show the right and wrong distances when using a greeting.
      (3) Show the right and wrong distances when discussing the past weekend.
      (4) Show the right and wrong distances when discussing after-school plans.

3. Use a game show format to quiz students about what each letter stands for and give examples of each. For example, ask what the "H" stands for in H.E.A.D. and to give you an example. Give tokens or pretend money for right answers. Make sure everyone gets to respond and earns a prize.

4. Bait the skill. This means doing something that requires students to demonstrate their understanding of the skills.

   a. Change the volume of your voice, stop eye contact, get too close, or do not let anyone else talk, and then ask the student for feedback about what you did wrong.

   b. Ask about the student's week or use another conversation starter and then look at her as if you are waiting for her to ask you something. If the student forgets to ask you a question in return, prompt her to do so.

5. Provide rewards for using the appropriate skills represented by the H.EA.D. acronym.

   a. Give verbal praise for correct or partially correct tone of voice, eye contact, alternating turns talking, and maintaining an appropriate distance.

   b. Give tokens, pennies, or points for periods in which the student used the skills. When he gets an agreed-upon number of tokens (e.g., five tokens), give a special reward (e.g., snack, stickers, or privileges to play special game).

Jed E. Baker, *Social Skills Training for Children and Adolescents with Asperger Syndrome and Social-Communication Problems*, 2003. Shawnee Mission, KS: Autism Asperger Publishing Company; www.asperger.net

# T.G.I.F.

## (Means more than "Thank Goodness It's Friday" – It's about Having a Conversation)

**TIMING:** The time to start a conversation is when the other person is not talking or there is a pause in their conversation.

**GREETINGS:** A greeting is the first thing you say to someone when beginning a conversation.

| Hi. | Hello. | What's up? | How are you? |
|-----|--------|------------|--------------|

**INITIAL QUESTION:** An initial question is something you ask a person to start a conversation about a particular topic.

How was your _____? What are you _____? What will you be _____?

**FOLLOW-UP QUESTIONS:** These are the questions you ask to get more information about a topic and to keep the conversation going.

Who . . .?   What . . .?   What else . . .?   Where . . .?
When . . .?   How . . .?   Why . . .?

## Practice

Who will I try this with? _____

When? _____

What happened? _____

_____

How did I do? _____

Jed E. Baker, *Social Skills Training for Children and Adolescents with Asperger Syndrome and Social-Communication Problems*, 2003. Shawnee Mission, KS: Autism Asperger Publishing Company; www.asperger.net

# Suggested Activities for
# T.G.I.F.

1. For many students with good verbal rote memories, the acronym T.G.I.F. can serve to remind them of several important skills related to having a conversation. All the skills imbedded into this acronym appear as separate skills and are covered in more detail elsewhere in the book. For example, "Timing" is like the skill INTERRUPTING. "Greetings" is covered separately in the skill by the same name. "Initial Question" is dealt with in more detail in STARTING A CONVERSATION, and "Follow-Up Question" is covered more fully within the skill MAINTAINING A CONVERSATION. The decision on whether to teach these skills separately or all together using the acronym T.G.I.F. should be based on the student's verbal rote memory and subsequent ability to use acronyms to guide behavior.

2. Role-play each part of this skill separately:
   a. **Timing**
      (1) Demonstrate by asking how others are doing by interrupting an ongoing conversation instead of waiting for a pause.
      (2) Demonstrate by saying hello to someone who is busy working instead of waiting until the person is done or asking if it is an okay time to talk.
   b. **Greetings**
      (1) Role-play starting a conversation with someone you see for the first time during the day without saying hello.
   c. **Initial Question**
      (1) Role-play starting conversations about the past, present and future (see STARTING A CONVERSATION for greater detail on role-plays).
         (a) Ask about what the person did yesterday, over the weekend, or last week. Ask about what she is doing, eating, playing, reading, or watching. Ask about what she is going to do after school, tomorrow, over the upcoming weekend or vacation.
   d. **Follow-Up Questions**
      (1) Role-play keeping the conversation going with questions and comments that are on-topic (see MAINTAINING A CONVERSATION for more role-play ideas).
      (2) Pretend to interview a famous person and ask follow-up questions.
      (3) Put a mystery item in a bag and have students guess what is in it by asking follow-up questions.
      (4) Role-play typical conversations at school and home. Ask about what they did yesterday, over the weekend, or last week. Ask about what they are doing, eating, playing, reading, or watching. Ask about what they will do after school, tomorrow, over the upcoming weekend or vacation. Keep it going with follow-up questions.

3. Use a game show format to quiz students about what each letter stands for and examples of each. For example, ask what the "T" stands for in T.G.I.F. and to give you an example. Give tokens or pretend money for right answers. Make sure everyone gets to respond and earns a prize.

4. Bait the skill. This means doing something that requires the student to demonstrate an understanding of the skills. Begin a conversation with the student and wait for him to ask you questions back. Do not carry the conversation by asking questions; sit through the pause until he can come up with questions. Prompt him if necessary to keep the conversation going with questions or comments.

5. Provide rewards for using the appropriate skills represented by the T.G.I.F. acronym.
   a. Give verbal praise for correct or partially correct Timing, Greetings, Initial Questions, and Follow-Up Questions.
   b. Give tokens, pennies, or points for periods in which the student used the skills. When he gets an agreed-upon number of tokens (e.g., five tokens), give a special reward (e.g., snack, stickers, or privileges to play special game).

Jed E. Baker, *Social Skills Training for Children and Adolescents with Asperger Syndrome and Social-Communication Problems*, 2003. Shawnee Mission, KS: Autism Asperger Publishing Company; www.asperger.net

# Asking Someone to Play

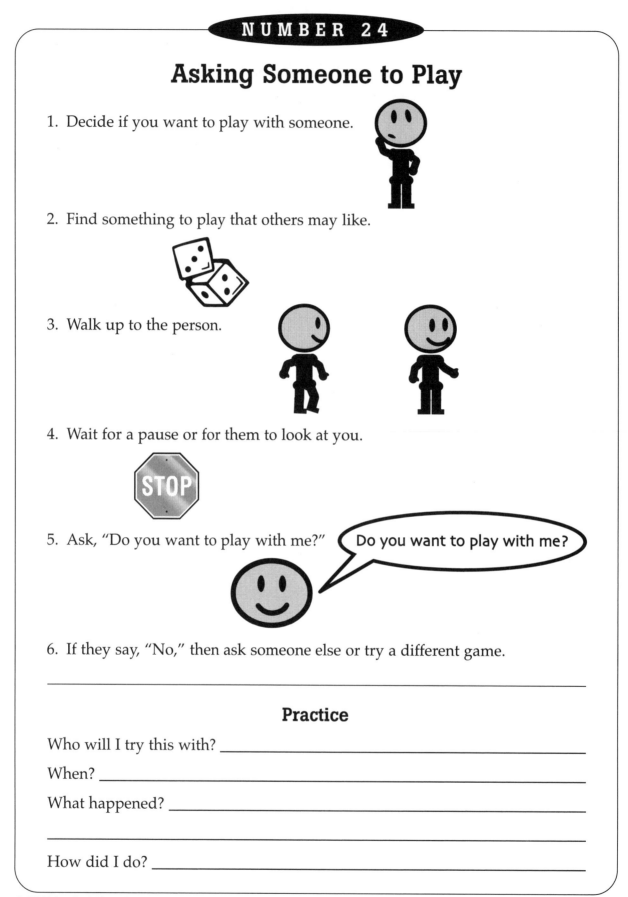

1. Decide if you want to play with someone.

2. Find something to play that others may like.

3. Walk up to the person.

4. Wait for a pause or for them to look at you.

5. Ask, "Do you want to play with me?"

   *Do you want to play with me?*

6. If they say, "No," then ask someone else or try a different game.

---

## Practice

Who will I try this with? _____

When? _____

What happened? _____

_____

How did I do? _____

Jed E. Baker, *Social Skills Training for Children and Adolescents with Asperger Syndrome and Social-Communication Problems*, 2003. Shawnee Mission, KS: Autism Asperger Publishing Company; www.asperger.net

# Suggested Activities for
# Asking Someone to Play

1. Role-play the steps for ASKING SOMEONE TO PLAY. Suggested role-plays involve the following scenarios:

   a. Pretend it is snack, free-play, or recess time at school and no one has started playing yet. Have the child initiate play with someone. Have the recipient say yes and also no sometimes so that the student must remember to ask someone else or get another game.

   b. Extend the role-play above to the point where no child will play any game and the child must seek the teacher's help rather than express anger at the other children, thereby risking loss of friendship.

   c. Pretend it's a play-date at someone's house. Role-play selecting games that the other child really likes and games that the other child does not like to highlight the importance of choosing games that others enjoy.

   d. Pretend that children are busy reading or finishing their work in school. Role-play waiting until they are done with their work versus asking them to play in the middle of their work.

2. Bait the skill. This means doing something that requires the student to initiate play. For example, purposely display an interactive game that the child really likes in front of him without asking to play. If he does not ask to play, prompt him to ask. For example, say, "If you want to play, ask me to play that game with you."

3. Correct inappropriate ways of asking others to play, such as demanding others to play or insisting on playing games that others do not like. Also prompt students who sit on the periphery, fearful of asking others to play.

   IMPORTANT NOTE: If you are going to encourage shy students to ask others to play, direct them to students whom you have previously coached to accept such offers (see Chapter 9 for details on coaching typical peers).

4. Provide rewards for appropriate ASKING SOMEONE TO PLAY.

   a. Give verbal praise for correct or partially correct ASKING SOMEONE TO PLAY.

   b. Give tokens, pennies, or points every time the student asks someone to play. When she gets an agreed-upon amount of tokens (e.g., five tokens), give a special reward (e.g., snack, stickers, or privileges to play a special game).

Jed E. Baker, *Social Skills Training for Children and Adolescents with Asperger Syndrome and Social-Communication Problems*, 2003. Shawnee Mission, KS: Autism Asperger Publishing Company; www.asperger.net

# Joining Others in Play

1. Walk up to the people playing.

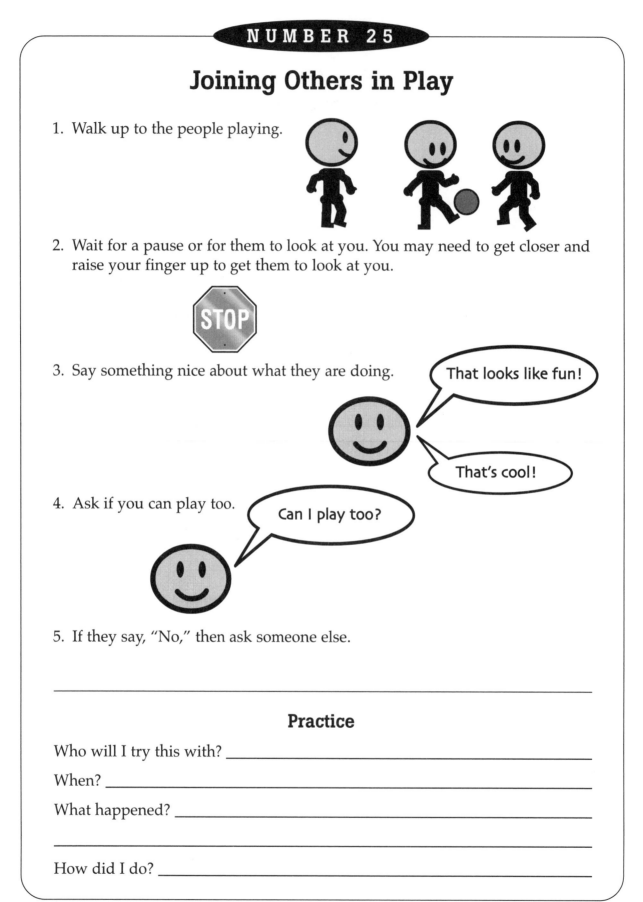

2. Wait for a pause or for them to look at you. You may need to get closer and raise your finger up to get them to look at you.

STOP

3. Say something nice about what they are doing.

That looks like fun!

That's cool!

4. Ask if you can play too.

Can I play too?

5. If they say, "No," then ask someone else.

## Practice

Who will I try this with? _____

When? _____

What happened? _____

_____

How did I do? _____

Jed E. Baker, *Social Skills Training for Children and Adolescents with Asperger Syndrome and Social-Communication Problems*, 2003. Shawnee Mission, KS: Autism Asperger Publishing Company; www.asperger.net

# Suggested Activities for
# Joining Others in Play

1. Role-play the steps for JOINING OTHERS IN PLAY. Suggested role-plays involve the following scenarios:

   a. Have two children play a recess game (e.g., two-square) and a third student wanting to join in. Have students say yes to join in and sometimes also no, so student has to remember to go ask someone else.

   b. Have siblings invite friends over to play a game. Have the student ask to join in.

   c. Have peers play a game with a teacher, and have the student ask to join in.

2. Bait the skill. This means doing something that requires the student to join in. For example, purposely play something that the child really likes in front of her without asking her to join in. Prompt or wait for her to ask to join in.

3. Correct inappropriate ways to join in, such as barging in on a game and taking over. Also prompt students who sit on the periphery, fearful of joining in.

   IMPORTANT NOTE: If you are going to encourage shy students to join in, direct them to students whom you have already coached to allow the student to join in to ensure success (see Chapter 9 on coaching typical students).

4. Provide rewards for appropriate JOINING OTHERS IN PLAY.

   a. Give verbal praise for correct or partially correct JOINING OTHERS IN PLAY.

   b. Give tokens, pennies, or points every time the student joins in. When he gets an agreed-upon number of tokens (e.g., five tokens), give a special reward (e.g., snack, stickers, or privileges to play special game).

Jed E. Baker, *Social Skills Training for Children and Adolescents with Asperger Syndrome and Social-Communication Problems*, 2003. Shawnee Mission, KS: Autism Asperger Publishing Company; www.asperger.net

# Compromising

1. Find out what the other person wants to do.

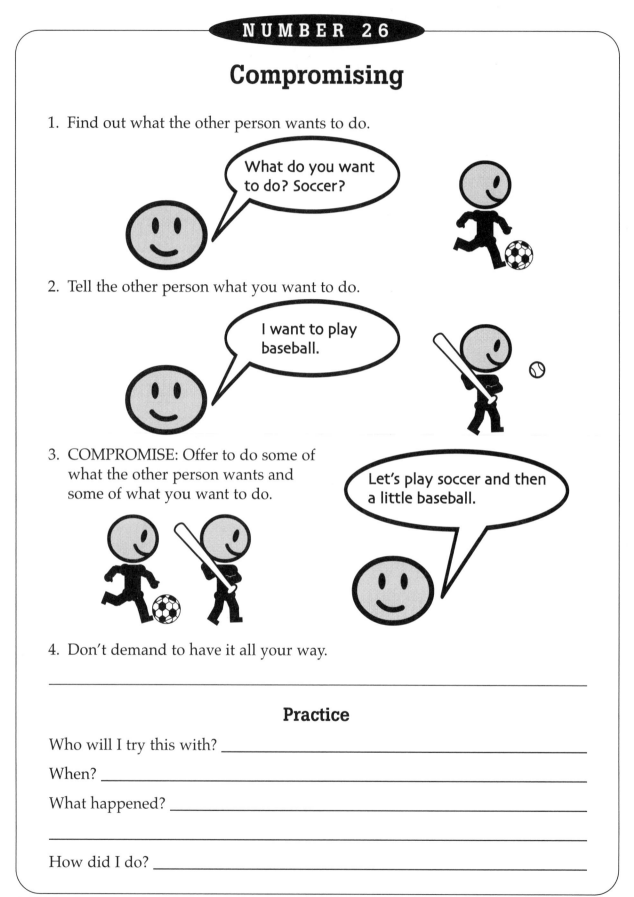

   What do you want to do? Soccer?

2. Tell the other person what you want to do.

   I want to play baseball.

3. COMPROMISE: Offer to do some of what the other person wants and some of what you want to do.

   Let's play soccer and then a little baseball.

4. Don't demand to have it all your way.

---

## Practice

Who will I try this with? _____

When? _____

What happened? _____

_____

How did I do? _____

Jed E. Baker, *Social Skills Training for Children and Adolescents with Asperger Syndrome and Social-Communication Problems*, 2003.
Shawnee Mission, KS: Autism Asperger Publishing Company; www.asperger.net

# Suggested Activities for Compromising

1. Role-play the steps for COMPROMISING. Suggested role-plays involve the following scenarios:

   a. Two children both want to play with the same toy.
   b. Two children are going to play together but they both want to play different games.
   c. Siblings are arguing over who will get to watch what they want on TV.
   d. Two children want the last piece of cake.

2. Bait the skill. This means doing something that requires the student to compromise. For example, purposely say you want to do something other than what the student wants to do and say, "I wonder if we could compromise?"

3. Correct demands by the student to have it all her way. Have the student suggest a compromise.

4. Provide rewards for appropriate COMPROMISING.

   a. Give verbal praise for correct or partially correct COMPROMISING.
   b. Give tokens, pennies, or points every time the student compromises. When she gets an agreed-upon number of tokens (e.g., five tokens), give a special reward (e.g., snack, stickers, or privileges to play special game).

## Sharing

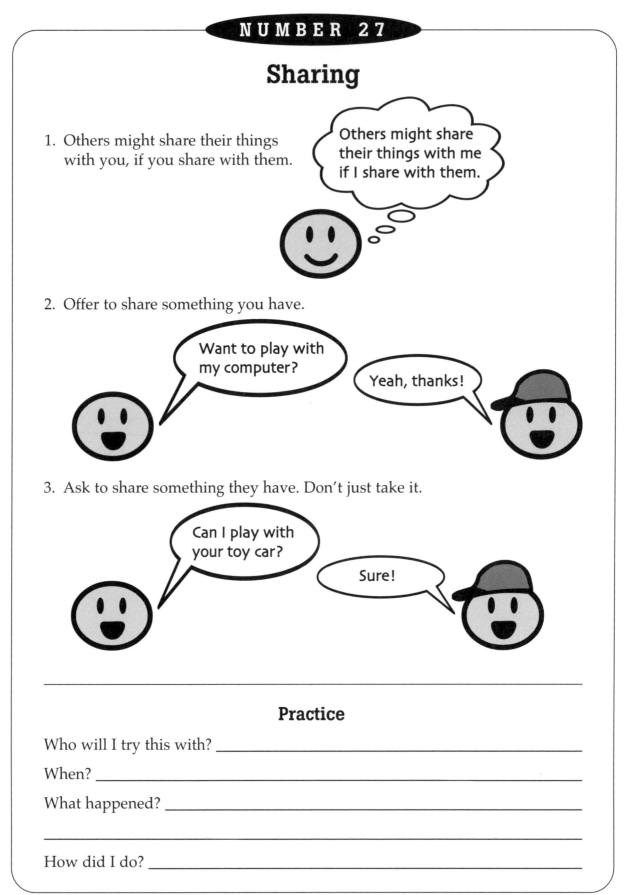

1. Others might share their things with you, if you share with them.

   *Others might share their things with me if I share with them.*

2. Offer to share something you have.

   *Want to play with my computer?*

   *Yeah, thanks!*

3. Ask to share something they have. Don't just take it.

   *Can I play with your toy car?*

   *Sure!*

### Practice

Who will I try this with? _____

When? _____

What happened? _____

_____

How did I do? _____

Jed E. Baker, *Social Skills Training for Children and Adolescents with Asperger Syndrome and Social-Communication Problems*, 2003.
Shawnee Mission, KS: Autism Asperger Publishing Company; www.asperger.net

# Suggested Activities for Sharing

1. Role-play the steps for SHARING. Suggested role-plays involve the following scenarios:

   a. Two children (peers or siblings) both want to play with the same set of building blocks or some other toy in the classroom or at home.

   b. One child wants to play with a game that the other child owns at home or in school.

   c. Students (or siblings) do an art project without having separate materials so that they must share.

   d. During snack time, one student has nothing to eat.

2. Bait the skill.

   a. Have students (or siblings) do an art project without giving separate materials to each. Have only one set of markers, one bottle of glue, etc., so that they must share.

   b. Give out snacks and pretend to run out, forcing students to share with each other. In case they do not share, have enough snacks on hand after all.

3. Correct unwillingness to share. Some children more readily share materials or toys when they are told that it is temporary – that they will get the materials right back again.

4. Provide rewards for appropriate SHARING.

   a. Give verbal praise for correct or partially correct SHARING.

   b. Give tokens, pennies, or points every time the student shares. When she gets an agreed-upon number of tokens (e.g., five tokens), give a special reward (e.g., snack, stickers, or privileges to play special game).

Jed E. Baker, *Social Skills Training for Children and Adolescents with Asperger Syndrome and Social-Communication Problems*, 2003. Shawnee Mission, KS: Autism Asperger Publishing Company; www.asperger.net

## Taking Turns

1. Taking turns means you let other people play with something while you wait. Then you play while they wait.

2. You may have to wait, but you will win a friend if you take turns.

## Taking Turns Going First

1. Use this skill to decide who goes first when playing a game or using a toy.

2. Pick a way to decide who will go first:

   a. Play **"Rock, scissors, paper, shoot."** This is appropriate for two people. In this game, each person forms a rock, scissors, or paper with their right hand behind their back. After saying "rock, scissors, paper, shoot," they simultaneously show their hand to the other. Rock beats scissors, scissors beats paper, paper beats rock.

   b. Play **"The odd finger is it."** This game is appropriate for more than two people. In this game, everyone forms one or two fingers behind their back. After they say, "the odd finger is it," all show their hands. The person who has a different number of fingers out than everyone else gets to go first. Keep playing until only one person has a different number of fingers than everyone else.

   c. **Toss a coin.** One person calls heads or tails while the coin is in the air.

   d. Play **"Eeny, meany, miny, moe, catch a tiger by the toe, if he hollers, let him go, eeny meany, miny, moe."** Someone points to each player in turn while saying each word, and the person who is being pointed to at the last word (*moe*) gets to go first.

3. Next time you play a game, someone else gets to go first. If you wait your turn, the other person will be happy and want to play with you.

---

## Practice

Who will I try this with? _____

When? _____

What happened? _____

_____

How did I do? _____

Jed E. Baker, *Social Skills Training for Children and Adolescents with Asperger Syndrome and Social-Communication Problems*, 2003.
Shawnee Mission, KS: Autism Asperger Publishing Company; www.asperger.net

# Suggested Activities for
# Taking Turns

1. Role-play the steps for TAKING TURNS. Children can decide to let others go first or use a fair way to decide (see TAKING TURNS GOING FIRST). Suggested role-plays involve the following scenarios:

   a. Two or more children want to use the one computer available at home or in school.

   b. Two or more children want to use some playground equipment that only one person can go on at a time.

   c. Children need to decide who will go first in a board game. Then they need to decide what color or game piece they want, using a fair way to decide (see TAKING TURNS GOING FIRST).

   d. Role-play the same items as above, but pretend it is another day and that the person who went first the previous day should now go second or last.

2. Bait the skill. Say you want something you see that the student is about to ask for so that you must take turns. Say you want to go first or demand the special game piece that the student wants so you will have to use a fair means to decide.

3. Correct those who don't give others a turn. Remind them that giving others a turn is temporary; they will be able to get to play again, or go first the next time.

4. Provide rewards for appropriate turn-taking.

   a. Give verbal praise for correct or partially correct turn-taking.

   b. Give tokens, pennies, or points every time the student takes turns. When she gets an agreed-upon number of tokens (e.g., five tokens), give a special reward (e.g., snack, stickers, or privileges to play special game).

Jed E. Baker, *Social Skills Training for Children and Adolescents with Asperger Syndrome and Social-Communication Problems*, 2003. Shawnee Mission, KS: Autism Asperger Publishing Company; www.asperger.net

# Playing a Game

1. Find out the rules of the game.

   a. "What is the object of the game?"
   b. "How do you play?"

2. Decide who goes first.

   a. Let others go first to make friends.
   b. Decide through a game of chance, like flipping a coin, rolling dice, or playing "Rocks, Paper, Scissors, Shoot."

3. Wait your turn during the game.

---

## Practice

Who will I try this with? _____

When? _____

What happened? _____

_____

How did I do? _____

Jed E. Baker, *Social Skills Training for Children and Adolescents with Asperger Syndrome and Social-Communication Problems*, 2003. Shawnee Mission, KS: Autism Asperger Publishing Company; www.asperger.net

# Suggested Activities for Playing a Game

1. Role-play the steps for PLAYING A GAME. Suggested role-plays involve the following scenarios:

   a. Use any standard board game to work through the skill steps.

   b. Have students take turns making up a new rule for a standard game until you have a new game. This requires that they pay close attention to the rules. In addition, it allows them to become more flexible about playing new games. You may want to give examples of new rules so they have a template for making their own rules. For example, you could play a game of tag where multiple persons are "it" and you have any number of "safe" zones where you cannot get tagged. Or you could play checkers where you can jump others at a right angle as well as the standard way.

2. Bait the skill.

   a. Start playing a standard game and do not tell students the rules unless they ask. Keep changing the rules until they protest, then remind them to get the rules prior to the game.

   b. As you play, insist on going first and occasionally go even when it is not your turn unless anyone protests. Then prompt others to take turns fairly.

3. Correct lack of turn-taking or forgetting to get the rules.

4. Provide rewards for GETTING THE RULES and TAKING TURNS.

   a. Give verbal praise for correct or partially correct game playing.

   b. Give tokens, pennies, or points every time the student plays fairly. When she gets an agreed-upon number of tokens (e.g., five tokens), give a special reward (e.g., snack, stickers, or privileges to play special game).

Jed E. Baker, *Social Skills Training for Children and Adolescents with Asperger Syndrome and Social-Communication Problems*, 2003. Shawnee Mission, KS: Autism Asperger Publishing Company; www.asperger.net

# Dealing with Losing

1. Say to yourself: "It's only a game, there will be other games."

2. Remember, although you lost the game, you can win a friendship (which is more important) if you show good sportsmanship.

3. To show good sportsmanship, you should tell the other person:

"Congratulations"          "Good game"

"You played a good game"

4. Shake the other person's hand and help him put away the game or materials.

---

## Practice

Who will I try this with? _____

When? _____

What happened? _____

_____

How did I do? _____

Jed E. Baker, *Social Skills Training for Children and Adolescents with Asperger Syndrome and Social-Communication Problems*, 2003.
Shawnee Mission, KS: Autism Asperger Publishing Company; www.asperger.net

# Suggested Activities for Dealing with Losing

1. To teach this skill, parents and teachers may need to temporarily exaggerate the idea that losing calmly is great and that winning a game is not that important. Adults should remind students just before they play a game that they are more interested in how the students deal with losing than whether they win the game. As the game is played, the adult can anticipate which child is losing and remind him that if he does not get mad, he will win a friend and may receive a reward for staying calm. The adult should show little enthusiasm when someone wins, and also show great enthusiasm when someone deals well with losing.

2. Role-play the steps for DEALING WITH LOSING. Suggested role-plays involve short games so that the skill can be practiced without waiting for a long game to end:

    a. Use a coin toss (heads or tails) or "odds or evens" (each student puts out one or two fingers after one child calls "odds" or "evens") to decide who will go first. Whoever loses should be coached through the steps of DEALING WITH LOSING. The one who lost is applauded for staying calm.

    b. "Tic-tac-toe" is another quick game that is good for practicing this skill. As a two-person game, it can be used for students to role-play in front of a larger group. It is imperative to applaud the student who loses and stays calm before she has a chance to get upset.

    c. "Musical chairs" and "Simon Says" are ideal quick group games. As students lose and are reminded to go through each step of DEALING WITH LOSING, they may be applauded as they sit out to await the next game. For the child who gets very upset, try to distract him rather than use reason. Repetition of the experience will eventually reduce the outbursts.

    d. For older children (4th grade and up), use board games or sports. The skills involved in DEALING WITH LOSING can be used not only when you lose the game, but also for any perceived loss in the game (e.g., striking out, a low roll of the dice, missing a shot, etc.).

3. Bait the skill by doing something that requires your student to deal with losing. For example, say, "I am going to try to beat you at this game to see if you can deal with losing. It is much harder to deal with losing than to win this game. Let's see if you can do it."

4. Redirect expressions of anger to the DEALING WITH LOSING steps when a student gets upset after losing. If the student continues to remain angry or becomes more upset, use a distraction (e.g., walk away from the game and engage him in something new).

5. Provide rewards for appropriate DEALING WITH LOSING.

    a. Give verbal praise for efforts to stay calm when a student is about to or has lost.

    b. Give tokens, pennies, or points every time the student deals appropriately with losing. When he gets an agreed-upon number of tokens (e.g., five tokens), give a special reward (e.g., snack, stickers, or privileges to play special game).

Jed E. Baker, *Social Skills Training for Children and Adolescents with Asperger Syndrome and Social-Communication Problems*, 2003. Shawnee Mission, KS: Autism Asperger Publishing Company; www.asperger.net

# Dealing with Winning

1. If you win a game, you can also win a friend if you show good sportsmanship.

2. "Sportsmanship" means:

    a. Do not brag or show off that you won. This makes others feel bad.
    b. Say, "Good game."
    c. If the others are upset because they lost, remind them that it is only a game and they might win next time.

---

## Practice

Who will I try this with? _____

When? _____

What happened? _____

_____

How did I do? _____

Jed E. Baker, *Social Skills Training for Children and Adolescents with Asperger Syndrome and Social-Communication Problems*, 2003. Shawnee Mission, KS: Autism Asperger Publishing Company; www.asperger.net

# Suggested Activities for
# Dealing with Winning

1. Just as in DEALING WITH LOSING, we need to remind students that the goal is not to win a game, but to win a friend. Highlight that we are interested in their ability to win friends as they play.

2. Role-play the steps for DEALING WITH WINNING. These suggested role-plays are the same as for DEALING WITH LOSING, and both skills should be role-played simultaneously. Use short games so that the skill can be practiced without waiting for a long game to end.

   a. Use a coin toss (heads or tails) or "odds or evens" (each student puts out one or two fingers after one child calls "odds" or "evens") to decide who will go first. Whoever loses should be coached through the steps of DEALING WITH LOS-ING while the other is coached through the steps of DEALING WITH WIN-NING. Both are applauded and praised for staying friends by not getting mad or bragging. No one is applauded for their skill in the game, as the game play itself is secondary to friendship skills.

   b. "Tic-tac-toe" is another quick game that is good for practicing this skill. As a two-person game, it can be used for students to role-play in front of a larger group. Again, both are applauded and praised for staying friends by not get-ting mad or bragging.

   c. "Musical chairs" and "Simon Says" are also ideal quick group games.

   d. For older children (4th grade and up), use board games or sports. The skills involved in DEALING WITH LOSING and DEALING WITH WINNING can be used not only when you win or lose the game, but also for any perceived win or loss during the game (e.g., striking out or hitting a home run, etc.).

3. Bait the skill by doing something that requires students to deal with winning in a gracious way. For example, as you lose a game, say, "You are so much better than I am. You are the greatest ever. I am terrible." See if the student can try to cheer you up rather than gloat over the victory.

4. Provide rewards for appropriate DEALING WITH WINNING.

   a. Give verbal praise for efforts to deal with winning.

   b. Give tokens, pennies, or points every time the student deals appropriately with winning. When she gets an agreed-upon number of tokens (e.g., five tokens), give a special reward (e.g., snack, stickers, or privileges to play special game).

Jed E. Baker, *Social Skills Training for Children and Adolescents with Asperger Syndrome and Social-Communication Problems*, 2003.
Shawnee Mission, KS: Autism Asperger Publishing Company; www.asperger.net

# Ending a Play Activity

1. Decide if you do not want to play any more.
   a. Is it because you want to do something else?
   b. Is it because the person you were playing with did something you did not like?
   c. Is it because you do not like the other person?

2. Do not just walk away. Try to finish the game if the other person wants to finish.

3. Tell the person in a nice tone of voice why you do not want to play any more.
   a. If you want to do something else, say, "I want to stop because I want to play something else."
   b. If you do not like what the other person did, say, "I do not want to play any more because of what you did."
   c. If you do not like the other person, make an excuse that you have other things you want to do. Say, "I have to stop because I have other things I want to do."

_____

## Practice

Who will I try this with? _____

When? _____

What happened? _____

_____

How did I do? _____

Jed E. Baker, *Social Skills Training for Children and Adolescents with Asperger Syndrome and Social-Communication Problems*, 2003.
Shawnee Mission, KS: Autism Asperger Publishing Company; www.asperger.net

# Suggested Activities for
# Ending a Play Activity

1. Role-play the steps for ENDING A PLAY ACTIVITY. Suggested role-plays involve the following scenarios:

   a. You are playing a game and it is getting boring. Practice telling the other person you want to play something else versus just walking away.

   b. After playing a game with someone you do not feel like playing with anyone, practice finishing the game and telling the person you want to take a break versus walking out in the middle of the game.

   c. Pretend you are playing a game and one person keeps cheating. Practice telling the person why you do not want to play any more in a calm way rather than getting mad.

   d. Pretend you were asked to play a game with someone you do not really like. Practice making an excuse that you do not feel like playing rather than telling the person you do not like him or her.

2. Correct inappropriate or abrupt endings. Have the student wait to finish the game and/or make an appropriate excuse.

3. Bait the use of the skill. Tell students you are going to test their ability to end games appropriately. Purposely play games that are tedious or begin to cheat and make the game frustrating until students appropriately end the game.

4. Provide rewards for appropriately ending the play activity.

   a. Give verbal praise for correct or partially correct ways to end a play activity.

   b. Give tokens, pennies, or points in instances in which the student ended a play activity appropriately. When she gets an agreed-upon number of tokens, give a special reward (e.g., snack, stickers, and privileges to play special game or watch special show).

Jed E. Baker, *Social Skills Training for Children and Adolescents with Asperger Syndrome and Social-Communication Problems*, 2003.
Shawnee Mission, KS: Autism Asperger Publishing Company; www.asperger.net

# Informal Versus Formal Behavior

| | Formal | Informal |
|---|---|---|
| Definition | Very polite and respectful. | Casual and relaxed. |
| People | People you do not know well. Authority figures: Older adults, parents, teachers, principal, group leaders, police, employers. | Good friends and close family members. |
| Greetings | "Hello. How are you?" | "What's up? How's it going?" |
| Asking Permission | Always ask permission. "May I get a drink?" | Sometimes you do not have to ask permission. "I'm going to get a drink." |
| Listening Position | Sit upright. Make eye contact. Quiet hands and feet. Do not interrupt. | May sit in a more relaxed way. Might interrupt a little. |
| Deciding What to Do | You can let the person know what you would like, but the authority figure gets to decide. | Compromise. Both can have some of what they want. |
| Telling Jokes or Acting Silly | Do not tell jokes or act silly in formal situations unless the authority figure does so first. | You can tell a joke if your friends want to hear it. You can act a little bit silly, but stop if your friends ask you to stop. |

## Practice

Who will I try this with? _____

When? _____

What happened? _____

How did I do? _____

Jed E. Baker, *Social Skills Training for Children and Adolescents with Asperger Syndrome and Social-Communication Problems*, 2003. Shawnee Mission, KS: Autism Asperger Publishing Company; www.asperger.net

# Suggested Activities for
# Informal Versus Formal Behavior

1. After teaching the skill through explanation, you can use a game show approach to review the situations described in the skill. A choice format is "Who Wants to Be a Millionaire?" (see Chapter 4 for a description). Students take turns answering questions that require them to show informal or formal behaviors in different situations. Suggested questions are detailed below.

    a. A student sees the principal of his school at the mall. How should he greet the principal?
    b. A student sees her friends at the mall. How could she greet them?
    c. A student is in class and wants to go get a drink of water. What can he say?
    d. A student is at his friend's house for dinner with his friend's parents. How should he ask for more dessert?
    e. A student is watching TV and eating snacks with her friends. What should she do if she wants more snacks?
    f. Show how students should look when they are listening in class.
    g. Show how students could look when they are listening to each other while playing in their living room.
    h. If one student wants to get some pizza and the other wants to go get hamburgers for lunch, and they are by themselves with their own money, how could they decide what to do?
    i. If one student and his parents want to get some pizza and another student who is a guest in their house wants to go get hamburgers for dinner, and the parents are paying, how could they decide what to do?
    j. Discuss to whom you can tell silly jokes. If a teacher tells silly jokes to her class, can the students tell silly jokes too? Should they keep telling after people say stop?

2. Correct inappropriate levels of informality when it occurs, highlighting who was there and why it is inappropriate.

3. Bait the skill. Act formal in a classroom or home situation when new guests come over, and then act very relaxed with familiar people at home or at a friend's home. See if the students can pick up on your behavior and use that to determine their own level of formality.

4. Provide rewards for appropriate levels of INFORMAL AND FORMAL BEHAVIOR.

    a. Give verbal praise for correct or partially correct levels of formality.
    b. Give tokens, pennies, or points for instances in which the student demonstrated the appropriate level of formality needed for a situation. When he gets an agreed-upon number of tokens, give a special reward (e.g., snack, stickers, and privileges to play special game or watch special show).

Jed E. Baker, *Social Skills Training for Children and Adolescents with Asperger Syndrome and Social-Communication Problems*, 2003. Shawnee Mission, KS: Autism Asperger Publishing Company; www.asperger.net

# Respecting Personal Boundaries

1. People have the right to be alone or to keep things to themselves. If you respect others' space and belongings, they will respect you.

2. Respecting others' space means:

    a. Keeping some physical distance from them. For example, stay about **an arm's length away**, unless invited to come closer.
    b. Allowing others to have time by themselves.
    c. Letting others talk and do things with other people. That is, don't push them to talk and do things only with you.
    d. Not asking them to talk about private information that they say they do not want to discuss.

3. Respecting others' belongings means:

    a. Not touching others' belongings unless given permission or invited to do so.
    b. Not taking or borrowing others' belongings without permission.
    c. Keeping others' property clean and in good condition if you borrow it.

---

## Practice

Who will I try this with? _____

When? _____

What happened? _____

_____

How did I do? _____

Jed E. Baker, *Social Skills Training for Children and Adolescents with Asperger Syndrome and Social-Communication Problems*, 2003. Shawnee Mission, KS: Autism Asperger Publishing Company; www.asperger.net

# Suggested Activities for
# Respecting Personal Boundaries

1. After teaching the skill through explanation, you can use group discussion with older students or a game show approach to review the situations described in the skill. A favored game show format is "Who Wants to Be a Millionaire?" (see Chapter 4 for a description). Students take turns answering questions that require them to describe different ways in which to respect others' boundaries. Suggested questions are detailed below.

   a. How far should people be from each other when talking or playing together?
   b. If friends want to do something by themselves when you want to get together with them, what should you do and why?
   c. If you ask your friend to get together and she says she can't meet with you because she is going somewhere with some other friends, what should you do or say? Why?
   d. If you ask your friend why he never discusses certain things (e.g., his parents, where he used to go to school, why he does not change in the locker room, why he is never available on Saturdays) and he says he does not want to discuss it, what should you do or say? Why?
   e. If you see one of your friend's belongings that you really want to pick up and look at, what should you do? Why?
   f. Is it okay to borrow something from your friend without asking him? Is it ever alright to do that (e.g., to borrow a pencil)?
   g. If you borrow your friend's CD player and it breaks, what should you do? Why?

2. Correct inappropriate violations of others' boundaries.

3. You can bait the skill of asking before touching others' belongings by purposely putting attractive items or snacks in reach of the students and see if they ask before they touch.

4. Provide rewards for appropriate respect for others' boundaries.

   a. Give verbal praise when you observe students respecting others' boundaries.
   b. Give tokens, pennies, or points for instances in which the student demonstrated respect for others' boundaries. When he gets an agreed-upon number of tokens, give a special reward (e.g., snack, stickers, and privileges to play special game or watch special show).

Jed E. Baker, *Social Skills Training for Children and Adolescents with Asperger Syndrome and Social-Communication Problems*, 2003.
Shawnee Mission, KS: Autism Asperger Publishing Company; www.asperger.net

# Facts Versus Opinions
# (Respecting Others' Opinions)

1. Definitions:

   a. **Facts** are ideas that are agreed upon by everyone. If one person disagrees, then the idea is an opinion, not a fact.

   b. **Opinions** are not agreed upon by everyone. People have different opinions.

2. Getting along well with others means:

   a. State your ideas as opinions not facts.

   b. Respect others' right to have their own opinion. "Well, that's your opinion, mine is different."

   c. Try to be flexible by doing things other people's way sometimes.

---

## Practice

Who will I try this with? _____

When? _____

What happened? _____

_____

How did I do? _____

Jed E. Baker, *Social Skills Training for Children and Adolescents with Asperger Syndrome and Social-Communication Problems*, 2003. Shawnee Mission, KS: Autism Asperger Publishing Company; www.asperger.net

# Suggested Activities for Respecting Others' Opinions

1. Role-play the steps for RESPECTING OTHERS' OPINIONS. Suggested role-plays involve the following scenarios:

    a. Discuss students' preferences for food, TV shows, and video games. As they discover differing preferences, instruct them to show respect for others' preferences by saying that they respect the others' preferences. In contrast, role-play insulting others' preferences (only the instructor should do this to keep it from provoking a fight). For example, show how it is not okay to say things like, "You favorite team stinks" or "You like that video game, that's for babies."

    b. As the instructor, share an opinion that you know will be in deep contrast to the opinions or values of the students and require them to say that they respect your right to your opinion even though they disagree with it. For example, for people who hate "liver and onions" say, "I think liver and onions is the best food." More challenging to tolerate is usually comments about religion and politics. You can say to a member of one political party that only the other political party is dealing with reality. Prompt them to calmly show respect for your right to your opinion, and then state how they disagree with it.

    c. Have each member of the group, class, or siblings at home make up new rules to old games. Take turns playing the game with each different set of rules so that the students can see there are many ways to play a game.

2. Bait the skill. Share provocative opinions like the ones above and prompt the students to show respect before they disagree. Similarly, purposely change the way a game or routine is conducted to help the student gain flexibility with different styles.

3. Correct the student when he demands that others agree that his is the only way to do something or that he has the only "allowable" opinion about something.

4. Provide rewards for RESPECTING OTHERS' OPINIONS.

    a. Give verbal praise for correct or partially correct respect for others' opinions.
    b. Give tokens, pennies, or points every time the student respects a different opinion or way to do something. When she gets an agreed-upon number of tokens (e.g., five tokens), give a special reward (e.g., snack, stickers, or privileges to play special game).

Jed E. Baker, *Social Skills Training for Children and Adolescents with Asperger Syndrome and Social-Communication Problems*, 2003. Shawnee Mission, KS: Autism Asperger Publishing Company; www.asperger.net

# Sharing a Friend

1. Sometimes your friends want to talk or hang out with others.

2. If you don't get mad but let your friends do what they want to do, they will feel happy and relaxed when they are with you.

3. If you get mad at your friends for talking or hanging out with others, they will feel uncomfortable. Instead of wanting to be with you, they will feel forced into being with you.

4. Decide if you want a friend who wants to be with you or just someone who feels forced to be with you. Friends are people you want to be with and who also want to be with you.

## Practice

Who will I try this with? _____

When? _____

What happened? _____

_____

How did I do? _____

Jed E. Baker, *Social Skills Training for Children and Adolescents with Asperger Syndrome and Social-Communication Problems*, 2003.
Shawnee Mission, KS: Autism Asperger Publishing Company; www.asperger.net

# Suggested Activities for Sharing a Friend

1. This skill lends itself more to discussion than role-play as the key is for students to distinguish between real friends and forced friendships, and then to work towards fostering real friendships. The following activity can help students understand the need to share friends.

   a. Have the student sit in an area of the classroom or home and play a boring game with you. Have another student ask him to play more interesting games while you demand that he only play with you. Discuss how willing he would be to play with you again.
   b. Do the activity again, instead letting the student play a short game with others. After a while, come back to him and offer to play a fun game with him. Talk about the differences in willingness to play the second time compared to when he was forced to play with you.

2. Bait the skill. When the student is playing with a friend, try to entice the friend away to play with you. Prompt the student to share his friend and then his friend will return.

3. Correct instances of demanding that friends do not play with others. Remind the student that friends may want to come back if he lets them go.

4. Provide rewards for SHARING A FRIEND.

   a. Give verbal praise for correct or partially correct sharing of friends.
   b. Give tokens, pennies, or points every time the student shares a friend. When she gets an agreed-upon number of tokens (e.g., five tokens), give a special reward (e.g., snack, stickers, or privileges to play special game).

Jed E. Baker, *Social Skills Training for Children and Adolescents with Asperger Syndrome and Social-Communication Problems*, 2003. Shawnee Mission, KS: Autism Asperger Publishing Company; www.asperger.net

# Getting Attention in Positive Ways

1. Attention is when people look at and listen to you.
   a. Positive attention is when people look at and listen to you and like what you are doing. Using positive ways to get attention helps you make and keep friends.
   b. Negative attention is when people look at and listen to you but do not like what you are doing. Negative ways to get attention can cause you to lose friends.

| Positive Ways | Negative Ways |
|---|---|
| Listen to others and ask questions about what they are discussing. | Don't do all the talking. |
| Start a conversation about somebody else's interests. | Don't just talk about your interests. |
| Compliment others. | Don't insult others or bring up sensitive topics (topics that make others uncomfortable). |
| Ask to play something another person wants to do. | Don't tell everyone what they should play. |
| Ask to get together. If the person you ask says no, ask someone else. | Don't get mad at others if they do not want to talk or get together with you. |
| Only tell a joke if others want to hear it. Say, "Do you want to hear a joke?" | Don't say silly jokes over and over again. |
| Tell the truth. | Don't make up any stories that are not true. Don't try to get others' sympathy by pretending to be hurt. |

## Practice

Who did I do this with? _____

When did I try this? _____

What happened? _____

How did I do? _____

Jed E. Baker, *Social Skills Training for Children and Adolescents with Asperger Syndrome and Social-Communication Problems*, 2003. Shawnee Mission, KS: Autism Asperger Publishing Company; www.asperger.net

# Suggested Activities for
# Getting Attention in Positive Ways

1. The amount of information in this skill may be overwhelming for younger students. Sometimes it is wise to focus on only one example of positive and negative attention. If a student has a problem with getting attention in negative ways, focus on what that student does (e.g., being too silly all the time) and one thing she could do instead (e.g., asking to play what the other children like to play). For older students who have already learned the skills to initiate play, start conversations, avoid sensitive topics, and talk briefly, this skill is a good way to review many of the positive things that facilitate friendship.

2. After teaching the skill through explanation, use a game show approach to review the situations described in the skill. A favored game show format is "Who Wants to Be a Millionaire?" (see Chapter 4 for a description). Students take turns answering questions that require them to describe ways to get attention and maintain friendships. Suggested questions are detailed below.

   a. Does getting attention mean that others will like you? (No, getting attention in negative ways will push people away.)

   b. Will being silly all the time make people like you more? (No, if people tell you to stop being silly, you should do so to prevent them from getting annoyed with you.)

   c. Name and show one positive way to get attention.

   d. Show a negative way to get attention and then tell what you could do instead to get attention in a positive way.

   e. Show another positive way to get attention and tell what you did.

   f. Show another positive way to get attention and tell what you did.

3. Role-play the positive and negative ways to get attention. Students can take turns acting out the different positive and negative ways while the rest of the group guess what they are doing. This can be facilitated by writing each negative and positive way to get attention on separate slips of paper. Each student can select a slip of paper and then enact what it says to do.

4. Redirect negative ways to get attention to appropriate ways to maintain friendships. Some students may need a loss system that gives them warnings for inappropriate remarks until they lose a privilege or get a "time-out."

5. Bait the skill by simply stating "stop" when students get too silly, reminding them that if they stop they will maintain their friendships.

6. Provide rewards for getting attention in positive ways or avoiding negative ways to get attention.

   a. Give verbal praise when students get attention positively or avoid too much silliness.

   b. Give tokens, pennies, or points for periods in which the student got attention positively or avoided too much silliness. When he gets an agreed-upon number of tokens, give a special reward (e.g., snack, stickers, and privileges to play special game or watch special show).

Jed E. Baker, *Social Skills Training for Children and Adolescents with Asperger Syndrome and Social-Communication Problems*, 2003. Shawnee Mission, KS: Autism Asperger Publishing Company; www.asperger.net

# Don't Be the "Rule Police"

1. Most of the time, don't tell people what to do.  It is not your job to make others follow the rules. If you tell others what rules to follow or tattle on them, they will be annoyed with you.

2. But there are some **exceptions** when it is okay for you to tell people what rules to follow.

   a. When you are the teacher, boss, or put in charge of others.
   b. When people ask you what the rules are.
   c. When people break a rule that could cause great danger to themselves or others.
   d. If people do something to hurt you, you can use an "I" statement or tell on them.

## Practice

Who will I try this with? _____

When? _____

What happened? _____

_____

How did I do? _____

Jed E. Baker, *Social Skills Training for Children and Adolescents with Asperger Syndrome and Social-Communication Problems*, 2003. Shawnee Mission, KS: Autism Asperger Publishing Company; www.asperger.net

# Suggested Activities for
# Dont't Be the "Rule Police"

1. For younger children and those with difficulties comprehending language, it may be more appropriate to teach WHEN TO TELL rather than DON'T BE THE "RULE POLICE," which is a little more abstract. Both review much of the same material. After teaching the skill through explanation, you can use a game show approach to review the situations described in the skill. A favored game show format is "Who Wants to Be a Millionaire?" (see Chapter 4 for a description). Students take turns answering questions that require them to discriminate between situations that require them to tell others what to do or to say nothing. Suggested questions are detailed below.

    a. Why should you not tell others what to do?
    b. If someone is chewing gum in school, which is breaking a school rule, what should you do? (Probably nothing. This situation is not dangerous despite being a rule violation.)
    c. If someone is drawing when the teacher tells everyone to read a book, what should you do? (Probably nothing, because it is not your job to tell on the other person.)
    d. If someone is lighting toilet paper on fire in the bathroom, what should you do? (Tell an adult what is happening because it is dangerous. You might want to avoid using the child's name or avoid direct confrontations in this dangerous situation.)
    e. If everyone on the lunch line in the cafeteria is supposed to take just one carton of milk but someone takes two, what would you do? (If there will still be enough milk for everybody, then maybe do nothing.)
    f. If a classmate is annoying you by whispering to you when the teacher is talking, what can you do? (Probably tell the classmate to stop because he is directly annoying you.)
    g. If a classmate is annoying another classmate by tapping him on the shoulder, what should you do? (Probably nothing, because this is not dangerous and does not directly impact you.)

2. Role-play the situations above or actual situations that occurred in which the students have inappropriately told others what to do.

3. Redirect instances of BEING THE "RULE POLICE" by asking the student, "Was it dangerous? Was the person hurting you? Are you in charge? If not, then do not tell them what to do."

4. You can bait the skill by breaking nondangerous rules in front of students (e.g., chewing gum, or not following a direction).

5. Provide rewards for refraining from telling others what to do.

    a. Give verbal praise when students refrain from telling others what to do.
    b. Give tokens, pennies, or points for instances in which someone broke a rule and the student acted appropriately by doing nothing or by telling. When he gets an agreed-upon number of tokens, give a special reward (e.g., snack, stickers, and privileges to play special game or watch special show).

Jed E. Baker, *Social Skills Training for Children and Adolescents with Asperger Syndrome and Social-Communication Problems*, 2003. Shawnee Mission, KS: Autism Asperger Publishing Company; www.asperger.net

# Offering Help

1. Think of the advantages of helping others:

   a. Others may help you if you help them.
   b. People who see you helping others will think you are nice and may want to be friends with you.
   c. You can feel good about yourself for being helpful to others.

2. Look for signs that others may need help:

   a. They are having trouble with their work.
   b. They are having trouble carrying something heavy.
   c. They are missing a pencil or piece of paper that you could lend them.
   d. They are being ignored and need someone to invite them to play or talk.
   e. Their hands are full so they cannot open a door.

3. Say, "Let me help you," and then give them the help.

4. If they say they do not want help, then leave them alone.

5. Be careful not to be overly helpful to teachers when they do not need the help because other kids may get angry with you for trying to be the "teacher's favorite."

## Practice

Who will I try this with? _____

When? _____

What happened? _____

_____

How did I do? _____

# Suggested Activities for Offering Help

1. Role-play the skill steps using the following situations or situations that actually occurred in the students' daily lives.

   a. A classmate is having trouble with work.
   b. A parent or teacher is having trouble carrying something heavy.
   c. A classmate is missing a pencil or piece of paper that you could lend them.
   d. A friend is being ignored and needs someone to invite them to play or talk.
   e. A student, teacher, or parent has their hands full so they cannot open a door.
   f. Role-play any of the above situations again but with the change that the other person does not want the help.
   g. Role-play repeatedly offering to help a teacher in front of the other classmates when she does not ask for help. Remind the teacher about homework she assigned and other work she was going to assign. Review with the students how other classmates would feel about this behavior.

2. Prompt others to help when they are ignoring those who may need it.

3. You can bait the skill by acting like you need help without directly asking for it. For example, struggle to open a door with your hands full, or complain that you cannot figure out how to put something together.

4. Provide rewards for OFFERING HELP.

   a. Give verbal praise when students offer help.
   b. Give tokens, pennies, or points for instances in which students offer help. When they get an agreed-upon number of tokens, give a special reward (e.g., snack, stickers, and privileges to play special game or watch special show).

Jed E. Baker, *Social Skills Training for Children and Adolescents with Asperger Syndrome and Social-Communication Problems*, 2003. Shawnee Mission, KS: Autism Asperger Publishing Company; www.asperger.net

# When to Tell on Someone

1. Try not to tell on others most of the time because it may make them feel mad and sad.

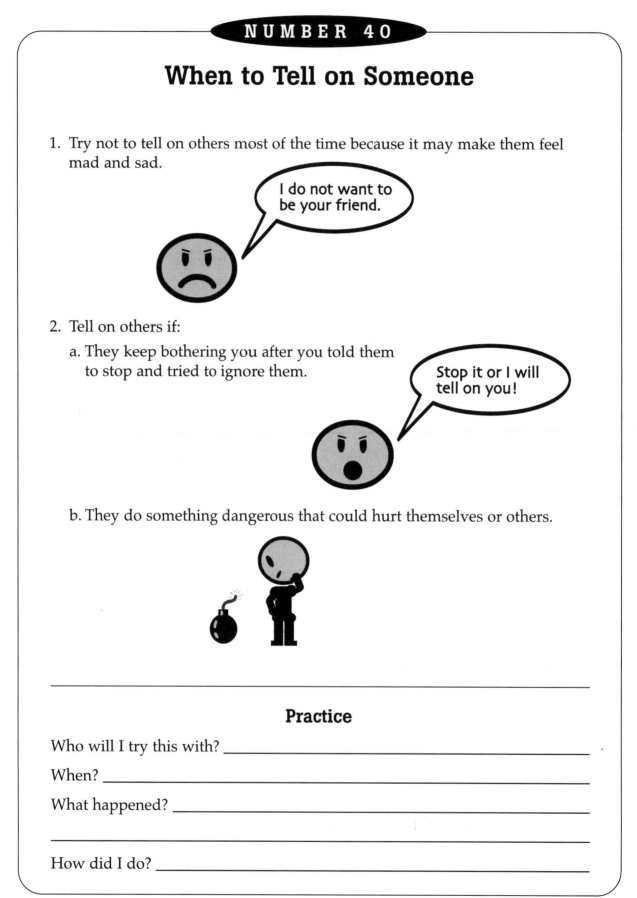

I do not want to be your friend.

2. Tell on others if:

   a. They keep bothering you after you told them to stop and tried to ignore them.

   Stop it or I will tell on you!

   b. They do something dangerous that could hurt themselves or others.

---

## Practice

Who will I try this with? _____

When? _____

What happened? _____

_____

How did I do? _____

Jed E. Baker, *Social Skills Training for Children and Adolescents with Asperger Syndrome and Social-Communication Problems*, 2003. Shawnee Mission, KS: Autism Asperger Publishing Company; www.asperger.net

# Suggested Activities for
# When to Tell on Somebody

1. This is very similar to DON'T BE THE "RULE POLICE" but often more appropriate to teach preschoolers through second graders. After teaching the skill through explanation, role-play actual situations that occur in the classroom or at home in which the students tell on each other or use the situations described below. For children who can imagine hypothetical situations, you can use a game show approach to review the situations described in the skill. A favored game show format is "Who Wants to Be a Millionaire?" (see Chapter 4 for a description). Students take turns answering questions that require them to discriminate between situations that require them to tell others what to do or to say nothing. Suggested questions are detailed below.

   a. If someone keeps tapping you with a pencil, what should you do? (Tell them to stop first; if they do not, only then can you tell on them.)
   b. If someone is chewing gum in school, which is breaking a school rule, what should you do? (Probably nothing; this situation is not dangerous despite being a rule violation.)
   c. If someone is drawing when the teacher tells everyone to read a book, what should you do? (Probably nothing, because it is not your job to tell on the other person.)
   d. If somebody is throwing toilet paper at you in the bathroom, what should you do? (Tell them to stop; if they don't, then tell an adult.)
   e. If everyone in the classroom is supposed to take just one piece of candy for Halloween, but someone takes two, what would you do? (If there will still be enough treats for everybody, then maybe do nothing.)
   f. If a classmate is annoying you by whispering to you when the teacher is talking, what can you do? (Probably tell the classmate to stop because he is directly annoying you; only tell if he does not stop.)
   g. If a classmate is annoying another classmate by tapping him on the shoulder, what should you do? (Probably nothing, because this is not dangerous and does not directly impact you.)

2. Redirect instances of tattle-telling by asking, "Was it dangerous? Was the person hurting you? Did you tell them to stop first?"

3. You can bait the skill by breaking nondangerous rules in front of students or gently bothering them (e.g., chewing gum or tapping them on the shoulder over and over).

4. Provide rewards for refraining from telling others what to do.

   a. Give verbal praise when students refrain from telling others what to do.
   b. Give tokens, pennies, or points for instances in which someone broke a rule and the student acted appropriately by doing nothing or by telling. When he gets an agreed-upon number of tokens, give a special reward (e.g., snack, stickers, and privileges to play special game or watch special show).

Jed E. Baker, *Social Skills Training for Children and Adolescents with Asperger Syndrome and Social-Communication Problems*, 2003. Shawnee Mission, KS: Autism Asperger Publishing Company; www.asperger.net

# Modesty

1. Modest means that you present your abilities as "good," but not great. It means that you do not brag about your talents or accomplishments in front of others.

2. Think of the advantages of acting modestly.

   a. When you are modest, people have more respect for you.
   b. Others will feel that you are equal to and not better than they are, so they will feel good to be around you.

3. Modesty looks and sounds like . . .

   a. Handing in your homework without saying to the whole class, "I did all of the work."
   b. Answering some but not every one of the questions the teacher asks the class.
   c. Thinking, but not saying, what all your talents and accomplishments are unless someone asks you.

## Practice

Who will I try this with? _____

When? _____

What happened? _____

_____

How did I do? _____

Jed E. Baker, *Social Skills Training for Children and Adolescents with Asperger Syndrome and Social-Communication Problems*, 2003. Shawnee Mission, KS: Autism Asperger Publishing Company; www.asperger.net

# Suggested Activities for
# Modesty

1.  In teaching this skill, make sure students do not begin to be self-deprecating. They can still present themselves in a positive light without bragging and avoid putting themselves down. Role-play the skill using the following situations or other situations that actually occurred in the students' daily lives:

    a.  Have each student write down some of their strengths and talents (e.g., schoolwork, sports, musical, or artistic talents). Have each student practice describing their abilities to the other students in a modest fashion versus bragging about them. Correct any negative self-statements.

    b.  Role-play a student answering all the questions in a classroom lesson. Discuss how the other students feel about that student.

    c.  Pretend one student is having trouble with homework. Practice offering help in a bragging versus modest way.

    d.  Pretend a student is talking about a time when he had trouble playing a sport, musical instrument, or completing some school or home task. Show how another student could respond in a bragging way (e.g., "I am much better than you at that" or "I can help you because I am much better than you") versus a supportive way (e.g., "Yeah, that happened to me once too" or "Do you want any help with that?").

2.  Correct arrogant behavior by reminding students how others will feel if you say such things.

3.  Bait the skill by acting like you are having trouble with something that you know they are really good at (e.g., "I am having so much trouble with this spelling"). Prompt students to offer help rather than brag.

4.  Provide rewards for MODESTY.

    a.  Give verbal praise when students demonstrate MODESTY.

    b.  Give tokens, pennies, or points for instances in which a student demonstrated modest behavior. When she gets an agreed-upon number of tokens, give a special reward (e.g., snack, stickers, and privileges to play a special game or watch a special show).

Jed E. Baker, *Social Skills Training for Children and Adolescents with Asperger Syndrome and Social-Communication Problems*, 2003. Shawnee Mission, KS: Autism Asperger Publishing Company; www.asperger.net

# Asking Someone Out on a Date

1. Initiate a conversation (small talk) using the GETTING TO KNOW SOME-ONE NEW skill or CONVERSATION STARTERS skill.

    a. Think of what you have in common with the person to find an initial question.

    b. Ask follow-up questions (Who, What, Where When, Why, How) and make on-topic comments.

    c. Introduce yourself. Say, "By the way, my name is _____, what's your name?"

2. Initiate 1-3 conversations before you ask the person out.

    a. Get to know whether you share any common interests. For example, ask, "What are you studying?  What kind of work do you do? What do you do for fun?"

    b. Try to find out, indirectly, if the person is available.   For example, if she tells you what she likes to do, you could ask, "Do you do that with family, friends, a boyfriend?"

    c. Without asking, try to determine if the person is interested in talking with you again.  Look for signals of interest: Is she always making excuses to leave or does she initiate conversation with you?

3. During one of the later conversations, ask if the person wants to get together with you some time.

4. Ask the person out to a place that she would like to go.
    a. Go to a restaurant, movie, roller rink, park, or any other place of interest.

5. Pick the person up or plan to meet in a place that is convenient for her/him.

    a. Surprise her/him with a box of candy or flowers when you meet.

6. Pay for the meal, movie, or activity unless the date insists on paying her/his own way.

7. During the date, you can:

    a. Compliment your date on how nice she/he looks.

    b. Ask about: the person's interests, where she/he grew up, work or school, family composition (e.g., does she/he have any siblings).

    c. Talk **briefly** about your own interests.

Jed E. Baker, *Social Skills Training for Children and Adolescents with Asperger Syndrome and Social-Communication Problems*, 2003. Shawnee Mission, KS: Autism Asperger Publishing Company; www.asperger.net

# Suggested Activities for
# Asking Someone Out on a Date

1. The first part of this skill it essentially a repeat of the GETTING TO KNOW SOMEONE NEW skill. Therefore, all the activities and role-plays for that skill are relevant here as well. It is important that students understand that you must get to know someone a little before asking them out. Asking out strangers can lead to trouble, sometimes even with the law.

2. Many students with AS do not have opportunities to meet suitable romantic partners because of social skill difficulties. It may be helpful to first discuss or create a list of who is a suitable candidate to ask out. Examples of who one could and should not ask out include:

   a. In the school setting, it is not appropriate to ask out staff members.
   b. It may be productive to ask out other members of the group, or a club you are in, particularly because you may share similar experiences or similar interests.
   c. It may not be productive to ask out someone who is already dating someone or who is so popular that he or she does not have any desire to make new friends.
   d. Sometimes, teenagers chat with other teenagers on chat lines. This can be a less stressful means to begin getting to know someone new because you do not have to answer immediately or process nonverbal cues. If this is suggested as a means to meet possible dating partners, great care needs to be taken to warn students of the dangers of meeting strangers from the Internet. It would be wise to have parents supervise any plans made to meet people from the chat lines.

3. Give students a list of what not to do with regard to asking someone out with possible consequences for rule violations. Many students have inappropriately harassed or stalked fellow students for whom they had an attraction because they did not clearly understand the cues and rules governing dating. Be clear that they cannot ask out someone repeatedly after the person has said no. They are not to follow somebody around or write love notes if the person has indicated a disinterest. Disinterest by fellow students may be communicated with direct verbal statements of disinterest in getting together or by subtler cues such as making excuses not to talk with the student, or walking away whenever they see the student.

4. If possible, bring similar-aged groups together for socials, including some separate boys and girls groups. In this context, the students have a chance to meet other students who may also have social needs and therefore have some common experiences. Opportunities for dating are sometimes greater in this context than in the larger school environment.

Jed E. Baker, *Social Skills Training for Children and Adolescents with Asperger Syndrome and Social-Communication Problems*, 2003. Shawnee Mission, KS: Autism Asperger Publishing Company; www.asperger.net

# Appropriate Touch

1. **Appropriate** touch is when you touch people in ways that they want to be touched. **Inappropriate** touch is touching that makes people feel bad.

2. If you are not sure whether or not a certain kind of touch will upset others, ask before you touch.

   a. For example, you can say, "Is it okay to hug you?"

3. Here are some examples of different touches with different people. Even OK touches may require permission first. They are marked with a question mark.

|  | Mother | Friend | Boy/Girl Friend | Stranger |
|---|---|---|---|---|
| Tap Shoulder | OK | OK | OK | ? |
| Handshake | OK | OK | OK | ? |
| Hug | OK | ? | OK | Not OK |
| Kiss | OK | ? | ? | Not OK |
| Pat Behind | Not OK | Not OK | ? | Not OK |

_____

## Practice

Who will I try this with? _____

When? _____

What happened? _____

_____

How did I do? _____

Jed E. Baker, *Social Skills Training for Children and Adolescents with Asperger Syndrome and Social-Communication Problems*, 2003. Shawnee Mission, KS: Autism Asperger Publishing Company; www.asperger.net

# Suggested Activities for Appropriate Touch

1. Much of this skill should not be role-played as it might involve inappropriate touch. You can use a game show format to review what is and is not appropriate. A favored game show format is "Who Wants to Be a Millionaire?" (see Chapter 4 for a description). Students take turns answering questions that require them to decide if a touch is or is not appropriate. Sample questions are listed below.

   a. Go through the chart on the skill page and ask about each person with each kind of touch. For example, "Is it okay for you to shake hands with your mother?" For answers that are not so clear (indicated by the question marks on the chart), give bonus dollars for good comments.

   b. Like the set of questions above, go through the chart on the skill page and ask again about each person with each kind of touch, but this time ask if it is okay to ask permission to engage in the touch. For example, "Is it okay to ask a stranger if you can pat their behind?"

2. In considering the different kinds of touches, ask students how they would feel if one of their friends touched their mother, sister, brother, or father in an inappropriate way. Making the personal connection often helps them more fully take the perspective of potential victims of inappropriate touch.

3. When students frequently touch others in ways that make them uncomfortable, or coerce others into being touched in sexual ways, they should be referred to a professional mental health counselor for an evaluation to determine the best course of intervention. In some cases, the incident may need to be reported to state child protective agencies. When uncertainties arise as to what constitutes a reportable incident, consult with a state child protection agency.

Jed E. Baker, *Social Skills Training for Children and Adolescents with Asperger Syndrome and Social-Communication Problems*, 2003. Shawnee Mission, KS: Autism Asperger Publishing Company; www.asperger.net

# Dealing with Peer Pressure

1. Sometimes other children will ask or pressure you to do things. Decide if it is good or bad peer pressure.

   a. **Good peer pressure** is when friends ask you to do something that might help you or others.

   (1) Like encouraging you to be kind to others, do your school work, practice a sport or hobby, or help a friend.

   b. **Bad peer pressure** is when friends ask you to do something that will get you in trouble, hurt others, or when they insist they will only be your friend if you do it. This can include:

   (1) Playing a trick on someone.

   (2) Trying a drug, or doing something else that is dangerous.

2. If it is bad peer pressure:

   a. Look at the person and use a strong voice.

   b. Say no and refuse to do it.

   c. Explain why.

   d. Walk away.

3. If you are not sure whether someone is telling you to do something that is good or bad, ask a person you do trust for advice.

## Practice

Who will I try this with? _____

When? _____

What happened? _____

_____

How did I do? _____

Jed E. Baker, *Social Skills Training for Children and Adolescents with Asperger Syndrome and Social-Communication Problems*, 2003. Shawnee Mission, KS: Autism Asperger Publishing Company; www.asperger.net

# Suggested Activities for Dealing with Peer Pressure

1. Students often do not know when a peer is exerting positive or negative peer pressure and the desire to belong may lead them to follow even when they are unsure of whether it is okay. In addition to working on the skill steps for DEALING WITH PEER PRESSURE, teachers and parents must first address the following two issues:

   a. Have the student make a list of students and staff that he can trust to give helpful advice. These should be the people the student will seek out when a peer asks him to do something and the student does not know whether it is okay to do.

   b. Help the student make another list of people who care about and like him, and who do not ask the student to do dangerous or hurtful things. Explain that these are real friends and that those who would have him do dangerous or hurtful things just to feel accepted are not real friends.

2. Role-play or simply discuss situations that represent good or bad peer pressure, along with who to ask if the student is not sure of what to do. Suggested situations:

   a. Peer asking the student to join him in stealing candy from a store and explaining that everyone else does it. (Bad)

   b. Peer encouraging the student to finish schoolwork so he can go out and play. (Good)

   c. Peer encouraging the student to leave work so he can go out and play. (Bad)

   d. Peer asking for money in exchange for friendship. (Bad)

   e. A group of peers saying the student has to be tough and defy the teacher to be cool and accepted into their group. (Bad)

   f. Peer encouraging the student to keep practicing a sport or musical instrument. (Good)

   g. Peer telling the student that a friend wants to go out with her and that she should ask him out. (Unclear, go ask someone you trust)

   h. Peer telling the student that another student is mean and to avoid being friends with him. (Unclear, go ask someone you trust)

3. Bait the skill. Purposely tell the student to do something that would be hurtful and prompt or wait for her to assertively refuse or ask someone she trusts. NOTE: ONLY DO THIS WITH STUDENTS WHO UNDERSTAND IT IS PRETEND AND A TEST OF THEIR JUDGMENT.

4. Provide rewards for appropriate DEALING WITH PEER PRESSURE.

   a. Give verbal praise for correct or partially correct DEALING WITH PEER PRESSURE.

   b. Give tokens, pennies, or points for DEALING WITH PEER PRESSURE. When the student gets an agreed-upon number of tokens (e.g., five tokens), give a special reward (e.g., snack, stickers, or privileges to play a special game).

Jed E. Baker, *Social Skills Training for Children and Adolescents with Asperger Syndrome and Social-Communication Problems*, 2003. Shawnee Mission, KS: Autism Asperger Publishing Company; www.asperger.net

# Dealing with Rumors

1. Sometimes people say mean things about others that are false (not true).

2. Do not believe mean rumors about someone.

   a. If you are not sure whether it is true, you can ask someone you trust, like a teacher or parent. If you are not sure if it will get you in trouble, ask someone you can trust to give you the right information.

3. Do not spread a false rumor by telling others.  That will make others upset.

---

## Practice

Who will I try this with? _____

When will I do it? _____

What happened? _____

_____

How did I do? _____

Jed E. Baker, *Social Skills Training for Children and Adolescents with Asperger Syndrome and Social-Communication Problems*, 2003.
Shawnee Mission, KS: Autism Asperger Publishing Company; www.asperger.net

# Suggested Activities for Dealing with Rumors

1. Students with AS often do not know whether to believe a rumor, and therefore may need advice from a trusted friend or adult. Suggest they make a list of students and staff whom they can trust to give helpful advice.

2. Role-play or simply discuss situations that represent different types of rumors. If possible, use situations in the students' lives where they were uncertain of the truth of the rumor. For each situation, discuss how they would feel if the rumor was told about them, reinforcing the importance of not spreading rumors. Suggested situations include:

   a. Peer tells a student that another student wears diapers.
   b. Peer tells a student that their teacher is an alien from Mars.
   c. Peer tells a student that there will not be school for a week because of a special teacher convention.
   d. Peer tells a student that the teacher was just kidding about the test she said they would have tomorrow.
   e. Peer tells a student that a terrorist attack is going to occur in the school tomorrow.

3. Bait the skill. First tell students that in the next several hours you may test their ability to deal with rumors. Some time later, tell students something false, but nothing that would cause danger. For example, say that you are going to fly to the moon tomorrow. Wait only about 30 minutes to see if the student tells anyone else or decides to ask for advice about the truth of such a statement.
   NOTE: ONLY DO THIS WITH STUDENTS WHO UNDERSTAND IT IS PRETEND AND A TEST OF THEIR JUDGMENT.

4. Provide rewards for appropriate DEALING WITH RUMORS.

   a. Give verbal praise for correct or partially correct DEALING WITH RUMORS, like if they ask your advice before spreading a rumor, or simply do not spread a rumor.
   b. Give tokens, pennies, or points for DEALING WITH RUMORS. When the student gets an agreed-upon number of tokens (e.g., five tokens), give a special reward (e.g., snack, stickers, or privileges to play a special game).

Jed E. Baker, *Social Skills Training for Children and Adolescents with Asperger Syndrome and Social-Communication Problems*, 2003.
Shawnee Mission, KS: Autism Asperger Publishing Company; www.asperger.net

# Calling a Friend on the Telephone

Say hello and give your name. "Hello, this is _____ calling."

Ask for your friend. "Is _____ there?"

| If you friend is home | If your friend is not there |
|---|---|
| Say, "Hi, how are you?" | Say, "Can I leave a message?" |
| Say why you called: "I wanted to ask you something." "I wanted to know if you wanted to get together." "I was bored and just wanted to talk with you." | If the answer is yes, give your name and telephone number and any message you want to leave. |
| Start a new topic: "So what have you been doing lately?" "What are you doing now?" "What are you going to be doing _____?" "Did you hear about _____?" Ask follow-up questions and make on-topic comments. WHO, WHAT, WHERE, WHEN, WHY, HOW | "This is _____ and my telephone number is _____. Please tell _____ that I called." |
| When you want to get off the phone, wait for a pause and then say, "Well, I have to go do some other things right now. It was good to talk with you. See you later." Then wait for the other person to say goodbye before you hang up. | Say, "Thank you. Goodbye now." |

Jed E. Baker, *Social Skills Training for Children and Adolescents with Asperger Syndrome and Social-Communication Problems*, 2003. Shawnee Mission, KS: Autism Asperger Publishing Company; www.asperger.net

# Suggested Activities for
# Calling a Friend on the Telephone

1. This skill can be role-played simultaneously with the skill ANSWERING THE TELEPHONE. Suggested situations include:

   a. Student asks someone about a homework assignment. They go on to discuss what they have been doing and their weekend plans.

   b. A student calls a peer just because she is bored and wants to see what her friend is doing.

   c. A student calls a friend to ask about a video game.

   d. A student calls a friend to ask about a video game but only his parents are home.

2. Students often have great fear of using the telephone with peers. They can begin practicing by first writing a letter, using e-mail, then calling the group leader (therapist, teacher, parent) on the phone, then another member of the group, and finally a peer outside of the group training.

3. Bait the skill. Tell students to make a decision about what snack or activity they want the next time you meet and have them call you to tell you their decision.

4. Provide rewards for appropriate CALLING A FRIEND ON THE TELEPHONE.

   a. Give verbal praise for correct or partially correct CALLING A FRIEND ON THE TELEPHONE. You can first reward letter writing, e-mails, and then phone calls.

   b. Give tokens, pennies, or points for CALLING A FRIEND ON THE TELEPHONE. When the student gets an agreed-upon number of tokens (e.g., five tokens), give a special reward (e.g., snack, stickers, or privileges to play a special game).

Jed E. Baker, *Social Skills Training for Children and Adolescents with Asperger Syndrome and Social-Communication Problems*, 2003. Shawnee Mission, KS: Autism Asperger Publishing Company; www.asperger.net

# Answering the Telephone

Say "Hello."

↓

Get the caller's name, "Who is calling please?"

↓

Find out why the person is calling. "Who are you trying to reach?"

| You | Someone who is home | Someone who is out | A salesperson |
|-----|---------------------|--------------------|---------------|
| Say, "Hi, how are you? What have you been doing?" | Say, "Hold on. I will go get them." Put the phone down. | Say, "They cannot come to the phone right now. Can I take a message?" | Say, "Sorry, I am not interested." |
| Ask follow-up questions and make on-topic comments. | Go tell the person at home that he or she has a telephone call from _____. Don't yell this information from another room. | Say, "Hold on, I need to get a pen a paper." Ask for the caller's name, telephone number, and any **message** that the person wants to leave. | Don't give the caller any information about you or your family. |
| When you want to get off the phone, wait for a pause and then say, "Well I have to go. It was good to talk with you. See you later." Then wait for them to say goodbye before you hang up. | Give the phone to the person at home. | Repeat the message to check if it is correct. Say, "Let me make sure I got this right." If the caller says it's right, then say, "Okay, goodbye." Wait for the them to say "goodbye" before you hang up. | Say, "Goodbye." Then hang up the phone. |

Jed E. Baker, *Social Skills Training for Children and Adolescents with Asperger Syndrome and Social-Communication Problems*, 2003. Shawnee Mission, KS: Autism Asperger Publishing Company; www.asperger.net

# Suggested Activities for
# Answering the Telephone

1. Role-play ANSWERING THE TELEPHONE. This skill can be role-played simultaneously with the skill CALLING A FRIEND ON THE TELEPHONE. Suggested situations include:

   a. Student answers a call from a peer asking about a homework assignment. They go on to discuss what they have been doing and their weekend plans.
   b. A student answers a call from a peer who called just because she was bored.
   c. A student answers a call from a friend who called to ask about a video game.
   d. A student answers a call from an adult who wants to talk to his parent. Role-play this twice, once pretending that the parent is home and another that the parent is not home.

2. Students often have great fear of using the telephone with peers. They can begin practicing gradually by answering letters, e-mails, calls from the group leader (therapist, teacher, parent) on the phone, then another member of the group, and finally a peer outside of the group training.

3. Bait the skill. Tell students to make a decision about what snack or activity they want the next time you meet and tell them you will call them to see what their decision was.

4. Provide rewards for appropriate ANSWERING THE TELEPHONE.

   a. Give verbal praise for correct or partially correct ANSWERING THE TELE-PHONE. You can first reward letter writing, Emails, and then phone calls.
   b. Give tokens, pennies, or points for ANSWERING THE TELEPHONE. When the student gets an agreed-upon number of tokens (e.g., five tokens), give a special reward (e.g., snack, stickers, or privileges to play a special game).

Jed E. Baker, *Social Skills Training for Children and Adolescents with Asperger Syndrome and Social-Communication Problems*, 2003. Shawnee Mission, KS: Autism Asperger Publishing Company; www.asperger.net

# Recognizing Feelings
# (Building Awareness of Feelings)

## Journal Page

Date: _____

What happened (draw or write):

What I felt when this happened (write or draw):

What I thought when this happened:
*Examples. Thoughts about others: They did not mean it. It was on purpose. They like me.*
*They do not like me.*
*Thoughts about me: I am okay. Something is wrong with me. I am successful. I am a failure.*

How I tried to deal with this feeling:
*Examples. I tried to talk to a friend. I tried to talk to the person bothering me. I asked for*
*help. I did something fun until I felt better. I tried to change my thoughts.*

Jed E. Baker, *Social Skills Training for Children and Adolescents with Asperger Syndrome and Social-Communication Problems*, 2003.
Shawnee Mission, KS: Autism Asperger Publishing Company; www.asperger.net

# Suggested Activities for
# Recognizing Feelings

Some children have difficulty recognizing the facial expressions, tone of voice, and situations that may be associated with different feelings or moods. For those students, direct instruction and practice is imperative. They should work through all the activities described below until they can consistently identify feelings.

1. Look through magazines and cut out photos of people showing basic emotions like happy, sad, mad, and scared.
   a. Show and explain to the student how shape of mouth, eyes, eyebrows, and body position correspond to different feelings.
   b. After you have taught the student what to look for in the pictures, have him try to pick out pictures corresponding to happy, sad, mad, and scared feelings.
   c. After you have worked with these basic feelings, try to expand to less obvious feelings like being proud, nervous, guilty, confused, disgusted, surprised, etc.
   d. Engage the student in a discussion of what makes the people in the pictures feel the way they do.

2. Watch clips of video or TV without sound and guess the feelings portrayed. (Video is easier as it can be paused to highlight facial expressions and body position.)
   a. Engage in a discussion of why the people in the video feel the way they do.

3. Use a mirror or video to help the student watch herself as she tries to enact different feelings.  Children often think they are accurately portraying a feeling even when their faces and bodies do not correspond to the intended feeling. Give the child feedback until she can accurately display the feelings.

4. Use a Feelings Thermometer (see p. 175) to learn different words to describe gradations of emotion.  For example, happy might include words like "fine" or "okay" on the low temperature side, to "excited" or "ecstatic" at the high-temperature end.
   a. Fill out a Feelings Thermometer for happy, sad, angry, and scared.

5. Play "counting to 10" feeling charades:
   a. Take turns counting to 10 while pretending to enact different feelings.  See if the others can guess what feeling it is.  Since you will only count to 10, there are no words that indicate the feelings.  One can only guess by attending to nonverbal cues and tone of voice.
   b. Repeat this activity while hiding your face so observers can only use your tone of voice to guess.

Jed E. Baker, *Social Skills Training for Children and Adolescents with Asperger Syndrome and Social-Communication Problems*, 2003. Shawnee Mission, KS: Autism Asperger Publishing Company; www.asperger.net

6. Play activity charades:

    a. Use two sets of cards – one with feeling words and one with various activities (e.g., bowling, eating, writing, watching TV, etc.).

    b. Each person takes a feeling and an activity card and tries to act out the activity while feeling as indicated on the card.

    c. Observers must guess what the person is doing, what he is feeling, and why he feels that way.

7. Play the game "hot and cold" without words.

    a. Hide an object (snack, special treat) in the room while the student(s) are not there. When they return, instruct them that they must look at your face to see where the object is. Make an increasingly happy face when they are close to the treat and an increasingly sad or angry face when they are far from the treat.

    b. Coach students to keep checking your face for clues for how close they are rather than searching the room without referencing your face.

8. Play a board game and give extra points or turns if students can correctly identify your feelings and intentions during the game.

    a. For example, while playing a board game, steal the students' game piece when they are not looking and demonstrate a mad or playful (happy) face. When they notice, ask them whether they think you are playing (happy face) or trying to annoy them (mad face). Make sure that they look at your face to decide rather than merely guessing. If they can correctly identify your feeling, give them an extra turn or point. Remind them how important it is during games with other children to determine when others are just being playful versus trying to upset you.

    b. Periodically get upset during a game when you are losing or miss a turn. If the students can recognize your feeling, give them an extra point or turn. If they can also say something positive like, "You will do better next time" or "You can go again," give them another extra point or turn. Remind them that this is how they win the friendship game, by recognizing others' feelings and trying to make them feel better.

9. Help students keep a journal of what makes them happy, mad, sad, scared, and other feelings. This can later serve as topics to discuss during talk-time of a small group for elementary-aged children through adulthood.

    a. Use the structure on the Journal Page to make entries into the journal.

    b. Use the journal entries as topics of conversation during small group talk-time. Encourage group members to show understanding for another member's journal entry (see skill SHOWING UNDERSTANDING FOR OTHERS' FEELINGS). Also encourage members to help each other brainstorm coping strategies to deal with situations reviewed in journals.

Jed E. Baker, *Social Skills Training for Children and Adolescents with Asperger Syndrome and Social-Communication Problems*, 2003. Shawnee Mission, KS: Autism Asperger Publishing Company; www.asperger.net

# Feelings Thermometer

1. Label each main group of feelings.

2. Write the feelings that belong in the group in order from the least amount of feeling to the most amount of feeling.

3. See "happy" as an example. Fill in the words for sad, angry, and scared.

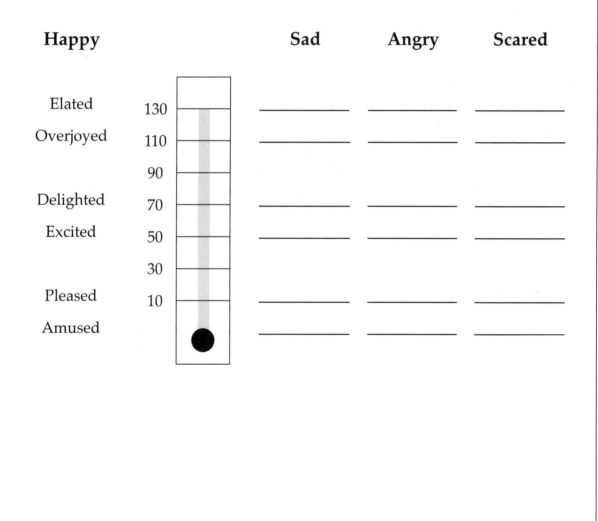

| Happy | | Sad | Angry | Scared |
|---|---|---|---|---|
| Elated | 130 | _____ | _____ | _____ |
| Overjoyed | 110 | _____ | _____ | _____ |
| | 90 | | | |
| Delighted | 70 | _____ | _____ | _____ |
| Excited | 50 | _____ | _____ | _____ |
| | 30 | | | |
| Pleased | 10 | _____ | _____ | _____ |
| Amused | | _____ | _____ | _____ |

Jed E. Baker, *Social Skills Training for Children and Adolescents with Asperger Syndrome and Social-Communication Problems*, 2003. Shawnee Mission, KS: Autism Asperger Publishing Company; www.asperger.net

# Keeping Calm

1. Stop and count to 10.

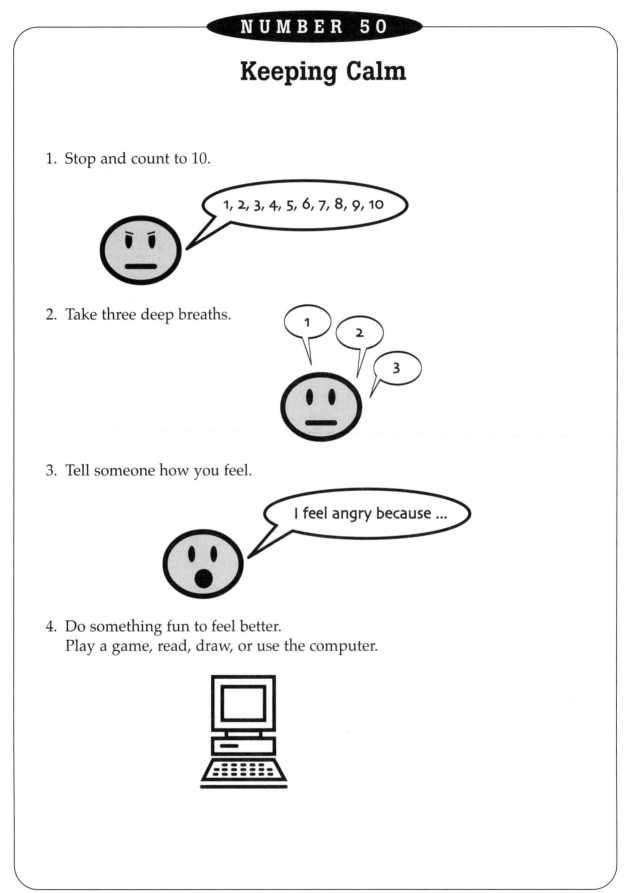

1, 2, 3, 4, 5, 6, 7, 8, 9, 10

2. Take three deep breaths.

1

2

3

3. Tell someone how you feel.

I feel angry because ...

4. Do something fun to feel better.
   Play a game, read, draw, or use the computer.

Jed E. Baker, *Social Skills Training for Children and Adolescents with Asperger Syndrome and Social-Communication Problems*, 2003.
Shawnee Mission, KS: Autism Asperger Publishing Company; www.asperger.net

# Suggested Activities for Keeping Calm

1. There are two approaches to dealing with anger and upset: Calming down when already upset and avoiding getting upset by dealing with the triggers that cause upset. Combine both approaches by giving students a procedure to use when they are upset and teaching them how to deal with common triggers so they do not get upset in the first place.

   a. KEEPING CALM is only intended to give students a procedure to use when they are already upset and need to calm down.

   b. Teach them how to avoid getting upset in the first place by learning how to deal with common triggers to upset. This involves learning other skills shown in this manual, like DEALING WITH MAKING A MISTAKE, DEALING WITH LOSING, ACCEPTING NO FOR AN ANSWER, DEALING WITH TEASING, and ACCEPTING CRITICISM. You must anticipate for students when they might come in contact with a trigger and remind them ahead of time what to do if the trigger occurs. For example, before playing a game you might say, "You might lose this game, but if you do not get mad, you can win a friend and I will give you a treat if you can deal with losing the game."

2. Role-play the steps for KEEPING CALM. These practice sessions must occur frequently (e.g., daily) when the student is not upset to ensure the student will be able to use a calming routine when she is upset. Suggested role-plays:

   a. Pretend the student cannot get something he wants (e.g., toy, treat, privilege).

   b. Pretend the student must stop playing with a favored activity (e.g., must stop the computer or TV to come to dinner).

   c. Pretend the student broke a favorite object (e.g., a toy, game, video device).

   d. Pretend the student loses when playing a game.

3. Bait the skill. This means doing something that requires the student to show how to calm down. For example, purposely frustrate the child by refusing to give him something. Prompt or wait for him to calm down. Do this only after he has learned to calm down and be sure to pick situations that will only mildly frustrate the student. For example, if the student does not usually get upset over being told she cannot watch TV, choose this situation to practice. As she gets more adept with the calming procedure, choose a slightly more frustrating situation.

4. Try to distract students when they are too upset to listen to you. Do not give in to what they want if they are tantruming because they want a particular toy or activity. Instead, try to distract them by another activity and change in the physical environment (e.g., take them out of the sight from the person or thing that is upsetting them).

5. Provide rewards for appropriate KEEPING CALM (i.e., using the skill or not needing the skill because they did not get upset).

   a. Give verbal praise for correct or partially correct KEEPING CALM.

   b. Give tokens, pennies, or points every time the student keeps calm or for periods in which he does not get upset. When he gets an agreed-upon number of tokens (e.g., five tokens), give a special reward (e.g., snack, stickers, or privileges to play special game).

Jed E. Baker, *Social Skills Training for Children and Adolescents with Asperger Syndrome and Social-Communication Problems*, 2003. Shawnee Mission, KS: Autism Asperger Publishing Company; www.asperger.net

# Problem Solving

1. Keep calm. Tell yourself, "I can solve this problem if I stay calm."

2. Decide what the problem is.

   a. Are you frustrated because you could not do something you wanted?
   b. Are you upset because someone did something to you?

3. Brainstorm. Think about possible solutions.

4. Think about the consequences. What will happen if you try different solutions?

5. Pick the best solution.

---

## Practice

Who will I try this with? _____

When? _____

What happened? _____

_____

How did I do? _____

Jed E. Baker, *Social Skills Training for Children and Adolescents with Asperger Syndrome and Social-Communication Problems*, 2003.
Shawnee Mission, KS: Autism Asperger Publishing Company; www.asperger.net

# Suggested Activities for Problem Solving

1. Teaching problem solving involves two major steps. First, you need to increase the students' motivation to keep calm when a problem arises. Only then will they be motivated to engage in problem solving. Second, students need to understand that if they hold back their frustration, they will in fact get some of what they want. The activities below may help make this point.

   a. Review with students times when their anger got in the way of solving a problem. You can use their journal entries if they have been keeping them or information from teachers and parents. Point out how their anger delayed the solution to the problem. Also point out how they did solve the problem. They need to be convinced that they can solve the problem so they do not need to get overly frustrated.

   b. If they have no journal entries to work from, review and role-play the following scenarios that show how anger delays problem solving:
      (1) You lose something, like a card from a game or another special item. In anger you break other special items compounding the problem and still not leading to finding the original item.
      (2) You cannot go to the video arcade because your parents have to stay home and wait for a repair person. If you have a tantrum, your parents will ground you from all activities. If you stay calm, your parents will let you do something else you want to do, or you may suggest that a friend's parent drive you to the arcade. (See ACCEPTING NO FOR AN ANSWER for similar role-plays.)
      (3) You make one mistake with homework and in anger you rip up all your homework, leaving you much more to do. Alternatively, you make a mistake, stay calm, ask for help and correct the problem. Now you go play because you are done with your work. (See DEALING WITH MISTAKES for similar role-play ideas.)

2. To role-play the problem-solving steps, use real past experiences from memory or journal entries. Alternatively, you can use the situations above. My experience with students with abstract thinking difficulties is that they have difficulty learning these general steps of problem solving. They do better learning the more concrete steps that help solve specific problems. The following is a list of other skills in this manual that relate to more specific problem areas: DEALING WITH MISTAKES, DEALING WITH LOSING, COMPROMISING, GETTING ATTENTION IN POSITIVE WAYS, DEALING WITH FAMILY PROBLEMS, ACCEPTING NO FOR AN ANSWER, ACCEPTING CRITICISM, ASSERTING YOURSELF, DEALING WITH BEING LEFT OUT, TRYING WHEN WORK IS HARD, TRYING SOMETHING NEW, DEALING WITH PEER PRESSURE, DEALING WITH RUMORS, RESPECTING PERSONAL BOUNDARIES, and DON'T BE THE "RULE POLICE."

3. Bait the skill. This means doing something that requires the student to solve a problem.

   a. For example, during a game, take the students' game piece or cheat in some way. Remind them that if they stay calm, they can solve the problem, and then coach them through its solution. Perhaps they will assert themselves, or playfully cheat as well, or just laugh and say give it back.

   b. See suggestions for skills listed in item 2 above.

4. Redirect emerging frustration into problem solving by reminding students that we can solve the problem if we stay calm.

5. Provide rewards for appropriate PROBLEM SOLVING.

   a. Give verbal praise for correct or partially correct PROBLEM SOLVING.

   b. Give tokens, pennies, or points every time the student stays calm and attempts to solve a frustrating problem. When she gets an agreed-upon number of tokens (e.g., five tokens), give a special reward (e.g., snack, stickers, or privileges to play special game or watch special show).

Jed E. Baker, *Social Skills Training for Children and Adolescents with Asperger Syndrome and Social-Communication Problems*, 2003. Shawnee Mission, KS: Autism Asperger Publishing Company; www.asperger.net

# Talking to Others When Upset

1. It is better to talk about your feelings than to act angry and upset. You will not get in trouble for talking about your feelings, but you might get in trouble for acting angry or upset.

2. Find someone who makes you feel good.

3. Ask, "Can I talk to you for a moment?"

4. If the person says yes, tell her how you feel. If she says no, talk to her later or find someone else to talk to in the meantime.

## Practice

Who will I try this with? _____

When? _____

What happened? _____

_____

How did I do? _____

Jed E. Baker, *Social Skills Training for Children and Adolescents with Asperger Syndrome and Social-Communication Problems*, 2003. Shawnee Mission, KS: Autism Asperger Publishing Company; www.asperger.net

# Suggested Activities for
# Talking to Others When Upset

1. Role-play the steps for TALKING versus ACTING OUT feelings. Suggested role-plays involve the following scenarios:

    a. You come to school angry because your brother teased you before school. Role-playing the wrong way involves showing "acting out" behaviors like refusing to work, banging on the table, using a disrespectful tone of voice with peers and teachers, or teasing others. Role-play the correct way by asking to talk with the teacher and explaining what happened before school. Maybe the teacher will let you draw for a while until you feel better since you explained why you were mad.

    b. You were at recess and no one would play with you. The right way to role-play is to ask to talk with an adult or trusted friend and share your upset. Maybe they will play with you or talk to the other students for you because you told how you feel. If you act out how you feel, role-play getting in trouble with the teachers.

    c. If students keep a journal, use journal entries as a basis for a role-play.

2. Bait the skill. This means doing something that requires the student to tell you she is upset.

    a. Role-play this during playtime by cheating, stealing a game piece, and prompting the student to say how he feels rather than hitting, throwing or some other acting-out behavior.

3. Correct acting-out behavior. Coach students to say in words how they feel. Some children may need to walk away and get calm before they can physically produce the words, as anger can tighten the chest and make talking difficult.

4. Provide rewards for appropriate TALKING TO OTHERS WHEN UPSET.

    a. Give verbal praise for correct or partially correct TALKING TO OTHERS WHEN UPSET.

    b. Give tokens, pennies, or points every time students talk about their feelings. When they get an agreed-upon number of tokens (e.g., five tokens), give a special reward (e.g., snack, stickers, or privileges to play special game or watch special show).

Jed E. Baker, *Social Skills Training for Children and Adolescents with Asperger Syndrome and Social-Communication Problems*, 2003. Shawnee Mission, KS: Autism Asperger Publishing Company; www.asperger.net

# Dealing with Family Problems

1. Typical family problems include:

   a. Parents arguing, fighting, yelling, or criticizing.

   b. Brothers and sisters provoking, picking on you, or taking your stuff.

   c. Less attention because of work, divorce, separation, illness, or death.

2. Ways of confronting family problems.

   a. GOOD WAYS include:

      (1) **Asserting yourself**. Tell the person how you feel using an "I" message so you do not provoke further conflict.

      (2) **Talking to another adult** who can try to talk with the person who is upsetting you or help you find another solution.

      (3) **Ignore** or laugh at any teasing to reduce its impact.

      (4) **Using your sense of humor** to calm the other person down.

   b. BAD WAYS include:

      (1) **Fighting**, yelling, or criticizing back. This will provoke further problems.

      (2) **Taking it out on others** by teasing, criticizing or hurting others.

3. Ways to escape or take a break from the problem.

   a. GOOD WAYS include:

      (1) Calling a friend to get together.

      (2) Listening to music or watching TV in your room away from others.

      (3) Taking a walk, but letting people know where you are going.

      (4) Playing some other game to get your mind off the problem.

   b. BAD WAYS include:

      (1) Running away. This causes more problems.

      (2) Trying or threatening to hurt yourself. This also causes more problems.

---

## Practice

Who will I try this with? _____

When? _____

What happened? _____

_____

How did I do? _____

Jed E. Baker, *Social Skills Training for Children and Adolescents with Asperger Syndrome and Social-Communication Problems*, 2003.
Shawnee Mission, KS: Autism Asperger Publishing Company; www.asperger.net

# Suggested Activities for
# Dealing with Family Problems

1. This is a skill suitable for preadolescents through adulthood. Although you can role-play any of the situations listed in step 1 of the skills, it is often more productive first to have students identify what problems they might be dealing with, develop a plan to deal with them and then role-play as described below.

   a. Give students a piece of paper with three headings: Problem, Ways to Confront the Problem, Ways to Escape the Problem.
   b. Have students identify some of the family problems they are dealing with and write them under the "Problem" heading.
   c. Next have students explore which positive strategy from skill step 2 (Confronting Family Problems) might help them deal with the problem. Have them write this under the "Ways to Confront the Problem" heading.
   d. Then have them identify which positive strategy from skill step 3 (Ways to Escape the Problem) might be helpful to them.
   e. Now take turns role-playing some of the students' situations and their plans to deal with them.

2. Redirect inappropriate behavior to deal with problems using suggested positive ways.

3. Provide rewards for appropriate DEALING WITH FAMILY PROBLEMS.

   a. Give verbal praise for correct or partially correct use of the positive strategies described in the skill.
   b. Give tokens, pennies, or points for dealing positively with family problems. When the student gets an agreed-upon number of tokens (e.g., five tokens), give a special reward (e.g., snack, stickers, or privileges to play a special game).

Jed E. Baker, *Social Skills Training for Children and Adolescents with Asperger Syndrome and Social-Communication Problems*, 2003. Shawnee Mission, KS: Autism Asperger Publishing Company; www.asperger.net

# Understanding Anger

1. What makes us angry?

**Trigger**  Something that happens. For example, teasing, losing a game, making a mistake, not getting what we want, waiting too long for things.

**Thoughts**  How we understand what happened. For example, if someone bumps into us, we might think it was on purpose or by accident.

**Feelings**  Angry, happy, sad, scared.

2. Develop a plan to deal with the triggers to your anger.
   a. Make a list of the trigger situations to your anger so you can prepare for them.
   b. Change your thoughts.  Think of positive ways to understand the situation.
      (1) Maybe the other person is trying to help.
      (2) Maybe the other person did not mean it.
      (3) Maybe the other person is just playing or trying to get attention.
      (4) If you made a mistake, that's okay. It will help you to learn.
      (5) If you cannot do something now, maybe you can do it later if you stay calm.
      (6) If you lose something, you may win something if you stay calm.
      (7) Use the 20-year rule: Whatever it is, it probably won't matter 20 years from now.
   c. Distract yourself from the trigger situations.
      (1) Remove yourself from the situation.
      (2) Count to 10.
      (3) Take deep breaths.
      (4) Think of pleasant images.
      (5) Listen to music. Watch TV.
      (6) Play a game. Draw. Read.
      (7) Talk to a friend.
      (8) Avoid the triggers.
   d. Assert your feelings. Tell the person how you feel in a positive way. Use an "I" message.

      I feel _____
                        (Feeling word)

      when you _____
                   (Descibe the other person's actions. Don't insult.)

      because _____.
                   (Describe why you feel that way.)

      What I want you to do is _____.

Jed E. Baker, *Social Skills Training for Children and Adolescents with Asperger Syndrome and Social-Communication Problems*, 2003.
Shawnee Mission, KS: Autism Asperger Publishing Company; www.asperger.net

# Suggested Activities for Understanding Anger

1. Since there is a lot of information in UNDERSTANDING ANGER we can use a game show format to review the material. A favored game show format is "Who Wants to Be a Millionaire?" (see Chapter 4 for a description). Students take turns answering questions for pretend cash. Sample questions are listed below.

   a. What is a trigger?
   b. What do thoughts have to do with your feelings?
   c. How can changing your thoughts change your feelings?
   d. If you made a mistake and got mad, how could you change your thoughts to alter your anger?
   e. If someone teased you, what could you think in order to be less mad?
   f. What is the 20-year rule?
   g. How can you distract yourself when you are angry?
   h. Name two other ways to distract yourself when angry.
   i. What is the difference between passive, aggressive and assertive?
   j. How could you assert yourself if a teacher accused you of cheating?
   k. How could you assert yourself if someone will not pick you for a team in gym?
   l. How could you assert yourself if your parents will not let you out on the weekend even though you did all your homework?

2. When students become angry, we can prompt them to use some aspect of the skill like change their thoughts, distract themselves, or assert themselves.

3. Bait the skill. Tell students that you are going to get them slightly angry and then prompt them to use a strategy from the skill. The goal is not to make them angry, just to keep them thinking about how to use the skill. So do not do something that would make them very angry.

4. Provide rewards for appropriate dealing with anger.

   a. Give verbal praise for correct or partially correct dealing with anger.
   b. Give tokens, pennies, or points for dealing with anger. When the student gets an agreed-upon number of tokens (e.g., five tokens), give a special reward (e.g., snack, stickers, or privileges to play a special game).

Jed E. Baker, *Social Skills Training for Children and Adolescents with Asperger Syndrome and Social-Communication Problems*, 2003. Shawnee Mission, KS: Autism Asperger Publishing Company; www.asperger.net

# Anger Record

Date: _____     Name: _____

**Trigger:** Write or draw the situation that triggered your anger. Was it teasing, making a mistake, losing something, not getting something, or something else?

**Thoughts** that made me angry:

**Feelings:** How angry was I?

| Just a Little | Somewhat | Pretty Angry | Really Angry |

**Change my thoughts:** Write or draw ways to think about the situation that won't make you angry.

**Ways to distract myself:** Write or draw ways to get your mind off what is bothering you.

**Plans to assert myself or other plans to change my feelings:** Write or draw "I" messages or other ways to reduce your anger.

Jed E. Baker, *Social Skills Training for Children and Adolescents with Asperger Syndrome and Social-Communication Problems*, 2003. Shawnee Mission, KS: Autism Asperger Publishing Company; www.asperger.net

# Suggested Activities for Using the Anger Record

1. The skill sheet UNDERSTANDING ANGER is the lesson. The ANGER RECORD is used to practice the skill independently.

2. The ANGER RECORD can serve as a journal for students to keep track of incidences when they were angry. They can fill out all or just the top section on their own and then bring it to group, class or individual therapy to review and discuss what happened, what they thought, and how they could handle such a situation in the future.

Jed E. Baker, *Social Skills Training for Children and Adolescents with Asperger Syndrome and Social-Communication Problems*, 2003. Shawnee Mission, KS: Autism Asperger Publishing Company; www.asperger.net

# Dealing with Making a Mistake

1. Say to yourself, "It's okay to make a mistake. Mistakes help us to learn."

2. Think about what you can do to learn from your mistake.

    a. Try it again until you get it right.
    b. Ask for help.
    c. Apologize if your mistake upset someone else.

3. Pick your best choice.

### Practice

Who will I try this with? _____

When will I do it? _____

What happened? _____

_____

How did I do? _____

Jed E. Baker, *Social Skills Training for Children and Adolescents with Asperger Syndrome and Social-Communication Problems*, 2003. Shawnee Mission, KS: Autism Asperger Publishing Company; www.asperger.net

# Suggested Activities for
# Dealing with Making a Mistake

1. Your students' ability to deal with a mistake depends on your ability to demonstrate that you value dealing with mistakes more than doing things perfectly.

   a. To reinforce this concept, ask the student to purposely make a mistake this week so she has an opportunity to work on DEALING WITH MAKING A MISTAKE.

   b. Show enthusiasm when the student makes a mistake rather than getting upset. Say, "Great, you made a mistake. This is an opportunity to learn. What can you say to yourself to deal with this mistake." Then praise appropriate DEALING WITH MAKING A MISTAKE steps.

2. Role-play the steps for DEALING WITH MAKING A MISTAKE. Suggested role-plays:

   a. Pretend the student makes a mistake when doing schoolwork (e.g., reading, math, or writing). You review the work and say he did something wrong and prompt him to correct it.

   b. Pretend the student makes a mistake when doing artwork (e.g., cutting, drawing, molding clay). Review the work and say he did something wrong and prompt him to correct it.

   c. Pretend the student makes a mistake during an athletic game (e.g., not catching a ball, not hitting or kicking a ball, not running fast enough). Point out that she is "out" or dropped the ball and prompt her to deal with the mistake.

   d. Pretend the student drops or breaks something that belongs to somebody else. Prompt her to apologize and deal with the mistake.

3. Bait the skill. This means doing something that requires the student to show how to deal with a mistake. For example, ask the child to make a mistake in the coming week. Purposely give her some difficult tasks to do and tell her you are more interested in how she deals with mistakes than whether or not she can avoid mistakes – you actually hope she will make a mistake.

4. Provide rewards for appropriate DEALING WITH MAKING A MISTAKE.

   a. Verbally praise correct or partially correct DEALING WITH MAKING A MISTAKE.

   b. Give tokens, pennies, or points every time the student deals with a mistake or for periods in which he does not get upset. When he gets an agreed-upon number of tokens (e.g., five tokens), give a special reward (e.g., snack, stickers, or privileges to play special game).

Jed E. Baker, *Social Skills Training for Children and Adolescents with Asperger Syndrome and Social-Communication Problems*, 2003. Shawnee Mission, KS: Autism Asperger Publishing Company; www.asperger.net

# Trying When Work Is Hard

1. Try to do some of it.

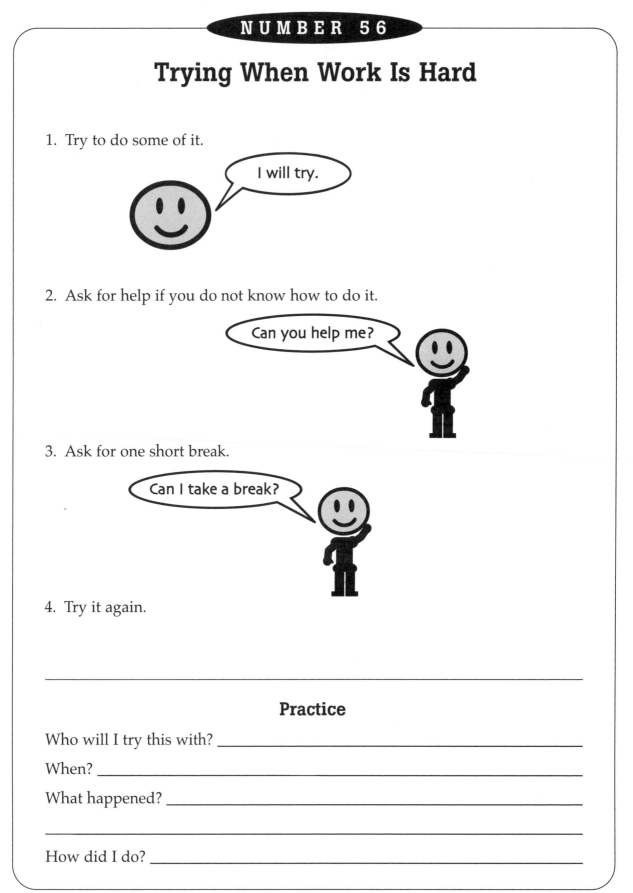

I will try.

2. Ask for help if you do not know how to do it.

Can you help me?

3. Ask for one short break.

Can I take a break?

4. Try it again.

_____

## Practice

Who will I try this with? _____

When? _____

What happened? _____

_____

How did I do? _____

Jed E. Baker, *Social Skills Training for Children and Adolescents with Asperger Syndrome and Social-Communication Problems*, 2003.
Shawnee Mission, KS: Autism Asperger Publishing Company; www.asperger.net

# Suggested Activities for
# Trying When Work Is Hard

1. Students often refuse to try work because it truly is too hard or because they have developed a "learned helplessness" attitude whereby they think they cannot do something because they had trouble with it in the past. In addition to working on the skill steps for dealing with difficult work, teachers and parents must first address the following two issues:

   a. If the work is too hard, modify it by changing the nature of the work to simpler steps or changing the quantity of work. Sometimes just asking students to do smaller amounts at a time, followed by a break or reward, can get them started.

   b. For students who have developed a "learned helplessness" attitude, helping them do the work involves building their confidence in their own ability. Prove to them that they are able to do the work by starting with something they definitely can do and showing tremendous encouragement and praise as they do it.

2. Role-play the steps for TRYING WHEN WORK IS HARD.
   NOTE: When role-playing, set a limit on how long the break can be and how many breaks are allowed. Allowing one 5-minute break per subject or period may be a good idea. It is not okay to keep taking breaks, but it is preferable to ask for one break than to have a tantrum when overly frustrated. Suggested role-plays:

   a. Give the student some work that is moderately challenging (i.e., she can do some, but not all of it).

   b. Ask the student to perform a physical activity (e.g., catching a ball or jumping rope) that is moderately challenging (i.e., he can do some, but not all of it).

3. Bait the skill. Purposely give the student something moderately difficult to do (i.e., he can do some, but not all of it). Prompt or wait for him to try it, ask for help, or ask for one break.

4. Provide rewards for appropriate TRYING WHEN WORK IS HARD (i.e., for trying to complete work).

   a. Give verbal praise for correct or partially correct TRYING WHEN WORK IS HARD.

   b. Give tokens, pennies, or points for each period in which the student tries to do work, or appropriately asks for help or one break.

      (1) You might give tokens after every period or unit of work. The more distracted the student is when doing work, the more frequently the tokens should be dispensed. If the tokens do not keep the student focused, try giving the tokens sooner.

      (2) Tokens can only be received for trying, asking for help, or for taking no more than one break. If students do not return from break, they cannot receive any more tokens.

      (3) When the student gets an agreed-upon number of tokens (e.g., five tokens), give a special reward (e.g., snack, stickers, or privileges to play a special game). The rewards are crucial, as they must be more powerful than the urge to escape frustrating work. It may take time to find out what they are, but every student finds certain things very rewarding.

Jed E. Baker, *Social Skills Training for Children and Adolescents with Asperger Syndrome and Social-Communication Problems*, 2003. Shawnee Mission, KS: Autism Asperger Publishing Company; www.asperger.net

# Trying Something New

1. Tell someone if you are afraid to try
   something new.

   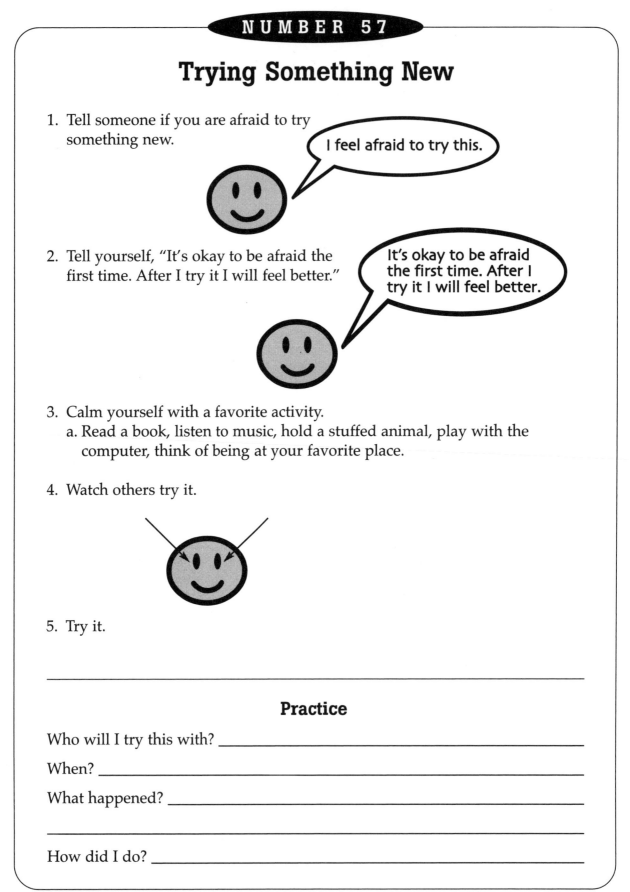

   I feel afraid to try this.

2. Tell yourself, "It's okay to be afraid the
   first time. After I try it I will feel better."

   It's okay to be afraid the first time. After I try it I will feel better.

3. Calm yourself with a favorite activity.
   a. Read a book, listen to music, hold a stuffed animal, play with the
      computer, think of being at your favorite place.

4. Watch others try it.

5. Try it.

## Practice

Who will I try this with? _____

When? _____

What happened? _____

_____

How did I do? _____

Jed E. Baker, *Social Skills Training for Children and Adolescents with Asperger Syndrome and Social-Communication Problems*, 2003.
Shawnee Mission, KS: Autism Asperger Publishing Company; www.asperger.net

# Suggested Activities for Trying Something New

1. Students often have numerous fears of trying something new because they may have had previous negative experiences with new situations and/or because they cannot easily adapt to new social situations where the rules are not clear. In practicing or role-playing this skill, it is best to gradually expose them to new material with the least frightening changes practiced first.

    a. One way to practice is to take a familiar game and slightly change the rules. Students can take turns changing the rules until you have a very different game. This activity not only practices dealing with something new, but also involves negotiation and creativity skills.

    b. Practice trying new schoolwork. Again, it is best to introduce it gradually, with more novel material coming after adjusting to mildly different material.

    c. With the use of video, pictures or others' testimony, you can introduce new places to go. New schools, after-school clubs, or vacation destinations can be gradually introduced with picture, video and verbal descriptions followed by visits to observe the location without staying there, followed by more active participation in the new location.

2. Bait the skill. Suggest new ways to get somewhere, new ways to play a familiar game, or new foods to try. Prompt students through the skill steps as necessary.

3. Provide rewards for appropriate TRYING SOMETHING NEW.

    a. Give verbal praise for correct or partially correct TRYING SOMETHING NEW.

    b. Give tokens, pennies, or points for instances in which the student tries something new, even if the student just tries part of the new experience (e.g., watches but does not participate). Gradually require the student to do more and more to get the tokens or rewards.

Jed E. Baker, *Social Skills Training for Children and Adolescents with Asperger Syndrome and Social-Communication Problems*, 2003. Shawnee Mission, KS: Autism Asperger Publishing Company; www.asperger.net

# Showing Understanding
# for Others' Feelings
## (Preschool-Elementary Age)

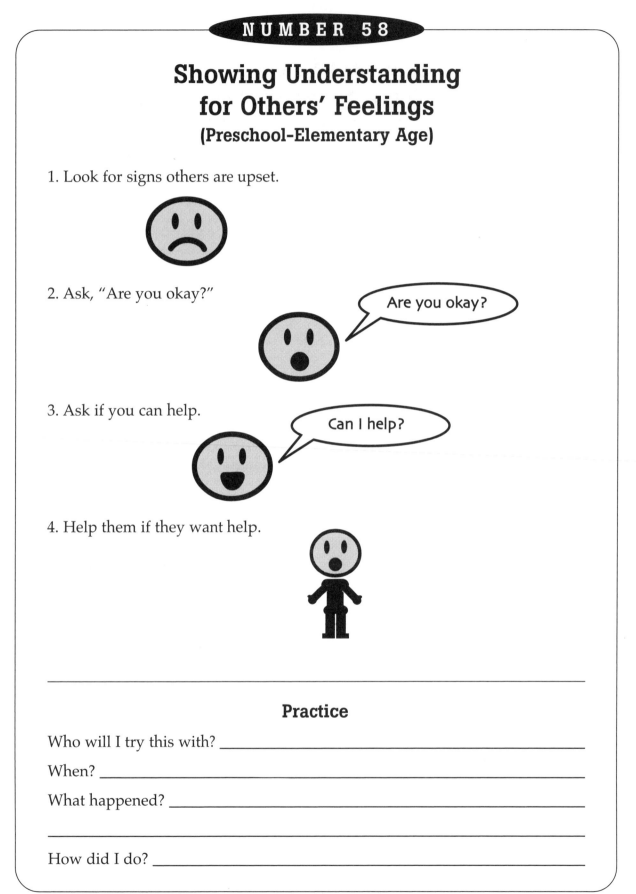

1. Look for signs others are upset.

2. Ask, "Are you okay?"

Are you okay?

3. Ask if you can help.

Can I help?

4. Help them if they want help.

---

## Practice

Who will I try this with? _____

When? _____

What happened? _____

_____

How did I do? _____

# Suggested Activities for
# Showing Understanding for Others' Feelings
## (Preschool–Elementary Age)

1. Role-play the steps for SHOWING UNDERSTANDING FOR OTHERS' FEELINGS. Suggested role-plays include the following scenarios:
   a. Pretend someone fell down and hurt himself and needs help getting up.
   b. Pretend someone lost something, got upset, and needs help finding it.
   c. Pretend someone is having a hard time with schoolwork and looks upset. Offer to help the student with her work.
   d. Pretend someone is sad because she did not get to play a game. Offer to help by playing something else.

2. Bait the skill. This means doing something that requires the student to show understanding. For example, purposely look upset, fall down, or lose something. Prompt or wait for the student to ask if you are okay and to offer help.

3. Correct inappropriate ways to show understanding, such as when the student does not see someone is obviously upset, or tries too hard to help when the other person does not want help.

4. Provide rewards for appropriate SHOWING UNDERSTANDING OF OTHERS' FEELINGS.
   a. Give verbal praise for correct or partially correct SHOWING UNDERSTANDING FOR OTHERS' FEELINGS.
   b. Give tokens, pennies, or points every time the student shows understanding. When he gets an agreed-upon number of tokens (e.g., five tokens), give a special reward (e.g., snack, stickers, or privileges to play a special game).

Jed E. Baker, *Social Skills Training for Children and Adolescents with Asperger Syndrome and Social-Communication Problems*, 2003. Shawnee Mission, KS: Autism Asperger Publishing Company; www.asperger.net

# Showing Understanding
# for Others' Feelings
### (Preadolescent-Adulthood)

1. Look for signs that the other person is upset.

2. Think about your choices.

   a. Ask the person if he is okay.

   b. Ask what happened.

   c. Share a time when you had a similar experience. Say, "I know how you feel because it happened to me . . ."

   d. Validate the other person's feelings. Say, "It makes sense that you feel that way given what happened to you."

   e. Refute any negative information. For example, if the other person feels ugly, say, "You are not ugly." If she feels her problems will never get better say, "I bet it will get better very soon."

   f. Ask the person if he wants to do something fun to get his mind off the problem.

   g. Ask if you can help.

3. Do not laugh at the person or make fun of him.

---

### Practice

Who will I try this with? _____

When? _____

What happened? _____

_____

How did I do? _____

Jed E. Baker, *Social Skills Training for Children and Adolescents with Asperger Syndrome and Social-Communication Problems*, 2003. Shawnee Mission, KS: Autism Asperger Publishing Company; www.asperger.net

# Suggested Activities for
# Showing Understanding for Others' Feelings
## (Preadolescent–Adulthood)

1. Role-play the steps for SHOWING UNDERSTANDING FOR OTHERS' FEELINGS. Suggested role-plays include the following scenarios:

    a. Pretend someone fell down and hurt himself and needs help getting up.
    b. Pretend someone lost something, got upset, and needs help finding it.
    c. Pretend someone is having a hard time with schoolwork and looks upset. Offer to help the student with her work.
    d. Pretend someone is sad because she did not get to play a game. Offer to help by playing something else.

2. Another good way to practice this skill is a game I call "Make Me Happy." Children take turns acting out situations (see below or use actual situation that happened to them) that might make them upset while others have to guess what the situation was. This part of the game is like charades and can be played with or without allowing the child who is acting to speak. Once a child has guessed what the situation is, all the other children have to take turns making a statement to make someone happy in such a situation. The statements can be pulled from the list of ways to show understanding on the skill sheet. Sample situations and supportive responses include the following:

    a. Someone fails a test. ("I know how you feel, it happened to me lots of times." "You'll probably do great next time." "That test wasn't even fair." "Want me to help you study next time?")
    b. No one will dance with someone at a school dance. ("I can never find anyone to dance with either." "They do not know what they are missing; you are a good dancer." "Let's play a game instead of trying to dance with them.")
    c. Someone is teased by being called ugly. ("You are not ugly." "I get teased too sometimes. Don't believe what they say.")
    d. Someone's parent is very ill. ("Sorry to hear that. Is there anything I can do to help?" "I know someone who was sick with the same thing and was fully cured." "Want to do something fun to get your mind off it for a while?")

3. Bait the skill. This means doing something that requires the student to show understanding. For example, purposely look upset, fall down, or lose something. Prompt or wait for the student to ask if you are okay and to offer help.

4. Correct inappropriate ways to show understanding, such as when the student does not see someone is obviously upset, or tries too hard to help when the other person does not want help.

5. Provide rewards for appropriate SHOWING UNDERSTANDING FOR OTHERS' FEELINGS.

    a. Give verbal praise for correct or partially correct SHOWING UNDERSTANDING FOR OTHERS' FEELINGS.
    b. Give tokens, pennies, or points every time the student shows understanding. When he gets an agreed-upon number of tokens (e.g., five tokens), give a special reward (e.g., snack, stickers, or privileges to play a special game).

Jed E. Baker, *Social Skills Training for Children and Adolescents with Asperger Syndrome and Social-Communication Problems*, 2003. Shawnee Mission, KS: Autism Asperger Publishing Company; www.asperger.net

# Cheering up a Friend

1. Look for signs that your friend is upset.

2. Ask, "Are you okay?" "What happened?"

3. Ask, "Do you want me to try to cheer you up?"

4. If the person says yes, think about your choices to cheer her up:
   a. Try to make her laugh with a joke or a funny face.
   b. Offer to play a game or do something fun.
   c. Offer words of encouragement like, "It will get better" or "I'll help you."

## Practice

Who will I try this with? _____

When? _____

What happened? _____

_____

How did I do? _____

Jed E. Baker, *Social Skills Training for Children and Adolescents with Asperger Syndrome and Social-Communication Problems*, 2003. Shawnee Mission, KS: Autism Asperger Publishing Company; www.asperger.net

# Suggested Activities for Cheering up a Friend

1. This skill is really a part of the previous skill, SHOWING UNDERSTANDING FOR OTHERS' FEELINGS. Thus all the situations described for that skill can be used to role-play this skill. For example:

   a. Pretend someone fell down and hurt himself and needs help getting up.
   b. Pretend someone lost something, got upset, and needs help finding it.
   c. Pretend someone is having a hard time with schoolwork and looks upset.
   d. Pretend someone is sad because she did not get to play a game.

2. For children about 10 years old through adulthood, a good way to practice this skill is a game I call "Make Me Happy." Children take turns acting out situations (see below or use an actual situation that happened to them) that might make them upset while others have to guess what the situation was. This part of the game is like charades and can be played with or without allowing the child who is acting to speak. Once a child has guessed what the situation is, all the other children have to take turns making a statement to make someone happy in such a situation. The statements can be pulled from the list of ways to show understanding on the skill sheet. Sample situations and supportive responses include the following:

   a. Someone fails a test. ("I know how you feel, it happened to me lots of times." "You'll probably do great next time." "That test wasn't even fair." "Want me to help you study next time?")
   b. No one will dance with someone at a school dance. ("I can never find anyone to dance with either." "They do not know what they are missing; you are a good dancer." "Let's play a game instead of trying to dance with them.")
   c. Someone is teased by being called ugly. ("You are not ugly." "I get teased too sometimes. Don't believe what they say.")
   d. Someone's parent is very ill. ("Sorry to hear that. Is there anything I can do to help?" "I know someone who was sick with the same thing and was fully cured." "Want to do something fun to get your mind off it for a while?")

3. Bait the skill. This means doing something that prompts the student to cheer someone up. For example, purposely look upset, fall down, or complain about something. Prompt or wait for the student to ask if they can sheer you up.

4. Provide rewards for appropriate CHEERING UP A FRIEND.

   a. Give verbal praise for correct or partially correct CHEERING UP A FRIEND.
   b. Give tokens, pennies, or points every time the student cheers someone up. When he gets an agreed-upon number of tokens (e.g., five tokens), give a special reward (e.g., snack, stickers, or privileges to play a special game).

Jed E. Baker, *Social Skills Training for Children and Adolescents with Asperger Syndrome and Social-Communication Problems*, 2003. Shawnee Mission, KS: Autism Asperger Publishing Company; www.asperger.net

# Asserting Yourself

1. "Assertive" means to try to get what you want without hurting others.

2. Decide if you need to be assertive.
   a. Someone is asking you to do something that is dangerous or makes you feel bad.
   b. You want or need someone to do something.

3. Tell the other person what you want in an assertive way.
   a. Use a firm but friendly voice, make eye contact, and show good posture.
   b. Use an "I" statement:

   "I feel _____

   when you _____

   because _____.

   What I want you to do is _____."

---

## Practice

Who will I try this with? _____

When? _____

What happened? _____

_____

How did I do? _____

Jed E. Baker, *Social Skills Training for Children and Adolescents with Asperger Syndrome and Social-Communication Problems*, 2003. Shawnee Mission, KS: Autism Asperger Publishing Company; www.asperger.net

# Suggested Activities for Asserting Yourself

1. Role-play the steps for ASSERTING YOURSELF. Suggested role-plays include the following scenarios:

   a. Pretend someone keeps bumping into you.
   b. Pretend someone borrows some money and does not pay you back when they said they would.
   c. Pretend someone demands to play a game that you do not want to play.
   d. Pretend you are doing a group project in school and no one is listening to your ideas.
   e. Pretend someone borrows your pencil and you need it back.
   f. Pretend the teacher or parent gives everyone a snack except you.

2. Bait the skill. This means doing something that requires students to assert themselves:

   a. Take their book bag when they need it.
   b. Give every one a snack, or a chance to do a favored activity except one student until she makes an assertive statement.

3. Correct inappropriate ways to express frustration like aggressive or passive responses. Redirect to be assertive.

4. Provide rewards for appropriate ASSERTING YOURSELF.

   a. Give verbal praise for correct or partially correct ASSERTING YOURSELF.
   b. Give tokens, pennies, or points every time the student asserts herself. When she gets an agreed-upon number of tokens (e.g., five tokens), give a special reward (e.g., snack, stickers, or privileges to play a special game).

Jed E. Baker, *Social Skills Training for Children and Adolescents with Asperger Syndrome and Social-Communication Problems*, 2003. Shawnee Mission, KS: Autism Asperger Publishing Company; www.asperger.net

# Accepting No for an Answer

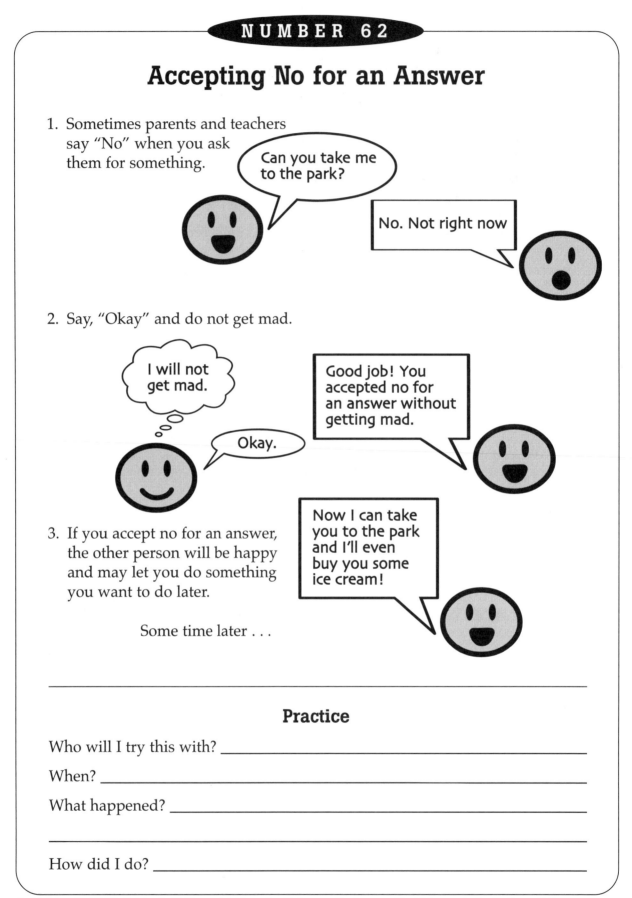

1. Sometimes parents and teachers say "No" when you ask them for something.

   Can you take me to the park?

   No. Not right now

2. Say, "Okay" and do not get mad.

   I will not get mad.

   Okay.

   Good job! You accepted no for an answer without getting mad.

3. If you accept no for an answer, the other person will be happy and may let you do something you want to do later.

   Now I can take you to the park and I'll even buy you some ice cream!

   Some time later . . .

---

## Practice

Who will I try this with? _____

When? _____

What happened? _____

_____

How did I do? _____

Jed E. Baker, *Social Skills Training for Children and Adolescents with Asperger Syndrome and Social-Communication Problems*, 2003. Shawnee Mission, KS: Autism Asperger Publishing Company; www.asperger.net

# Suggested Activities for Accepting No for an Answer

1. Your students' ability to accept no depends on your ability to demonstrate what is in it for them.

   a. To help in this change in perception, remind the students of the rewards and opportunities that await them if they can accept no and wait for what they want. For example, offer to get them double of what they want later (e.g., after a minute, an hour, a day, or a week depending on the child's ability to wait), if they can accept no for an answer. Or offer to get them something else if they can accept no for an answer.

   b. As the students' ability to wait increases, gradually lengthen the time before you provide any reward for waiting. Eventually fade out the need for any external reward, providing praise only for accepting no.

2. Role-play the steps for ACCEPTING NO FOR AN ANSWER. Suggested role-plays include the following scenarios:

   a. Pretend the student wants to sharpen her pencil or get a drink of water in school. You as the teacher say, "No, not right now." If the student accepts no, say, "Okay, then you can go later and you can have a reward for accepting no."

   b. Pretend the student asks a parent to go to the park, the movies or a friend's house, and the parent says, "No, not right now." If the student accepts no, say, "Okay, then you can go later and you can have a reward for accepting no."

   c. Pretend the student wants expensive toys, games, shoes, or clothing and you say, "No, you cannot have that." If the child accepts no, then say, "Okay, you can have something else that you want and you can have a reward for accepting no."

3. Bait the skill. This means doing something that requires the student to show how to accept no. For example, tell the child you might test him and then show him a favorite food, game, or toy and wait for him to ask for it. Then say, "No, you cannot have it." If the child accepts no, then say, "Great job. You accepted no, so you can have it now."

4. Provide rewards for appropriate ACCEPTING NO FOR AN ANSWER.

   a. Give verbal praise for correct or partially correct ACCEPTING NO FOR AN ANSWER.

   b. Give tokens, pennies, or points every time the student accepts no. When he gets five tokens, give a special reward (e.g., snack, stickers, or privileges to play special game).

Jed E. Baker, *Social Skills Training for Children and Adolescents with Asperger Syndrome and Social-Communication Problems*, 2003. Shawnee Mission, KS: Autism Asperger Publishing Company; www.asperger.net

# Dealing with Teasing
## (K–4th Grade)

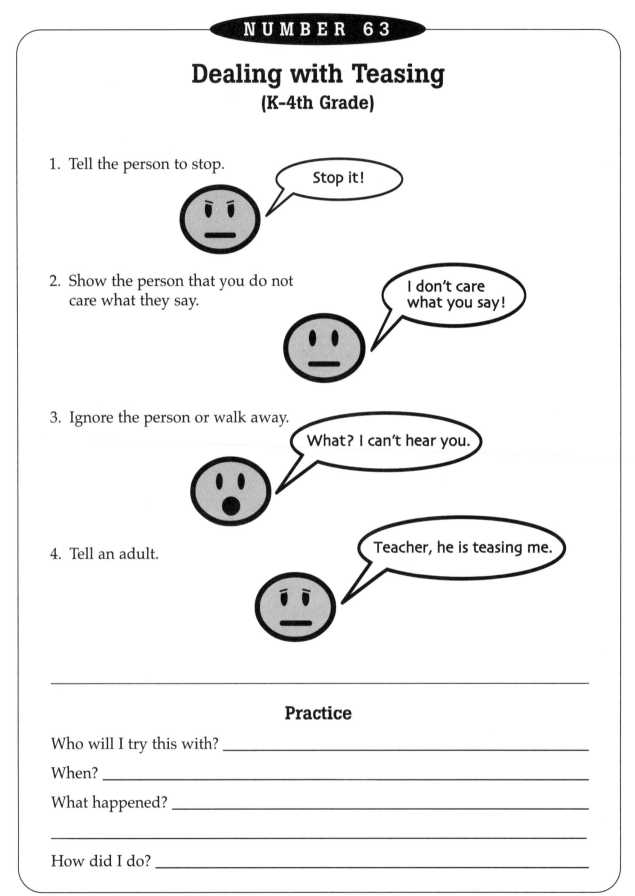

1. Tell the person to stop.

   Stop it!

2. Show the person that you do not care what they say.

   I don't care what you say!

3. Ignore the person or walk away.

   What? I can't hear you.

4. Tell an adult.

   Teacher, he is teasing me.

_____

## Practice

Who will I try this with? _____

When? _____

What happened? _____

_____

How did I do? _____

Jed E. Baker, *Social Skills Training for Children and Adolescents with Asperger Syndrome and Social-Communication Problems*, 2003. Shawnee Mission, KS: Autism Asperger Publishing Company; www.asperger.net

# Suggested Activities for Dealing with Teasing

1. Dealing with teasing is a two-way street. It involves training both the student and peers. Even if the student learns all the right ways to deal with teasing, peers may still tease unless they receive sensitivity training to be more accepting of all students. Peers can be rewarded for not teasing and demonstrating positive behaviors toward fellow students. This skill only focuses on what the student who gets teased should do.

   a. Encourage the student to try to confront the teaser herself rather than tell the teacher. "Telling" should be the last resort unless a child is physically threatened. Then he should immediately tell an adult.

2. Role-play the steps for DEALING WITH TEASING.
   NOTE: NEVER TEASE A STUDENT UNLESS SHE HAS GIVEN YOU PERMISSION TO PRACTICE. Always ask the student what she wants to be teased about as a way of practicing the skill. DO NOT ALLOW OTHER STUDENTS TO CHOOSE WHAT THE STUDENT SHOULD BE TEASED ABOUT, AS THIS WILL DO DAMAGE TO SELF-ESTEEM.

Suggested role-plays:

   a. The best role-play is one that mirrors what the student actually gets teased about. Ask students if there is anything they have been teased about so they can practice dealing with it.
   b. If the student is reluctant to discuss what he gets teased about, use less threatening words to practice (e.g., "I do not like your sneakers, hat, or shirt" instead of saying something about the student's personality, body type, or behavior).

3. Have the students create their own responses to teasing by filling out the bottom of the "More Words to Deal with Teasing" sheet.

4. Provide rewards for appropriate DEALING WITH TEASING.

   a. Give verbal praise for correct or partially correct DEALING WITH TEASING.
   b. Give tokens, pennies, or points every time the student deals with teasing or for periods in which she does not get upset. When the student gets an agreed-upon number of tokens (e.g., five tokens), give a special reward (e.g., snack, stickers, or privileges to play special game).

Jed E. Baker, *Social Skills Training for Children and Adolescents with Asperger Syndrome and Social-Communication Problems*, 2003. Shawnee Mission, KS: Autism Asperger Publishing Company; www.asperger.net

# Dealing with Teasing
## (5th Grade and up)

1. Think about why the person is teasing you.

   a. Is she just playing? Does she want attention?
   b. Is it a gesture of respect for your ability in a competition?
   c. Is it malicious? Find out by asking if the person is serious.

2. Try not to let it upset you. Say to yourself, "It does not matter what the other person says. What is important is what I think and what my friends think."

3. Think about your choices.

   a. Tell the person to stop.
   b. Walk away or ignore the person. "I can't hear you."
   c. Compliment the person. "You are too nice to want to tease me."
   d. Act as if it is just a joke. "Yeah, that's a pretty good one."
   e. Tell an adult if it is a physical threat, like when someone threatens to hurt you.
   f. If kids gang up on you, say, "Why does it take all you guys to deal with me. You guys can't deal with me alone?"
   g. Tease back in a joking way that does not provoke a fight.

4. Don't tease back using mean words or sensitive topics because that will provoke a fight.

## Practice

Who will I try this with? _____

When? _____

What happened? _____

_____

How did I do? _____

Jed E. Baker, *Social Skills Training for Children and Adolescents with Asperger Syndrome and Social-Communication Problems*, 2003. Shawnee Mission, KS: Autism Asperger Publishing Company; www.asperger.net

# More Words to Deal with Teasing

## Telling Them to Stop

"Stop!"

"I'm serious, cut it out!"

"Quit it!"

## Ignoring

Ignore (do not look or listen)

"Is someone talking?"

"What? What? What?"

"Talk to the hand because the ears don't hear."

## Talking Back

"So. So. So. So. So."

"I do not really care what you say."

"I've got better things to do than to listen to you."

"Grow up."

"Very mature."

"Takes one to know one."

"It's sad you have to tease others to feel good about yourself."

## Telling on Them

Do not be afraid to tell on them when they threaten or hurt you.

## Ganged up On

"Why does it take all of you to try to hurt one person's feelings?"

## What Words Do You Want to Use?

_____

_____

_____

_____

Jed E. Baker, *Social Skills Training for Children and Adolescents with Asperger Syndrome and Social-Communication Problems*, 2003. Shawnee Mission, KS: Autism Asperger Publishing Company; www.asperger.net

# Dealing with Being Left Out

1. Think about the possible reasons why you were left out.

2. If it was because no one knew you wanted to join in, then ask to join in.

3. If it was because the others do not want you to join in, then:
   a. Don't let these people influence how you feel about yourself. Some people reject you without ever getting to know you (they mistakenly "judge a book by its cover").
   b. Find others who are more willing to have you join in an activity with them.
   c. Ask an adult for help if no one will play with you.

4. Do some activity you enjoy.

## Practice

Who will I try this with? _____

When? _____

What happened? _____

_____

How did I do? _____

Jed E. Baker, *Social Skills Training for Children and Adolescents with Asperger Syndrome and Social-Communication Problems*, 2003. Shawnee Mission, KS: Autism Asperger Publishing Company; www.asperger.net

# Suggested Activities for
# Dealing with Being Left Out

1. Most of the responsibility for making sure that somebody is not being left out falls to the adults who surround the student (e.g., teachers and parents). We must create social opportunities for students, and this may involve sensitizing peers to the needs of the student and encouraging them to engage the student (see Chapter 9 on Sensitivity Training). However, we can also help the student learn how to avoid being left out as described in this skill.

2. Role-play the steps for DEALING WITH BEING LEFT OUT. Suggested role-plays include the following scenarios:
   a. Pretend a bunch of students are playing a game at recess and one student is sitting by herself. Role-play that the student says nothing to join in and then review that this is why she was left out. Role-play again that the student tries to join in but is turned away. Have her pretend to make positive self-statements as in the skill ("It does not matter what they think") and then go ask others to play. If that does not work, practice asking an adult for help finding someone to play with.
   b. Do the same as above, yet this time pretend you are looking for a partner or group to do a school project in class.

3. Have students make a list of students who may be more likely to let them join in. Also make a list of the adults to ask for help if students are left out of an activity they want or need to join.

4. Bait the skill. Tell students you are going to test their ability to deal with being left out. Begin an activity with a group or class and leave out a student in the hope that he will say something to try to join in.

5. Correct inappropriate ways to DEALING WITH BEING LEFT OUT like passively doing nothing or aggressively responding to others. Prompt students to ask to join or to ask someone else or get an adult to help of they are left out.

6. Provide rewards for appropriately DEALING WITH BEING LEFT OUT.
   a. Give verbal praise for correct or partially correct DEALING WITH BEING LEFT OUT (e.g., asks to join in, asks someone else, or asks for help).
   b. Give tokens, pennies, or points every time the student deals effectively with being left out (e.g., asks to join in, asks someone else, or asks for help). When he gets an agreed-upon number of tokens (e.g., five tokens), give a special reward (e.g., snack, stickers, or privileges to play a special game).

Jed E. Baker, *Social Skills Training for Children and Adolescents with Asperger Syndrome and Social-Communication Problems*, 2003. Shawnee Mission, KS: Autism Asperger Publishing Company; www.asperger.net

# Avoiding Being "Set Up"
## (See Also Dealing with Peer Pressure)

1. Sometimes other children ask or pressure you to do things. Decide if it is a good or bad thing they want you to do.

    a. **Good peer pressure** is when others ask you to do something that might help you or others, such as:
    (1) Encouraging you to be kind to others, do your school work, practice a sport or hobby, or help another friend.

    b. **Bad peer pressure** is when others ask you to do something that will get you in trouble, hurt others, or they say they will only be your friend if you do it, such as:
    (1) Playing a trick on someone.
    (2) Trying a drug, or doing something else that is dangerous.

2. If you know it is bad peer pressure:

    a. Look at the person, use a strong voice, and refuse to do it.
    b. Explain why.
    c. Walk away.

3. A "set-up" is when someone pretends to help you but is really trying to get you to do something that will hurt you. If you are not sure whether someone is telling you to do something that is good or bad, ask a person you trust for advice.

---

## Practice

Who will I try this with? _____

When? _____

What happened? _____

_____

How did I do? _____

Jed E. Baker, *Social Skills Training for Children and Adolescents with Asperger Syndrome and Social-Communication Problems*, 2003. Shawnee Mission, KS: Autism Asperger Publishing Company; www.asperger.net

# Suggested Activities for Avoiding Being "Set Up"

1. This skill involves all the steps of DEALING WITH PEER PRESSURE and adds information about what a "set-up" is. Thus, all the activities for DEALING WITH PEER PRESSURE can be used. Students often do not know when a peer is exerting positive or negative peer pressure, and the desire to belong may lead them to follow even when they are unsure of whether it is okay. In addition to working on the skill steps for DEALING WITH PEER PRESSURE, teachers and parents must first address the following two issues:

   a. Have the student make a list of students and staff whom he can trust to give helpful advice. These should be the people the student will seek out when a peer asks him to do something and the student does not know whether it is okay to do.
   b. Help the student make another list of people who care about and like him, and who do not ask the student to do dangerous or hurtful things. Explain that these are real friends and that those who would have him do dangerous or hurtful things just to feel accepted are not real friends.

2. Role-play or discuss situations that represent good or bad peer pressure, along with who to ask if the student is not sure of what to do. Suggested situations include:

   a. Peer asking the student to join him in stealing candy from a store and explaining that everyone else does it. (Bad)
   b. Peer encouraging the student to finish schoolwork so he can go out and play. (Good)
   c. Peer encouraging the student to leave work so he can go out and play. (Bad)
   d. Peer asking for money in exchange for friendship. (Bad)
   e. A group of peers saying the student has to be tough and defy the teacher to be cool and accepted into their group. (Bad)
   f. Peer encouraging the student to keep practicing a sport or musical instrument. (Good)
   g. Peer telling the student that a friend wants to go out with her and that she should ask him out. (Unclear, go ask someone you trust)
   h. Peer telling the student that another student is mean and to avoid being friends with him. (Unclear, go ask someone you trust)

3. Bait the skill. Tell the student to do something that would be hurtful and prompt or wait for her to assertively refuse or ask someone she trusts.
   NOTE: ONLY DO THIS WITH STUDENTS WHO UNDERSTAND IT IS PRETEND AND A TEST OF THEIR JUDGMENT.

4. Provide rewards for appropriate AVOIDING BEING "SET UP."

   a. Give verbal praise for asking for advice before doing something that may be a "set-up."
   b. Give tokens, pennies, or points for asking for advice before doing something that may be a "set-up." When the student gets an agreed-upon number of tokens (e.g., five tokens), give a special reward (e.g., snack, stickers, or privileges to play a special game).

Jed E. Baker, *Social Skills Training for Children and Adolescents with Asperger Syndrome and Social-Communication Problems*, 2003. Shawnee Mission, KS: Autism Asperger Publishing Company; www.asperger.net

# Giving Criticism in a Positive Way

1. Nobody likes to be criticized.

2. If the person is able to change what he is doing, say:

    a. "Can I make a suggestion?"
    If he says yes, then tell him in
    a nice way what you want
    him to do differently,

    OR

    *Can I make a suggestion? Why don't you do it this way instead of that way?*

    b. Make an "I" statement.

    "I feel _____

    when you _____

    because _____.

3. If the person **cannot** change what he is doing, do not say anything.
   IF YOU HAVE NOTHING POSITIVE TO SUGGEST, DON'T
   SAY ANYTHING AT ALL.

    a. Try to cope with it by ignoring it, distracting
    yourself, or suggesting a solution that does
    not involve the other student.

_____

## Practice

Who will I try this with? _____

When? _____

What happened? _____

_____

How did I do? _____

Jed E. Baker, *Social Skills Training for Children and Adolescents with Asperger Syndrome and Social-Communication Problems*, 2003.
Shawnee Mission, KS: Autism Asperger Publishing Company; www.asperger.net

# Suggested Activities for Giving Criticism in a Positive Way

1. Role-play or discuss situations where it would be appropriate to give critical feedback to another person and situations where it would not be appropriate. Use situations that have actually happened if possible. Other suggested situations include:

   a. A teacher asks a student to read aloud in class. The student reads very slowly and that begins to annoy another student. Role-play what that other student should do (e.g., do not say anything, but perhaps quietly read ahead if he cannot wait).

   b. A peer is in a wheelchair on a trip to the museum. Another student is annoyed that the child in the wheelchair is slowing them down. Role-play what this student can do and should not do (e.g., do not criticize, but perhaps ask if he can go ahead with another adult and meet the rest of the group later).

   c. A peer keeps interrupting a student when they are talking. Role-play what the student could do (e.g., use an "I" statement to express his annoyance at the interruptions).

   d. A peer throws a pencil at another student. Role-play what the student can say or do. Here it is okay to criticize in a positive way using an "I" statement.

2. Bait the skill. Do something that you can change (like constantly interrupting the student) or something that you cannot change (like telling them to walk with you to the park when you must walk slowly because of an injury). Prompt them to use an "I" statement for things you can change and to refrain from critical remarks for actions you cannot change.

3. Provide rewards for appropriately GIVING or REFRAINING from CRITICISM.

   a. Give verbal praise for using "I" statements or for refraining from criticism when the other person cannot change.

   b. Give tokens, pennies, or points for "I" statements or for refraining from criticism when others cannot change their behavior. When the student gets an agreed-upon number of tokens (e.g., five tokens), give a special reward (e.g., snack, stickers, or privileges to play a special game).

Jed E. Baker, *Social Skills Training for Children and Adolescents with Asperger Syndrome and Social-Communication Problems*, 2003. Shawnee Mission, KS: Autism Asperger Publishing Company; www.asperger.net

# Accepting Criticism

1. Stop and remind yourself to keep calm. If you get mad, it makes you look like you have to be perfect. No one is perfect; we all make mistakes. That is how we learn.

2. Decide if the criticism is **constructive** or **hurtful**.
   a. **Constructive** criticism points out what you did wrong but focuses on what you can do to improve.
   b. **Hurtful** criticism only points out what you did wrong and offers no idea of how to improve.

3. If it is constructive criticism, say, "Okay, I'll think about that."

4. If you are asked to correct work, do it rather than argue over it because then you will sooner be able to play or relax.

5. If it is hurtful criticism, treat it like teasing and try to ignore it.

---

## Practice

Who will I try this with? _____

When? _____

What happened? _____

_____

How did I do? _____

Jed E. Baker, *Social Skills Training for Children and Adolescents with Asperger Syndrome and Social-Communication Problems*, 2003. Shawnee Mission, KS: Autism Asperger Publishing Company; www.asperger.net

# Suggested Activities for Accepting Criticism

1. Role-play or discuss situations in which the student should accept criticism or correction. Use actual situations that have occurred or the following scenarios:

   a. A student is asked to stop interrupting so he and his classmates can continue to learn.

   b. A student is asked to stop biting his fingernails to prevent getting an infection.

   c. A student is told to correct her work before going to the playground. If she argues it will further delay going to the playground.

   d. A student is told that he draws badly. This should be treated as an insult and ignored or responded to as if it was teasing (see DEALING WITH TEASING).

2. Bait the skill. Tell students to correct a behavior or their academic work. Ask them if they perceived it as helpful or hurtful. Review why it might be helpful to be able to accept criticism.

3. Correct inappropriate reactions to criticism. Again, ask students if they perceived it as helpful or hurtful. Review why it might be helpful to be able to accept criticism.

4. Provide rewards for appropriate ACCEPTING CRITICISM.

   a. Give verbal praise for ACCEPTING CRITICISM.

   b. Give tokens, pennies, or points for ACCEPTING CRITICISM. When the student gets an agreed-upon number of tokens (e.g., five tokens), give a special reward (e.g., snack, stickers, or privileges to play a special game).

Jed E. Baker, *Social Skills Training for Children and Adolescents with Asperger Syndrome and Social-Communication Problems*, 2003. Shawnee Mission, KS: Autism Asperger Publishing Company; www.asperger.net

# Having a Respectful Attitude

| Dos | Don'ts |
|---|---|
| Respect personal distance: Keep an arm's length away. | **Do not touch** anybody. Do not get closer than an arm's length away. |
| Use "request" words. "May I …?" "Can I …?" "Would you mind …?" "Would it be okay if …?" | Do not use "demand" words. "Do this now!" "I will not …" "You should . . ." |
| Use a "request" tone of voice. | Do not use a "demand" tone of voice. |
| Compromise or accommodate others. | Do not demand to have it all your way. |
| Ask permission before touching anything that is not yours. | Do not touch others' belongings without permission. |
| When upset, ask to talk about your feelings. | Do not act out your feelings by using a disrespectful tone or words. |

## Practice

Who will I try this with? _____

When? _____

What happened? _____

_____

How did I do? _____

Jed E. Baker, *Social Skills Training for Children and Adolescents with Asperger Syndrome and Social-Communication Problems*, 2003. Shawnee Mission, KS: Autism Asperger Publishing Company; www.asperger.net

# Suggested Activities for Having a Respectful Attitude

1. Some children understand how to be respectful, but choose not to because of chronic anger or depression. These children need more than this skill. They should be referred to a competent mental health professional for an evaluation to determine all the factors that contribute to their condition. For those with occasional disrespectful attitudes and who may not fully understand how they are impacting others, this skill lesson can be quite helpful.

2. This skill is a composite of several previous skills like DON'T BE A SPACE INVADER, TONE OF VOICE, COMPROMISING, RESPECTING OTHERS' BOUNDARIES, and TALKING VERSUS ACTING OUT FEELINGS. Therefore, role-plays from each of these skills can be used to review this skill. The one new step in this skill is understanding the difference between requests and demands. Some sample role-plays are provided below.

   a. Review appropriate distance when talking with others, standing in line, or walking through the hallways.
   b. Role-play the difference between requesting and demanding something like a snack, a chance to go somewhere like the playground, to play a special game, or to stop working.
   c. Do the same role-play as above with a respectful versus disrespectful tone of voice. Use a tape recorder or video recorder so students can hear how they sound.
   d. Review compromising versus demanding to play what you want to play. Use different games to practice.
   e. Pretend someone is angry because they did not want to come to group, school, or because earlier in the day someone teased them. Role-play talking versus acting out how you feel. Be sure to point out how it is not fair to take your anger out on someone who did not cause it.

3. Correct disrespectful actions and redirect to the appropriate behavior (e.g., watch the tone, make a request rather than demand, keep your distance, etc.).

4. Provide rewards for appropriate HAVING A RESPECTFUL ATTITUDE.

   a. Give verbal praise for respectful behavior.
   b. Give tokens, pennies, or points for periods in which the student demonstrated a respectful attitude. When the student gets an agreed-upon number of tokens (e.g., five tokens), give a special reward (e.g., snack, stickers, or privileges to play a special game).

Jed E. Baker, *Social Skills Training for Children and Adolescents with Asperger Syndrome and Social-Communication Problems*, 2003. Shawnee Mission, KS: Autism Asperger Publishing Company; www.asperger.net

## CHAPTER 9

# Promoting Peer Acceptance Through Sensitivity Training and Incentive Programs

**A**s mentioned at the outset of this book, training "typical" peers is a crucial element of a comprehensive social skills program. Social difficulties are defined as both a skill deficit for the student with a social disability and a problem of acceptance of that student by peers. Thus, intervention must also focus on teaching typical peers how to be more accepting. In my experience, including typical peers as a focus for intervention yields better and faster results, as typical peers may learn to be understanding of the student with a disability more quickly than the student with a disability can learn to interact more appropriately with peers.

Training for typical peers involves at least two components: (a) sensitivity training lessons to be more accepting of students with special needs, and (b) activities and incentive programs to promote generalization and practice of sensitivity skills in the situations where they are needed.

## SENSITIVITY TRAINING LESSONS

Sensitivity training in this context involves going into the class of a child with a disability and explaining to peers how the student is different and how they can be helpful by including the child in conversation and play, offering help when she is upset, and standing up for her if someone teases. Parents and teachers often worry that such a lesson will promote teasing or rejection by highlighting the student's difficulties. This may be true for a student who has absolutely no noticeable behavioral differences from peers. However, in that case there is no need to conduct sensitivity training.

For many children with a social disability like AS, the typical peers already know the student's behavior is different (or even "annoying") and may have begun to tease, ignore, or reject the student. Therefore, it is crucial to conduct a sensitivity lesson to explain the "different" behaviors to the peers so that they do not believe the behaviors are intentionally meant to annoy others. In addition, it is important to highlight the talents and abilities of the student with AS so the typical peers can come to value the student as a "whole" person.

The following are some guidelines for conducting sensitivity lessons. The guidelines are followed by two sample lessons: one for kindergarten to second grade, and the other for third grade and up.

## Guidelines for Sensitivity Training

1. Get permission from the target student's parents to talk about their child to his class. Discuss the advantages and disadvantages of doing so. If the child has noticeable behavioral differences, particularly behaviors that upset the other children, the sensitivity training can only help by explaining differences and their causes. If there are no noticeable behavioral differences, there is usually no need to conduct sensitivity training.

2. Talk to the target student about his strengths and areas of difficulty. It is important that the student understands something about himself before he hears it from a peer. If possible, get permission from the student to explain to peers how he is the same and different from others in the class. If it is difficult for the student to make friends, play or talk to others, tell him that you will explain these difficulties to classmates and ask for their help in talking and playing more with him.

3. Conduct the sensitivity training lesson, preferably without the target student present.

4. Explore with the classroom teacher ways to reward or praise peers for being kind or sensitive to the target student and to each other (see next section).

## Activities and Incentive Programs to Promote Generalization and Practice of Sensitivity Skills

Several activities have been developed that can promote peer acceptance and reinforce skills taught during a sensitivity training (e.g., Wagner, 1998). The following is a description of three such programs. All involve ways to bring typical peers and students with disabilities together and to reward peers for their efforts.

### Lunch buddy program

In this program, students are asked to volunteer to eat lunch and play at recess with the target child. After the sensitivity training, the teacher asks for volunteers to help the target student(s). Then, on a rotating basis, volunteers are selected randomly to be a special lunch buddy on a given day. Their job is to engage the target child in conversation and play. Volunteers are taught concrete skills like how to get the target child's attention (e.g., calling her name, getting in front her, or tapping her on the shoulder) and what games the child knows and would be willing to play. Then volunteers are instructed to ask the target student questions to begin a conversation (e.g., "What are you eating? How is it? What are you going to do after school? How was your week?"). Peers are also asked to invite the student to play in the recess games that the student knows.

Lunch buddies may be rewarded for their participation in the program. For example, lunch buddy volunteers may get "good friend" cards from the lunch teachers each time they volunteer, which they can later exchange for a special treat or social praise (e.g., their name is displayed prominently in the class as a "good friend of the day"). It is also important to meet with the volunteers occasionally to support their efforts and discuss any difficulties they may have encountered in helping the target students.

## Peer buddy program

This is similar to the lunch buddy program, but rather than targeting lunch and recess time, this program focuses on helping the student with disabilities during class time with work or other school responsibilities. Again, peers are asked to volunteer on a rotating basis and rewarded for their participation.

## Classwide incentive program

This program does not single out the target student. Instead, an incentive system is created to reward all students for being helpful and kind toward each other. A user-friendly version of this system is modeled after the "marble jar" used by Lee Canter (1987). In this system, a marble or token is put into a jar every time a student exhibits the target skills. When the class accumulates enough marbles (typically 50 to 100), the whole class gets a reward (e.g., a party, extra art period, etc.). It is wise to focus on no more than two or three skills at a time, and to avoid removing marbles for misbehavior. I typically target three "kind" behaviors: (a) including others who appear left out, (b) standing up for others who are teased, and (c) helping others (e.g., if they are upset, hurt, need help with work, or need encouragement).

## Schoolwide incentive program

This is a schoolwide extension of the classwide system. Although it is a lofty goal, this has the power to promote kind and positive behaviors throughout the school. The structure of the program is as follows:

1. With permission from the school administrators (e.g., principal, perhaps superintendent if the program is to be districtwide), conduct a staff meeting with all the classroom teachers and ask them to provide sensitivity training about individual differences. Have the teachers tell their students that they will be praised and given tickets or tokens for demonstrating "kind" behaviors during lunch, recess, in the hallways and in class. The tickets/tokens will be accumulated in the classrooms and may be exchanged for classroom rewards as determined by individual classroom teachers. The kind behaviors typically targeted are:

   a. Include others in conversation and play if they appear to be by themselves.
   b. Stand up for others who are teased by telling the teaser to stop or by getting help.
   c. Offer help to others who look upset or hurt.

2. Meet with all teachers, building custodians and others who work at lunch and recess and ask them to:

a. Look for and coach children to engage in these "kind" behaviors. Direct them to include others, stand up for those who are teased, and to offer help.

b. Praise them if they demonstrate one of the "kind" behaviors listed above.

c. Give out a ticket/token to any student who demonstrates one of the kind behaviors listed. The goal is to praise or give out at least two tickets/tokens each lunch and recess period.

d. These skills can be taught to school staff in the same way they would be taught to students: didactic explanation, modeling, and role-playing with feedback. To do this, you need to set up situations to model and role-play (see Sample Training for All Lunch/Recess Personnel on p. 227).

# Sample Sensitivity Training
# for Kindergarten to Second Grade

1. What would it be like if everyone in the world were exactly the same? The world would be a boring place if everyone were the same.

2. We are all the same and different in some ways.

   a. How are we all the same? Discuss physical attributes like two arms and legs.
   b. How are we different? Discuss physical attributes like hair color, eye color, etc.

3. There are other interesting differences between us besides how we look.

   a. READING. Some people read very quickly. Others find it hard to read, but easier to throw or catch a ball.
   b. ATTENTION AND SITTING STILL. Some people find it easy to sit still for a long time and listen; others like to get up and move a lot and easily get distracted by other things.
   c. PLAYING. Some children have an easy time playing with others; others are a little shy about playing with others.
   d. TALKING TO OTHERS. Some children love to talk to their classmates; others are too shy to talk with others.

[If sensitivity training is about a particular student, discuss how that student is the same as everyone else in the class, but how he is different as well. For example, "Johnny is the same as many of you in that he has two arms and two legs, likes to read, and is very nice. But he is different in that he does not always know what to say to play with others." Be sure to include both the student's talents and difficulties. If the student demonstrates behaviors that annoy other students, make sure to explain how these behaviors are not done intentionally to bother the other children. For example, "Sometimes Johnny makes funny noises when the teacher asks him to do work. He does not do that to bother anyone, he just gets nervous about the work. So do not tell him to be quiet because that gets him mad. Instead, let the teacher talk to him."]

4. Sometimes children tease or don't play with children who they think are different. Is this fair? How would you feel if you were left out because you were different in some way?

5. What is it like to feel left out? Use sample exercise to illustrate.

   a. Ask the children to stand if they want to play the game "Simon Says." Tell anyone with white sneakers that they must sit down and cannot play yet. Then tell anyone with brown hair that they too must sit down and cannot play yet. Continue telling students with various attributes to sit down until no one is allowed to play.

b. Discuss how it feels to be left out of play because you have different-colored sneakers or different-colored hair or eyes. Discuss how much worse this would be if others teased those who were left out. Explain that this is how it is for children who feel left out because they do not know how to play or are shy. Tell the students how they can help by asking those who might be left out to play.

6. How We Can Help?
   a. If you see students being left out, ask them to talk and play with you. Try three times, and if they do not want to play or talk, then do not force them.
   b. If you see students getting teased, tell the teaser to leave the other person alone. If they will not leave the person alone, get help from a teacher.
   c. If someone looks upset, ask if you can help.

[If the sensitivity training is about a particular student, discuss concrete ways to help that student. For example, if the student does not respond to his name sometimes, explain to the peers how to get his attention. For example, say, "If Johnny does not respond to your question, tap him on the shoulder to get his attention. Say, 'Look at me Johnny.' Then ask your question again. If that does not work, try it again by getting right in front of him so he is looking at you. If that does not work, ask the teacher for help."]

7. Rewards for Kind Behavior
   a. When you are observed being kind in any of the ways described above, you will receive a _____. When you get _____ (number) of _____, you will get _____.

# Sample Sensitivity Training
# for Third Grade and Up

1. What are the five senses? Hearing, seeing, taste, smell, and touch.

2. Does anyone know what the "sixth sense" is? No, it is not about seeing dead people (reference to the movie called "The Sixth Sense"). The sixth sense is the "social" or "friend" sense (this notion was adapted from Tony Attwood, 1998). The friend sense has to do with:

   a. Knowing how to talk to other kids
   b. Knowing how to play with other kids
   c. Understanding how other people feel

3. Some of us have trouble with our "friend sense." This makes it hard to make friends. For example, we might have trouble:

   a. Knowing how to talk to other kids
   b. Knowing how to play with other kids
   c. Understanding how other people feel

[If sensitivity training is about a particular student, discuss how that student has trouble with his friend sense, despite his many special talents and abilities. Discuss both the student's intellectual strengths and his difficulties socializing. If he exhibits behaviors that annoy other students such as invading their space, make sure to explain how these behaviors are not done intentionally to bother the other children.]

4. People can be very successful and helpful to others even though they have difficulties with their "friend sense." A number of famous people have had trouble with their friend sense despite their terrific talents and successes. This includes Albert Einstein, Amadeus Mozart, Thomas Edison, Thomas Jefferson, and Temple Grandin, among others. (Review these individuals' special gifts and talents as well as their social difficulties.)

5. What is it like to have trouble with the friend sense? Use the following sample exercise to illustrate.

   a. Tell all the children they can be part of a special club if they can join in. In the club you get anything you want, including a special treat (bring snacks for this exercise).
   b. Send five students out of the room (preselected by the classroom teacher to be students who are resilient and unlikely to be embarrassed in front of the other students).
   c. Tell all the remaining students how they can join the club. They just have to say, "Can I join in" while showing the "secret" behaviors (scratching their heads, pulling their ear and coughing, in any order). Practice for 3 minutes with three or four volunteers until the students can do these secret behaviors subtly.

d. Ask the five students who left the room to return and tell them to try to join the group by asking if they can join in. After the first student asks, turn to the entire class and say, "Did he do it right? Can he join in?" The students, seeing that he did not pull his ear, scratch his head or cough, say, "No, he cannot join." Then ask one of the volunteers who knows the secret to ask to join in and tell the five students who were outside to watch carefully. After the student successfully joins and receives a special treat, ask the whole class, "Did he do it right?" They say "yes" as he demonstrates the secret behaviors. Then ask another one of the five students who had left the room to try to join in again. Take turns between the students who do and do not know the secret behaviors, rewarding those who successfully join in.

e. Ask the five students how they felt before they caught on to the secret behaviors. Discuss their feelings of anger, unfairness that others were being rewarded, embarrassment at not knowing what to do, loneliness, and so on. Then discuss how students who have trouble with their "friend sense" often do not know how to join in and this is the way they feel.

f. Make sure all the students are told how to join in and that everyone gets rewarded. Give ample praise and applause for the courage of the five students who were not originally told the secret of how to join this made-up club.

6. How We Can Help?
   a. If you see students being left out, ask them to talk and play with you. Try three times, and if they do not want to play or talk, do not force them.
   b. If you see students getting teased, tell the teaser to leave the other person alone.
   c. If someone looks upset, ask if you can help.

[If the sensitivity training is about a particular student, discuss concrete ways to help that student. For example, if the student does not respond to questions, explain to the peers how to get her attention or how to rephrase a question.]

7. Rewards for Kind Behavior
   a. When you are observed being kind in any of the ways described above, you will receive a _____. When you get _____ (number) of _____, you will get _____.

# Sample Training for All Lunch/Recess Personnel

I have conducted this kind of training with the lunch staff to gain their cooperation in a schoolwide incentive program for kind behaviors. The training can also be conducted by the school principal or special education staff. Typically, the lesson is conducted on a half day of school when the lunch staff is available. It is crucial to get approval from the principal or other administrator to make sure staff are paid for attending the training since most lunch staff are already underpaid for a very demanding job.

## Rationale

Lunch/recess time is the most social and least structured time of the school day. For many children that means they can relax and get a break from the demands of the day. The lack of structure and social nature of recess also makes it the prime time for social conflicts and possible behavioral problems. We want to implement a program that we expect will reduce behavioral problems and foster a kind and caring atmosphere during recess.

## Structure of Program

A. All children in the school were taught by their teachers to demonstrate three "kind" and "responsible" behaviors during lunch and recess. These behaviors are:
   1. **Include** others in conversation and play if they appear to be by themselves.
   2. **Stand up for** others who are teased by telling the teaser to stop or by getting help.
   3. **Offer help** to others who look upset or hurt.

B. We ask that all teachers and staff at lunch and recess:
   1. Look for and coach children to engage in these "kind" behaviors. Direct them to include others, stand up for those who are teased, and to offer help.
   2. Praise them if they demonstrate one of the "kind" behaviors listed above.
   3. Give out a ticket/token to any student you observe demonstrating one of the kind behaviors listed above.
   4. Try to praise or give out at least two tickets/tokens each lunch and recess period.

C. Students will take the tickets/tokens back to their classroom teachers who will praise them for their kind behavior. The tickets/tokens will be accumulated in the classrooms and may be exchanged for classroom rewards as determined by the individual classroom teachers.

## Coaching and Praising Kind Behaviors (Modeling and role-plays)

A. **Including others** (need three people, two to play and one who sits out):
   1. Notice the loner.
   2. Coach the others to ask the loner to play.
   3. Come up with your own game to include the loner and other kids.
   4. Praise and give out the tickets.

B. **Standing up for others who are teased or put down** (need three people, teaser, victim of teasing, and a bystander):
   1. Notice slight putdowns, even if told to you after the fact.
   2. Coach the bystander: "He needs your help, can you stand up for him?"

227

3. Help the victim: "Don't attend to that, you know it's not true."
4. Address the teaser: "Can you apologize for saying those things. I do not want anyone to tease you and I do not want you to tease anyone."
5. Praise and give tickets for standing up for the other person.

C. **Helping Others**
1. Look for these situations: Someone comes to the aid of someone who is hurt, someone encourages or compliments someone who is having trouble with something (e.g., "Good throw" or you played well).
2. Coach the students to help.
3. Praise and give tickets for helping fellow students.

## When Will the Program Start?

As soon as you get the word from your building principal and he/she gives you the special tokens/tickets.

## Exercise to Understand the Power of Watching Others Be Rewarded

Tell all staff that they can leave the training early when they get three tickets. Then tell all staff to talk among themselves about their week or their weekend plans. Once most staff members are talking, go around the room giving out tickets to anyone who is quiet and say, "I like how quiet you are. Here is a ticket." Keep giving out tickets to those who are quiet until most staff have caught on that being quiet results in a ticket. Then explain how watching others being rewarded is often an incentive to behave well. This is what we want at lunch and recess time – for children to behave positively because they see other children being rewarded for such behavior.

## What to Do with Negative Behaviors?

A. Prevent negative behaviors by telling children ahead of time what is expected:
1. Remind them to compromise before they argue.
2. Remind them to include everyone, and encourage each other.

B. Attend to those who do the positive (e.g., the bystanders, etc.).

C. Instead of criticizing them about what they should not have done, educate them about what they can do.
1. Suggest a compromise for those who cannot agree on what to play.
2. Explain how to express anger in words ("I" message) rather than fighting:

I feel _____

When you _____

Because _____

What I want you to do is _____ .

3. Explain how to deal with losing, "If you lose a game, you can still win a friend if you do not get mad."

D. When all else fails and the problem continues, take it to the _____ (class teacher, building principal).

# References

American Psychiatric Association. (2000). *Diagnostic and statistical manual of mental disorders* (4th ed. – Text revision). Washington, DC: Author.

Asperger, H. (1944). Die 'Autistischen Psychopathen' im Kindesalter. *Archiv fur Psychiatrie und Nervenkrankheiten, 117,* 76-136.

Attwood, T. (1998). *Asperger's Syndrome: A guide for parents and professionals.* London: Jessica Kingsley.

Baker, J. E. (2003). *Social skill picture books.* Arlington, TX: Future Horizons, Inc.

Barnhill, G. P. (2001). Social attribution and depression in adolescents with Asperger Syndrome. *Focus on Autism and Other Developmental Disabilities, 16,* 46-53.

Barnhill, G. P., Cook, K. T., Tebbenkamp, K., & Myles, B. S. (2002). The effectiveness of social skills intervention targeting nonverbal communication for adolescents with Asperger Syndrome and related pervasive developmental delays. *Focus on Autism and Other Developmental Disabilities, 17*(2), 112-118.

Barnhill, G. P., Hagiwara, T., Myles, B. S., Simpson, R. L., Brick, M. L., & Griswold, D. (2000). Parent, teacher, and self report of problem and adaptive behaviors in children and adolescents with Asperger Syndrome. *Diagnostique, 25*(2), 147-167.

Bieber, J. (Producer). (1994). *Learning disabilities and social skills with Richard LaVoie: Last one picked . . . first one picked on.* Washington, DC: Public Broadcasting Service.

Canter, L. (1987). *Assertive discipline.* New York: Harper and Row.

Church, C., Alisanki, S., & Amanullah, S. (2000). The social, behavioral, and academic experiences of children with Asperger syndrome. *Focus on Autism and Other Developmental Disabilities, 15,* 12-20.

Durand, V. M. (1990). *Severe behavior problems: A functional communication training approach.* New York: Guilford Press.

Ehlers, S., & Gillberg, C. (1993). The epidemiology of Asperger Syndrome – A total population study. *Journal of Child Psychology and Psychiatry, 34*(8), 1327-1350.

Faherty, C. (2000). *What does it mean to me: A workbook explaining self awareness and life lessons to the child or youth with high-functioning autism or Asperger's.* Arlington, TX: Future Horizons.

Gajewski, N., Hirn, P., & Mayo, P. (1998). *Social skill strategies: A social-emotional curriculum for adolescents* (2nd ed.). Eau Claire, WI: Thinking Publications.

Goleman, D. (1997). *Emotional intelligence.* New York: Bantam Books.

Gray, C., Dutkiewicz, M., Fleck, C., Moore, L., Cain, S. L., Lindrup, A., Broek, E., Gray, J., & Gray, B. (Eds.). (1993). *The social story book.* Jenison, MI: Jenison Public Schools.

Greenspan, S., & Wieder, S. (1998). *The child with special needs: Encouraging intellectual and emotional growth.* Reading, MA: Addison Wesley Longman.

Grodon, J., & LeVasseur, P. (1995). Cognitive picture rehearsal: A system to teach self-control. In K. A. Quill (Ed.), *Teaching children with autism* (pp. 287-306). Albany, NY: Delmar Publishing.

Howlin, P., Baron-Cohen, S., & Hadwin, J. (1999). *Teaching children with autism to mind-read: A practical guide.* London: Wiley.

Kim, J. A., Szatmari, P., Bryson, S. E., Streiner, D. L., & Wilson, F. J. (2000). The prevalence of anxiety and mood problems among children with autism and Asperger Syndrome. *Autism, 4,* 117-132.

Klin, A., Volkmar, F. R., & Sparrow, S. S. (2000). *Asperger Syndrome.* New York: The Guilford Press.

Koning, C., & Magill-Evans, J. (2001). Social and language skills in adolescent boys with Asperger Syndrome. *Autism, 5,* 23-36.

McGinnis, E., & Goldstein, A. (1997). *Skillstreaming the elementary school child: New strategies and perspectives for teaching prosocial skills.* Champaign, IL: Research Press.

Myles, B. S., & Simpson, R. L. (2001). Effective practices for students with Asperger Syndrome. *Focus on Exceptional Children, 34*(3), 1-14.

Myles, B. S., & Southwick, J. (1999). *Asperger Syndrome and difficult moments: Practical solutions for tantrums, rage, and meltdowns.* Shawnee Mission, KS: Autism Asperger Publishing Company.

Myles, B. S., Simpson, R. L., & Becker, J. K. (1994-1995). An analysis of characteristics of students diagnosed as having higher-functioning autistic disorder. *Exceptionality, 5*(1), 19-30.

Ozonoff, S., Pennington, B. F., & Rogers, S. J. (1991). Executive function deficits in high-functioning autistic individuals: Relationships to theory of mind. *Journal of Child Psychology and Psychiatry and Allied Disciplines, 32,* 1081-1105.

# REFERENCES

Ozonoff, S., Rogers, S. J., & Pennington, B. F. (1991). Asperger's syndrome: Evidence of an empirical distinction from high-functioning autism. *Journal of Child Psychology and Psychiatry and Allied Disciplines, 32,* 1108-1122.

Twachtman-Cullen, D. (1998). Language and communication in high-functioning autism and Asperger Syndrome. In E. Schopler, G. Mesibov, & L. Kunce, (Eds.), *Asperger Syndrome or high functioning autism?* (pp. 199-225). New York: Plenum Press.

Wagner, S. (1998). *Inclusive programming for elementary students with autism.* Arlington, TX: Future Horizons, Inc.

Wing, L. (1981). Asperger Syndrome: A clinical account. *Psychological Medicine, 11,* 115-129.

Winner, M. G. (2002). Assessment of social skills for students with Asperger Syndrome and high functioning autism. *Assessment for Effective Intervention, 27*(1&2), 72-80.

Wolfberg, P. J. (2003). *Peer play and the autism spectrum. The art of guiding children's socialization and imagination.* Shawnee Mission, KS: Autism Asperger Publishing Company.